HOW THEY STARTED DIGITAL

Other books in the How They Started series:

How They Started: How 30 good ideas became great businesses
How They Started Global Brands: How 21 good ideas became great global businesses
How They Started in Tough Times: How 25 companies started and thrived in an economic crisis
How They Started: How 9 good ideas became great businesses (Pocket Edition)

HOW THEY STARTED DIGITAL

*How 25 **good ideas** became **spectacular** digital businesses*

David Lester

crimson

How They Started Digital: How 25 good ideas became spectacular digital businesses

This first edition published in 2012 by Crimson Publishing Ltd

Westminster House
Kew Road
Richmond
Surrey
TW9 2ND

British Library Cataloguing in Publication Data
A catalogue record for this book is available from the British Library

ISBN 978 1 78059 089 9

Typeset by Mac Style, Nafferton, East Yorkshire
Printed and bound in the UK by Ashford Colour Press, Gosport, Hants

Contents

Acknowledgements

W**e must first thank all the founders** of the businesses featured who consented to give detailed, frank and insightful interviews about the very earliest days of their companies. Many revealed stories and information that have not been shared publicly before.

Many early-stage investors in these brands, founding team members, and other associates of the founders were also generous in sharing their memories and knowledge of the fledgling brands we feature in this book.

And we must also thank the companies, many of which are no longer run or owned by the original founders. These businesses, in numerous cases, provided additional supporting information and photography that they have kindly agreed to let us use here.

Finally, it is appropriate to thank those at Crimson Publishing, who have spent a considerable amount of time putting this book together – including Ian Wallis, Lucy Smith, Dawn Wilkinson and Beth Bishop.

Introduction

I am writing this days after Facebook has gone public, valued by the stock market at around $100 billion (£64.6 billion). That means this eight-year-old company is worth roughly 12 times more than long-established UK giants Marks & Spencer or Sainsbury's, and three times Barclays Bank.

Perhaps even more breath taking is that a few weeks ago Facebook spent around $1 billion (£646.1 million) buying a one-year-old business which had no revenue at all.

Clearly, we are living in a time when it is possible to create global businesses and very dramatic riches faster than anyone has ever been able to do before. It is not merely possible, but even likely that some of you reading this book will be setting up your own ventures which will themselves be worth vast amounts in one year's time. I hope this book will be helpful to any of you thinking about doing just that.

I suspect, though, that most of you reading this will either be seeking more modest goals for your own business, or will simply be fascinated to learn how some of this incredible success has happened so very quickly. This book has been commissioned with you all in mind, whichever category you fall into. *How They Started: Digital* is part of a successful series. We have already produced other How They Started books, telling the amazing and often remarkable stories of how ordinary people can take an idea and develop it into a thriving, successful company. The world is changing faster than ever before due to what can only be described as a digital revolution. And as surely the most fundamental shift to all nations' economies, we felt compelled to produce a How They Started book dedicated to the exciting array of digital businesses out there.

We have been very subjective in the companies we have selected here, aiming to offer variety. We have included a number of already enormous businesses, as well as several smaller, fast growing ventures. We have inevitably included many from North America, which unquestionably leads the world in so much of the digital world today, but have made a point of including many businesses thriving outside that region, too. Spotify is perhaps the largest European-founded company featured here.

We made a decision early on in our research not to write about Facebook – primarily because there is already so much coverage of it in the media that a chapter here would add little to anyone interested. However we are delighted to feature a number of extremely well-known names, most notably Twitter, Dropbox, TripAdvisor and Zynga, which are in the same category of 'hyper-success'. And for comparison and balance we have also included some slightly older digital businesses, such as Electronic Arts, Google, eBay and Microsoft.

We have had generous access, sometimes extraordinarily so, to one or more of the founders of almost all companies featured here. We are very grateful to all those who helped us in our research. We have worked hard to go beyond the very basic information on each company, aiming to bring you the inside story about what really went on, and why each company evolved the way it did.

As you read through these stories, you are sure to be struck by the fact that anyone with a good idea and the right drive can start a company today, more easily than ever before. It is easier to start, raise funds, get advice and expand across the world than it has ever been. This is already leading to many more people setting up on their own, and that seems certain to continue. The website I created, www.startups.co.uk, which is the UK's leading site supporting people setting up their own business, is seeing not only higher numbers of readers than ever, but also more and more services aimed at helping people set up. And the great news is that this applies to anyone setting up a small, part-time business, as a hobby or supplementing either student life or a meagre pension, as much as for the few aiming for something far more ambitious.

These are great times to start a business, whoever you are. While it is clear many of the businesses featured here have been started by 'software engineers' or young people brought up on all things digital, there are plenty of digital businesses featured here started by non-techies: Neon Play, the UK-based app developer, Wonga and Match.com for example.

I have been struck, too, by the degree to which the elite of California's Silicon Valley have been instrumental in the extreme growth enjoyed by most of the recent web-based mega-brands. The business press both in Europe and North America have featured numerous articles about the networks and influence of LinkedIn and Netscape's respective founders Reid Hoffman and Marc Andreeson, who have subsequently invested their accumulated wealth in or sat on the board of a staggering number of other ventures. Facebook's IPO (Initial Public Offering – the process of floating their shares on a Stock Exchange) is being widely predicted to lead to a new crop of exciting digital start-ups from Facebook employees made rich through valuable share options. For many companies a recommendation from one of these elite influencers has been a notable milestone in their gaining traction.

Gaining traction is absolutely crucial for any digital business which relies on the crowd. Imagine a TripAdvisor which had no reviews on even half the world's hotels, for example – it's unthinkable that such a site would survive today, let alone thrive. For businesses such as these, hyper-growth is not just a wonderful thing, but a requirement of success. If a business that relies almost entirely on the interaction between users/customers has a slow start, it is surely doomed to failure.

In the last five years, starting a digital business in Silicon Valley would have offered significant advantages over starting it in most other parts of the world. A question we will all need to wait some years to be able to answer is how much this will change over time. Will Moscow, Shanghai, London's Tech City or some other hubs be able to produce a world-leading digital business on a scale similar to Twitter, Dropbox or Google? I certainly hope so.

It is easy to observe Facebook or Google with their billions in revenue, profit and users and think them unbeatable. Yet I can't help but wonder the extent to which any of these businesses will fall away as quickly as they have grown. It seems logical that any business which can grow so very fast could be threatened by some other new start-up delivering an even better product or service. Looking back just 10 years brings up memories of a time when Yahoo! and AOL were among the global elite. One clear consequence of the ease of starting up seems to be a weakening of the barriers to entry which have historically kept successful companies at the top of their field for many years or decades. I have no doubt that 10 years from now we will all know a new group of household name digital businesses which have not been founded yet. Perhaps more interesting today is which of today's giants they will displace.

Already we can see signs that more and more students are keen to set up their own business than ever before. This is surely inevitable given weaker graduate employment prospects in many countries and the apparently easy riches available to digital entrepreneurs. While I welcome anything which makes it easier for anyone to start their own business and make it work, I fear this ease will lead to a number of people starting without proper research and consideration, which is likely to lead to a rise in early business failures.

I fervently hope that one, albeit secondary, consequence of reading this book will be that some people who had wondered whether to start or not will actually decide not to as it is not for them. It is all too easy to read the headlines about so many 20-somethings becoming multi-millionaires and conclude that it is easy; I hope that the stories in this book will show that not only is it far from easy, but will give a rich and full picture of what it is like to set something up from scratch and make it a success.

I hope you enjoy reading this book as much as I and the rest of the team who have worked on it have done. The stories are all remarkable, and all impressive. And for those of you starting or building your own digital venture, I wish you well, and hope to write about your story in a future edition of this book!

David Lester
May 2012

Spotify

Spotting the gap

Founders: **Daniel Ek and Martin Lorentzon**	
Age of founders: **25 and 39**	
Backgrounds: **Formerly head of social network Stardoll and music sharing site UTorrent; and founder of internet marketing company TradeDoubler**	
Founded in: **2008, Sweden**	
Headquarters: **London, UK**	
Business type: **Music streaming**	

The launch of Spotify in 2008 altered the face of the music industry for ever. The recent online consumer shift, with its many negative effects – the demise of record stores, and increase in music piracy – has perhaps found a saviour in this new business model. Before Spotify came along, millions of people were downloading music from pirate sites, breaking the law and denying record labels the remuneration they deserved; Spotify offered its users an alternative way to access the music they love, which stays within the law and compensates those who bring the material into being.

While some still see Spotify as part of the threat to the music industry, and not the solution to its problems, there can be little doubt about its commercial impact. Since its launch in October 2008, Spotify has garnered more than 10 million active users, and three million paying subscribers. An alliance has been forged with Facebook, opening the door to hundreds of millions of new fans. And it seems that Spotify is now on the verge of cracking America – a feat many of the biggest artists on its roster have failed to achieve.

Experience is everything

It was always likely that Daniel Ek would make his money from computers. Having received his first machine aged five, the Swedish prodigy began programming when he was just 8 years old, and built his own web development business at 14, undercutting local design firms by training his school friends to build web pages for him. At one stage Daniel, running the operation from his school computer lab, was making around £10,000 a month.

The young entrepreneur eventually sold this first business in 2002, aged 19, and, after flirting with an engineering course at Sweden's Royal Institute of Technology, decided to plough the profits back into business. In 2005 Daniel set up Advertigo, an advertising agency that caused a stir in the online community with its ability to decipher websites and target ads accordingly. Then, just a few months later, he was invited by Index Ventures to take control of Stardoll, a new social network for fashion-conscious teenage girls. Harnessing his experience of programming cost-effective websites, Daniel laid the foundations of a network that would eventually reach an audience of 100 million.

By now, the Swede was big news on the tech scene, and about to embark on a new adventure that would shape his future success. In 2006 he was invited to take charge of a company – UTorrent – that was the world's biggest file-sharing site at the time. UTorrent allowed users to download their favourite songs for free, using a peer-to-peer (P2P) network – basically a giant swap shop, which copies music files from one user's hard drive and pastes it onto another. UTorrent was the intermediary, and didn't actually store any music itself. This meant it could handle a huge amount of traffic, without having to pay for the storage space – an advantage Daniel would seek to recreate when he launched Spotify a few years later.

Meanwhile Martin Lorentzon was carving his own niche in the tech space. After studying at Gothenburg University, Martin began experimenting with the newly invented internet, and in 1996 moved to San Francisco to join the marketing team at Alta Vista, at that time a promising start-up and later one the most popular search engines in the world. After a short spell in this hugely stimulating environment, Martin took significant roles in Swedish telecom operator Telia and Cell Venture, a venture capital firm specialising in internet start-up investments.

In February 1999, at the age of 30, Martin launched TradeDoubler, a digital company designed to help small companies get traffic from other sites. The service was an instant hit; clients loved the fact that they could now track their campaigns down to the tiniest detail, and only had to pay for successful results. Soon, TradeDoubler was active in 15 countries. By 2007, it was achieving an annual revenue of €282 million (£234 million).

A meeting of minds

In late 2005, Martin moved from Germany back to Sweden, and met Daniel a few weeks later. Martin was particularly impressed by Daniel's businesses, and soon agreed to pay $1 million (£730,000) to incorporate Advertigo into the TradeDoubler network. But he was also impressed by Daniel's nous and creativity, so he proposed that they start a new business together.

In late 2006 Daniel gave him a week's ultimatum: leave TradeDoubler and put a million euros aside for the new start-up. Remarkably, Martin did just that – before the idea for Spotify was even on the table.

Martin's approach was ideally timed. Daniel recalls that, having been so successful so young, he was becoming disillusioned. In fact he even contemplated abandoning business altogether and becoming a professional musician. But on a new project with Martin, he felt he could do something equally creative. The pair became fast friends, and they were committed to going into business together; but Daniel had doubts that Martin would actually take the plunge and leave his safety net at TradeDoubler. So, in late 2006 Daniel gave him a week's ultimatum: leave TradeDoubler and put a million euros aside for the new start-up. Remarkably, Martin did just that, before the idea for Spotify was even on the table.

For a while, in between gangster film marathons, they tossed around ideas, rough visions for new tech companies. One of their favourite topics was music. During their brainstorming sessions they regularly listened to music, through Daniel's media HTPC machine (a computer capable of playing songs and movies) and really weren't impressed with its usability. Daniel recalls in an interview with news blog Mashable, 'I think that's why we got stuck on the idea of Spotify.'

The idea that took shape was also influenced by the state of the music industry at the time. Speaking at LeWeb 2011, Daniel explained: 'Sweden was known for piracy. We had [the illegal music sites] Kazaar and The Pirate Bay ... because there was ubiquitous broadband and it was super-fast, consumption existed before the services did. That meant that the pirate networks were the pioneers ... the innovators.'

'The vision was like: "what if you had iTunes, but you had all the world's music in it?"'

At this time Daniel was still working at UTorrent, a service that, to a certain extent, endorsed piracy – although the site itself was legal, millions of the files shared via its P2P network were not. But now he began to envision a business that would usurp the pirate sites, and offer users a legitimate way to download the free music they had become used to, while also rewarding the artists and record labels. At LeWeb, he explained, 'we felt that the number one and the most important thing was to create a product that was better than piracy. The vision was like: "what if you had iTunes, but you had all the world's music in it?"'

Fresh thinking

The answer Daniel and Martin came up with was something akin to an enormous jukebox, a site that would play users' requests on demand. Users would not be able to *download* any music, but they could listen to all their favourite tracks whenever they liked. The service would be available in a 'freemium' model, offering both free and subscription-based alternatives.

The free tier would allow users to listen to as much music as they liked without charge, provided they were willing to put up with regular advertising breaks. While users could access hours of music without spending a penny, advertisers would be able to tailor their placements to specific artists and albums, homing in on exactly the right demographic.

The paid level would offer users an ad-free experience and several other benefits, including faster streaming speeds, in return for a small monthly subscription. The founders always knew that the free model would account for the vast majority of Spotify's users, but this wouldn't harm profitability. In September 2009 Daniel claimed that, to be commercially viable, Spotify needed just 10% of users to sign up to the paid subscription.

Spotting the name

According to Daniel, the name of his business actually stems from a misinterpretation that occurred during the brainstorming stage. 'Martin and I were sitting in different rooms shouting ideas back and forth of company names. We were even using jargon generators. Out of the blue Martin shouted a name that I misheard as Spotify. I immediately googled the name and realised there were no Google hits for the word at all. A few minutes later we registered the domain name.'

The Spotify marketing team has since post-rationalised the name, injecting it with reason and logic. According to the marketeers, the name 'Spotify' is a conflation of 'spot' and 'identify', encapsulating the company's core purpose: to help music fans get instant access to the music they like.

The struggle for software

In April 2006, after months of tweaking and brainstorming their idea, Daniel and Martin founded Spotify. Drawing on their earlier business windfalls, the partners had plenty of money to play with – and invested $5.6 million

(£3.6 miliion) each in the new venture. From here, they began building the technology on which Spotify's fate would rest.

Daniel invited a project manager called Andreas Ehn, whom he'd met at Stardoll, to become Chief Technical Officer, and Spotify's first employee. Appointed in summer 2006, Andreas recruited a team of six developers from KTH, Stockholm's premier technology university. Work began in August in a small office in the heart of Stockholm, and straightaway the team was presented with a huge challenge. Daniel and Martin wanted their site to stream millions and millions of songs, but how could this be done without blowing the entire development budget on storage space?

To solve this problem, the developers created a new, hybrid system for locating music, based on a network similar to the one Daniel had overseen at UTorrent. In addition to its own remote servers, the Spotify search engine was built to search the user's personal hard drive – if they've played a song before, they'll have an encrypted copy on their machine which the program can use, therefore never requiring Spotify's servers for this particular song. The engine will also scan for other users with a copy of the track, and, if the search is successful, will transfer the file across. In effect, most of the time users are just taking songs from each other. This significantly reduces demand on the Spotify servers, and it is really quick.

Indeed, speed was always a key goal for the development team. With this in mind, the developers created a unique 'prefetching' tool, which guesses what you're going to listen to next, and queues up songs to ensure a seamless, instant segue from track to track.

The developers' need for speed has yielded startling results. According to Spotify, its songs now play with a gap of just 256 microseconds between songs – faster than any other music streaming service.

Conuincing the record labels

At first, Daniel believed Spotify could be built like a standard internet radio service, without the need to secure the support of the record labels. But gradually, after much persuading from those around him, he came round to the view that the labels were needed if Spotify was to become a legitimate, sustainable commercial enterprise.

So, as Spotify's designated frontman, Daniel began going out to meet the record labels in August 2006. To realise his dream of bringing the entire anthology of world music under a single umbrella, Daniel, who had never negotiated a music contract before, would have to strike deals with over 5,000 publishers.

He recruited two new employees to help him – Petra Hansson as Chief Legal Counsellor and Niklas Ivarsson as Head of Licensing – and also enlisted the help of Fred Davis, industry lawyer. But, even with additional help, the pitch was not an easy one. Originally, he had aimed to secure global music rights, but this was a dead end. Instead, he focused on securing European rights. And even this was a long shot.

The record companies had to be persuaded to release their music into a model which was totally unproven; furthermore, Daniel's projections about the number of paid subscribers Spotify could attract initially met with scepticism from some executives, who believed them overly ambitious. But in the face of growing piracy, Daniel and his team argued that the labels needed to partner with Spotify in order to connect, and profit from, the coming generation. The team pointed to the fact that music industry revenues were plummeting; having peaked at $27 billion (£16.76 billion) in 1999, income would fall to $14 billion (£8.69 billion) in 2008.

The record companies had to be persuaded to release their music into a model which was totally unproven.

Spotify promised to reconnect the labels with their disillusioned fans, and also generate priceless marketing information on millions of potential customers: their age, their location, their musical preferences. Spotify could show the labels exactly where, and when, their music was being played – great for marketing artists and tour schedules.

Daniel showed music execs a version of the site that used pirated music as its content, to show how the site would work. Seeing it in action, the USPs of the site started to click with the labels.

To seal the deal, Daniel offered the labels a percentage payment every time one of their tracks was streamed, as well as million-dollar advances for their lists. Furthermore, the major labels (Universal, Warner, Sony and EMI) were offered a stake of between 2% and 6% in Spotify. This proposal was crucial in securing the breadth of material that would become one of the site's key advantages over its competitors. And in the end it worked: a task that Daniel originally thought would take three months in fact took two years.

The additional advances Daniel and Martin had to pledge to make these deals meant that the duo had to plough another $5 million (£3.1 million) of their own money into the company to keep it going until it could generate revenue on launch in 2008.

Going live

Thanks to the tireless work of Spotify's development team, an invitation-only trial version of Spotify was ready by May 2007. The management team purchased a database of influential people's contact details, known as a 'seed list', and began sending out invitations – ensuring that their new product was experienced in precisely the right circles.

This private launch created real buzz around the product – Spotify's viral marketing strategy hinged on users spreading the word and creating an underground success. Furthermore, the developers were allowed to tweak and hone under the radar, their underground fan base providing a perfect sounding board for any enhancements. And crucially, the invitation-only model was scalable, and would never allow demand to exceed bandwidth.

This private launch created real buzz around the product – Spotify's viral marketing strategy hinged on users spreading the word and creating an underground success.

The tipping point

In autumn 2008, after months of negotiation, a list of labels including Sony, EMI, Warner and Universal signed agreements to release their music to Spotify. With the core of the catalogue now secure, Daniel and Martin could finally push the red button; so, after what the company blog describes as 'two years, thousands of lines of code, and even more cups of coffee', Spotify went live to the public on 7 October. Although free accounts were still only available to invited guests, paid subscriptions were now available to everyone. Those who'd joined up during the trial stage received a free account, and a new bunch of invitations to scatter.

> *Total spend for Spotify's first three years was, staggeringly, less than £5,000.*

Today, Daniel admits that he wanted to launch in 30 or 40 countries straightaway, but was held back by those around him, as well as the deal he'd been able to do with the record labels. In fact, Spotify launched in just six European countries: Sweden, Norway, Finland, France, Spain and the UK. This cautious approach was reflected in the publicity strategy. Although Sales Director Jon Mitchell and his team had begun pitching ads well before the launch, and had secured sponsorship agreements with the likes of Ford, little was done to expand the original viral marketing strategy once Spotify went public. According to Jon, the bought-in list used to select invitees was the only marketing expenditure in those early days (in fact total spend for Spotify's first three years was, staggeringly, less than £5,000).

Although marketing outlay was minimal, interest quickly grew. The music community loved it, and, with thousands of new users signing up every week, the investment community began to sit up and take notice.

Cranking it up a notch

In November 2008, Spotify received its first tranche of external funding – €15 million (£12.4 million) from VC investment firms Northzone and Creandum, giving the company a total valuation of over €70 million (£58.2 million). The funding allowed Spotify to ramp up every aspect of its operation: hire new engineers, expand the ad sales team, and increase its storage space. Scores of new publishers were welcomed into the network, from all sorts of genres – one agreement, with classical music label Naxos, brought in 100,000 new tracks.

Now Spotify could release the handbrake. On 10 February 2009, Daniel and Martin began opening up Spotify's free service to the general public, by removing the invitation-only barrier in the UK. Similar action was taken in the company's other territories, and interest exploded; Spotify passed one million users in early March, and reached six million by the summer.

Meanwhile the developers, having guarded their secrets with Masonic zeal for so long, were finally ready to open their doors. In early April 2009 the company announced the launch of libspotify, which enabled third-party developers to write programmes for Spotify. The management team hoped that, by opening its doors to the tech community, Spotify could turn itself from a single site into an overarching music platform – just as Facebook had made itself a platform for social interaction.

The grand alliance

But Facebook itself was now getting interested. Both CEO Mark Zuckerberg and President Sean Parker fell in love with the new service – particularly its ability to integrate social functions. On 25 August, both men decided to go public with their appreciation; Mark wrote in his own Facebook feed that 'Spotify is so good', while Sean, who Daniel references as an inspiration through his creation of file sharing site Napster, decided to write his disciple an email.

Sean told Daniel that Spotify's design was 'clean, elegant, tight, and fast', and said that 'direct integration with Facebook is a good idea', albeit not until Spotify raised its market profile another few notches. This initial missive laid the foundations of Spotify's relationship with Facebook, and with its president in particular; Sean became close friends with Daniel, firing out suggestions for tweaks to the Spotify software. In October 2010, the man portrayed by Justin Timberlake in the film *The Social Network* completed a $15 million (£9.3 million) investment through his venture capital company, Founders Fund.

In late September 2011, the union was sealed; Spotify announced that, henceforth, no one could sign up to the site without a Facebook login. As the partnership is still in its infancy, it's hard to accurately assess the benefit this partnership has brought.

Where are they now?

Today, Spotify is fast becoming a commercial behemoth. In 2010 advertising revenue reached £63.2 million, a year-on-year increase of nearly 60%, and Spotify has three million paying users worldwide. Meanwhile investment has been secured from a string of wealthy businesses and individuals, notably Li Ka-Shing, the world's 11th richest man, who has injected around $50 million (£31 million).

This huge increase in revenue has enabled Spotify to enter exciting new territories, including the mobile space, but also, significantly, the US market. The service launched in the USA in July 2011, and notched up 1.4 million users within two weeks. Many industry commentators scoffed at a 2010 Spotify report, which had forecast 50 million US users within a year; few people are laughing now. On 30 November 2011, Daniel announced that Spotify was relocating its headquarters to New York.

It's not all been plain sailing, however. Spotify has yet to return a profit; in 2010 the company reported losses of £26.5 million. Furthermore, a string of artists and record label bosses have condemned the company's operating practices. In April 2010, it was alleged that Spotify had paid Lady Gaga just £108 for the first one million plays of her debut smash, 'Poker Face', and several stars have subsequently criticised Spotify for providing meagre royalties. In November 2011, America's National Association of Recording Merchandisers published a damning report on Spotify, prompting one prominent distributor to pull more than 200 labels from the company's catalogue.

With new music sites, such as Rara, emerging all the time, Spotify will have to face down serious challenges in the months ahead. But Daniel and Martin have recently unveiled a raft of new features, including one that allows the user to request tracks via voice command. The plucky Swedes believe their music revolution is just getting started.

Mind Candy

Monsters, Inc.

Founder: **Michael Acton Smith**	
Age of founder: **30**	
Background: **Formerly founder of e-commerce site Firebox**	
Founded in: **2004, UK**	
Headquarters: **London, UK**	
Business type: **Virtual social network for children**	

Children will always be captivated by two things:** puzzle games and cuddly toys. Now Mind Candy, a company founded by entrepreneur Michael Acton Smith in 2004, is earning global success by blending these two timeless attractions.

Mind Candy's flagship game, Moshimonsters, allows children to adopt their own virtual monster, in a secure online environment. Users can win virtual currency to feed and clothe their monster by solving a series of brain-teasing puzzles, and interact with their friends via an inbuilt social network.

Having launched less than five years ago, Moshimonsters already boasts 60 million registered users, and the growth curve continues to steepen.

A first try online

Raised in Buckinghamshire, Michael's entrepreneurial side blossomed early. As a child, he flogged old toys at car boot sales in an attempt to make some pocket money. The young wheeler-dealer had ambition and determination from an early age, as he proved by running a full marathon at the age of 12.

After completing a geography degree at Birmingham University, Michael began mapping out business ideas during a post-graduation round-the-world backpacking trip, frantically scribbling product sketches and business plans on post-it notes.

In June 1998, Michael and his friend Tom Boardman decided to capitalise on the growing popularity of the web by setting up their own e-commerce business, Hotbox.co.uk. The site's aim was to introduce the public to cool, unusual and wacky products, including a chess set for drinking games that the founders had dreamt up at university.

The business began life in the attic of Tom's parents' house, and in early 2000 it moved to offices in Streatham, London. After realising that their site shared its name with a US adult entertainment engine, they decided to rebrand as Firebox.com. Now, the founders managed to convince Tom Teichman, chairman of early-stage technology investor SPARK Ventures, to invest around £1 million into the business, and embarked on an aggressive plan of expansion. In hindsight, Michael accepts it was too aggressive. 'We got sucked into the "get big quick" mantra. We set up an office in Sweden – God knows why. We took on board a very expensive marketing director, and grew to about 20 employees. Our costs and the revenues we were generating started getting completely out of line.

At one stage, insolvency lawyers even visited the company's offices; Michael remembers that 'we were told that we'd go to jail if we continued, as trading insolvently is a serious offence.'

'Then in March 2000, the whole thing collapsed, and from that moment no one wanted anything to do with internet companies. We were trying to raise money, but no one wanted to speak to us. Suddenly, it terrifyingly dawned on Tom and I that we were going to go bankrupt if we continued.' At one stage, insolvency lawyers even visited the company's offices; Michael remembers that 'we were told that we'd go to jail if we continued, as trading insolvently is a serious offence.'

Ultimately, Firebox survived, thanks to some fairly savage boot-strapping. Michael and Tom cut their staff roster from 20 to five, in a process described by the former as 'horrible, because many of the people were our friends from university'. The founders stopped paying themselves, and downscaled to a poky little office. Somehow, they managed to claw back enough money to pull back from the brink.

The product range, which initially focused on 'boy's toys', expanded into homeware, baby products, kitchen appliances and all manner of other product streams. Usage began to rocket, and commercial titans began to take notice – Channel 5 took a small equity stake, in exchange for advertising worth around £500,000, exposing Firebox to a huge new audience.

In 2002 Firebox reached profitability, and two years later it was named in the *Sunday Times* as the 13th fastest-growing privately owned business in the UK. Many other entrepreneurs would have sat back in their swivel chair, satisfied with their achievement in creating such a profitable and respected business.

But, for Michael, this wasn't enough. He recalls: 'the business was profitable, we had a great management team in place, but, like a lot of entrepreneurs, I started getting itchy feet, and I wanted to do new stuff. And one of my big passions had always been games.'

Stepping into the game

In May 2004 Michael stepped back from the day-to-day running of Firebox, safe in the knowledge that Christian Robinson, recently hired as Managing Director, could look after the business with Boardman. After taking the role of Non-Executive Director, he began ploughing some of the money he had made from the business into a new company – Mind Candy.

Michael's vision for Mind Candy was centred on an idea he had for an alternative reality game, Perplex City, aimed at 16- to 30-year-olds. The game would weave real-world events into an online fantasy realm, with enough scope and mystery to dominate users' daily lives. Looking back on this initial plan, Michael recalls, 'As a kid I'd read a book, *Masquerade* by Kit Williamson, who buried treasure in the British countryside then wrote clues as to its whereabouts. I wanted to do the same – sending clues through every conceivable media, from podcasts, websites, mobile phones, actors, skywriting, anything you can name.'

SPARK Ventures, led by Michael's old friend Tom Teichman, headed up a group of private investors to provide the £700,000 investment he needed to get his idea off the ground. Michael used it to rent offices in Shoreditch, London, and began dreaming up a fictional metropolis, spinning a back-story of danger and intrigue. The plot's crucial event was the theft of a priceless artefact, 'the Cube', from Perplex City, and its subsequent burial on earth. Gamers would be challenged to find the Cube for themselves, solving cryptic puzzles to unlock clues.

Michael soon set about building a design team capable of realising his vision, scouring Britain's universities for their brightest minds. Naomi Alderman, a former Oxford student who had earned critical acclaim for her short stories, was recruited as lead writer, while PhD student Adrian Hon was plucked from his neurosciences course at Oxford and installed as Director of Play.

When the new team set about building their virtual world, no detail was left unexplored. The designers drew up maps of Perplex City, studying maps of real cities, before sending their designs off to a specialist cartographer based in Sydney. Back in Shoreditch, Naomi and her team studied Old English in order to create guides and diaries redolent of the period.

The game begins

After months of development, Perplex City launched in July 2005, with an advert in the *Guardian* demanding the return of the missing Cube. Mind Candy sold puzzle cards at £10 a pop, and offered £100,000 to anyone who found the Cube – giving this fantasy world a very serious prize.

The game was an instant hit, with 13,000 users signed up by January 2006, and 70,000 by the end of the year. Critical acclaim duly followed; Perplex City was even nominated for a BAFTA in 2006.

Back in November 2005 Index Ventures had ploughed £1.5 million into Perplex City, the first-ever significant investment by a venture firm in the alternative reality space. In October 2006, Index teamed up with Accel and SPARK Ventures to complete another funding round of £4.5 million, ahead of a major expansion in the Perplex City product range.

The game was an instant hit, with 13,000 users signed up by January 2006, and 70,000 by the end of the year.

But that expansion never came. The developers had planned to launch a new season of Perplex City in early 2007, but, on the eve of the launch, they announced the project was being suspended. Many outsiders were astonished. How, they asked, could a game that had been in the running for a BAFTA just months earlier be struggling?

Perplexing problems

But to those on the inside, this news had been coming for months. Divinia Knowles, Mind Candy's Chief Operating Officer and Chief Financial Officer, believes the project 'was amazing as a media buzz, and it was a huge PR success. Commercially, it was a bit of a dead dog!'

Michael was extremely reluctant to go overboard with commercial partners; he once said that the last thing he wanted was 'to build an ad agency'. But many believed that Perplex City could have done with a harder commercial edge. Without a clear sales plan – or even sales director – in place, retailers seemed baffled by Perplex City, unable to decide whether it was a puzzle book or playing cards – and received conflicting messages from the products the company were producing.

The choice was stark: wind up the business, or channel the money left over from Perplex City into an alternative business venture.

Perhaps most significantly, the game was far too complicated; it eventually encompassed more than 1,200 puzzles, and clues were written in everything from hieroglyphics to Singaporean barcodes.

By the time Michael went to his board in early 2007 to notify them of his decision to can Perplex City, almost all the external investment had dried up. Of the £6.4 million raised, all but £600,000 was gone. The choice was stark: wind up the business, or channel the money left over from Perplex City into an alternative business venture.

A monstrous resurrection

For Michael the answer was relatively simple. During the final weeks of Perplex City, he began working on a new concept for Mind Candy – something far simpler, aimed primarily at children. The idea for this game was built upon a pet rock he had lovingly nurtured as a child.

Michael envisioned a game in which users could nurture and interact with their own pet monster, tickling and hugging it and receiving intelligent emotional responses in return.

Like Perplex City, users would be invited to take part in a series of quirky and colourful puzzles, with virtual currency available on completion of each challenge. Users could spend the virtual cash on feeding and

The first Moshimonster sketch.

17

Michael had begun to sketch a whole world of Moshimonster characters.

clothing their monster – perfect for kids too young to have any real money of their own. The game would also have a social element: you could make friends with other users and their monsters.

Michael successfully presented his idea to the Mind Candy management team, unfurling all manner of sketches and diagrams. The figures certainly lent weight to his vision: pet-rearing game Webkinz was enjoying soaring popularity, and would have more than four million active users by the end of 2007. Meanwhile, children's social network Neopets had been bought by Viacom for $160 million (£102 million) in 2005.

Piecing the puzzle together

Having convinced the management team, Michael launched his new project during the final days of Perplex City, in mid-2007. The venture began under the working title 'Puzzle Monsters', but Michael knew this wasn't memorable enough. So he came up with a catchy, child-friendly title for his new venture: Moshimonsters.

But having a good name was one thing. To make the new game a success, an internal change was required – the existing Perplex City staff simply did not have experience in working on a children's project, nor did some of them particularly want to. Therefore, the management team had to replace and restructure much of their team to ensure they could fulfil the objectives of the new game.

Financially, Mind Candy also had to be especially prudent, having already spent the majority of the money received from external investors for Perplex City. They lived on the remaining £600,000 for a long time – cost-saving constantly, and keeping the development team as small as possible.

Rather than buying in costly technology from other developers, the Moshimonsters architects created their own brand-new infrastructure, which would allow them to develop the game further, as the user base grew. Meanwhile, designers worked on the 'front end' of the site (the bit that users would actually see) and created six different types of monster for players to choose from, as well as a virtual room for each user to house their pet, and a virtual landscape for them to roam around.

Rather than buying in costly technology from other developers, the Moshimonsters architects created their own brand-new infrastructure, which would allow them to develop the game further, as the user base grew.

Releasing the monsters

By November 2007, the monsters were ready to meet the public, and a trial version of the site was launched at the Virtual Worlds Forum in London. Michael, only too aware that neither of his previous business ventures had taken off smoothly, was initially cautious. He knew he didn't have much cash, and that the developers were still tinkering. So the team came up with a novel, but risky, way of ensuring their site did not get overloaded too early.

To launch the site, Mind Candy created a range of little toys, a bit like phone charms, which kids could attach to their mobile phone. When the phone was switched on, the toys would glow in the dark. Each toy came with a code, which allowed the user to sign up to moshimonsters.com. For the first couple of months, this was the only way a child could get into the site.

But Michael has always been a man in a hurry – his business career has been characterised by a desire for rapid growth. Inevitably, he soon began to regret his cautious strategy. With hindsight, he admits that this early approach just didn't work: retailers wouldn't stock the toy, and the site was getting around two sign-ups a day.

So in April 2008, Michael gambled. He made Moshimonsters free to access, with a view to ultimately launching a subscription-based member service where some features of the site were only accessible behind a paywall. The plan was to get enough children using the site to prove its worth and to secure another round of funding. Then, when they had several million users, they could turn the paywall on.

The free-access model certainly proved popular. By summer 2008, sign-ups were running at 5,000 a day. But the second round of funding failed to materialise – the recession was starting to bite, and investors were reticent. By January 2009, Mind Candy was down to the last dregs of its cash. Over that Christmas period, the management team had begun to worry about paying their staff, although these fears were never communicated to the rest of the company.

With time and money running out, the development team were asked to put up the paywall ASAP. On 16 January 2009, after hurriedly signing up a little-known e-commerce company as payment provider, Mind Candy launched its

The Mind Candy HQ reflects the fun virtual world Michael and his team have created.

brand-new members-only tier: existing users could now buy a virtual passport to access new parts of the Moshimonster universe, and give their monster a brand-new colour, in exchange for a monthly subscription fee.

But still the money problems remained – with development costs mounting, the new stream of membership income could only plug gaps. So, with desperation beginning to creep in, the management team went out to pitch for investment. Things appeared to be going well; they soon managed to land two promising investment contracts. But, over a couple of months, both parties vanished without trace.

Just when it looked as though Michael would have to scrap his second game in the space of two years, Moshimonsters was saved. In December 2008, Michael met a business angel whose children played Moshimonsters, and who believed in the business enough to invest. Although the amount has never been disclosed, it was enough to put Moshimonsters' finances on a secure footing – and support the business during an explosive period of growth.

Moshimonsters has lift-off

Having been on the brink of bankruptcy at the start of 2009, Moshimonsters was on the verge of global domination by the end of it. Monthly registrations jumped from 4.6 million in July to 9 million by November. Despite being in the throes of the recession, which ate into parental finances, Moshimonsters' growth rate continued to increase; by summer 2010, more than 22 million children had signed up.

Having been on the brink of bankruptcy at the start of 2009, Moshimonsters was on the verge of global domination by the end of it.

It's difficult to find a single catalyst for the Moshimonsters boom. The developers certainly deserve a considerable share of the credit, having made a number of enhancements to the game. The monsters were given their own pets, Moshlings, adding a layer of enticing complexity for users, and a myriad of attractions were added, such as a funky underground disco.

Likewise, Michael and his subscription team were intelligent in their pricing strategy. The 12-month package, the most desirable from Mind

Candy's perspective, was priced at £29.95, just £6 more than the six-month alternative, dangling the carrot of value in front of interested parents.

Furthermore, having begun as a relatively individual experience, Moshimonsters was transformed into a full-blown social network during 2009. Right from the start, the site had possessed the rudiments of a social platform, modelled after Club Penguin, a hugely successful kids' gaming world. Users were greeted with a newsfeed on the homepage, and messages from other players were displayed on a pinboard. But, in one key aspect, the first iteration of the game was singular and lonely: when kids left their houses to roam Moshimonsters' streets, they couldn't see any other users.

Michael realised he needed to rectify this. So, in April 2009, the engineers spent half a day building a feature that would enable users to see other users' monsters as they roamed their virtual neighbourhood, giving the sense that you were sharing your online world with others. The names of users who were logged in, or had recently logged in, were also displayed on a noticeboard.

The number of friend requests on Moshimonsters jumped 10-fold within hours of this new community feature going live. Furthermore, the new feature created a real 'fad factor' around the game; kids would join simply because their friends were on it. Children who were too young to use mainstream sites such as Facebook now had a means to message their friends, and Moshimonsters established itself as a secure social network for kids.

Moshimonsters staff hard at work in the design studio.

The new feature created a real 'fad factor' around the game; kids would join simply because their friends were on it.

As the gaming experience improved, so the PR and publicity campaign began to accelerate. While Michael was keen to focus primarily on product, in spring 2009 Moshimonsters' management team could see the need to advertise the product more fully. They appointed a full-time head of marketing, and in May began advertising in channels such as Google and Facebook, with TV ads following shortly.

Michael now admits he was initially reluctant to ramp up the PR, believing that TV ads were 'incredibly expensive and wasteful', and fiendishly difficult to track. But he was persuaded to spend £10,000 on a weekend advertising campaign on Nickelodeon and other kids' channels. The weekend campaign brought in £60,000, and by 2010 Mind Candy was advertising in 15 countries – establishing itself as a genuinely global phenomenon.

Where are they now?

Since that 2009 explosion, Mind Candy's monsters have conquered the globe with their cuddly charm. Moshimonsters is now active in 150 countries, and the brand is spreading all the time. In January 2012 Mind Candy released a range of miniature figures, Bobble Bots, based on the Moshimonsters characters. There is also a magazine, and the company now sells merchandise in eight countries.

Moshimonsters now has 34 million users signed up worldwide, and Mind Candy expects to make a profit of £62 million in 2012; but one gets the distinct impression that Mind Candy is just getting started.

Explaining Moshimonsters' huge success, Michael explains that, with technology, 'you can create something that literally overnight causes a huge sensation.' The monsters may be make-believe, but their commercial potential is very, very real.

Electronic Arts

Winning the game

Founder: **Trip Hawkins**	
Age of founder: **28**	
Background: **MBA and former Apple Computer executive**	
Founded in: **1982, USA**	
Headquarters: **USA**	
Business type: **Multi-platform games**	

Not many entrepreneurs spend 11 years planning their business's start. But from his first foray into business at age 17, Trip Hawkins knew he wanted to start his own. He just didn't know what it would do. Then, in 1971, he got a glimpse of an early prototype microcomputer at a friend's house, and an idea began to take shape. In the future, he realised, home computers would be commonplace.

From that initial flash of insight, the biggest company in digital gaming would arise. Trip knew it would take time for home computers to catch on, but he began to chart a course that would position him to profit from the coming electronic age.

He chose a date for his business launch: 1982. Just as planned, Trip did start a home-based, one-man business that year. That company became Electronic Arts, which now employs 7,600 people and made a profit of $677 million (£425 million) in 2010. How did it happen? Trip puts it down to a couple of personality traits: persistence and fearlessness.

'I was feeling completely sure of myself and totally confident about what my plans were, and pretty bulletproof', Trip recalls.

The very first game

Trip's interest in games began in childhood – and so did his interest in business. While still a teenage student at Harvard University, he borrowed $5,000 (£3,100) from his father to create a board game centred on his love of sport, AccuStat Football. The money allowed Trip to create several hundred copies of the tabletop game.

The game, although loved by those who played it, was a commercial failure, teaching Trip indelible business lessons that would shape his future plans.

'It was a thorough business experience for me, as I had to design, manufacture, have a marketing plan, and even assemble the product', Trip recalls. 'It helped me realise I was going to be an entrepreneur, but I was also disappointed that I failed. It made me a lot more careful and thoughtful before I started EA.'

At Harvard, Trip graduated with a self-designed degree in strategy and applied game theory, then added a Stanford MBA in 1978. Trip chose his first employer, Apple Computer, deliberately. He had seen the Apple II debut at a computer fair the year before, and wanted to work for a home-computer company.

The Jobs years

In Steve Jobs, Trip found a mentor who would greatly shape his outlook. It was early days at Apple: the company, based in California, had just 50 employees when Trip joined.

Trip's responsibilities at Apple grew over his four years there, but he never lost sight of his primary goal: to develop his business acumen and wait for personal computers (PCs) to become more popular and powerful. From Steve, he'd learned to think of himself as creative and unstoppable.

The time was growing ripe for his start-up. One gaming company, Brøderbund, debuted in 1980. Trip heard from one investor who was interested in funding a game start-up. He worried he was getting behind the curve.

> *In Steve Jobs, Trip found a mentor who would greatly shape his outlook. ... From Steve, he'd learned to think of himself as creative and unstoppable.*

His dream of starting a company had crystallised into what Trip thought of as his 'big idea'. Most software companies, he'd realised, treated developers like serfs instead of fostering their creativity. He wanted to start a game company that would operate like a music label.

'By this time, I had experience working with prima donna software development geniuses and realised these are really creative people', he recalls. 'I began to realise I could work with them as independent artists, and treat them as artists.'

Enter the crocodile

At just this time, Trip read about venture capitalist Don Valentine of Capital Management (which would soon become Sequoia Capital) in an airline magazine. The article said that Don was so intimidating that one young entrepreneur actually fainted in his office during a pitch. His management style was likened to that of a crocodile, lying in wait before rearing up to rip everyone's ideas apart.

While this might have caused most would-be business owners to pitch to someone else, the article prompted Trip to call Don and ask for a meeting.

He admired Don's attitude and thought he could get frank advice from him, which was exactly what Trip wanted. He wasn't afraid of Don's bite.

Knowing Trip's track record at Apple, Don readily agreed to a meeting, and Trip arrived at the venue with some trepidation. He had no written business plan yet for the company he had christened Amazin' Software, and Apple was gearing up to launch the Lisa computer. He thought Don would urge him to fulfill his commitments at Apple and finish his launch work. But that wasn't Don's opinion at all.

'He said I should quit Apple right away', Trip says. 'He offered me free office space, which is like saying, "If you pull this together, I'll want to fund it." It was the encouragement I needed to take the final step.'

Amazin' Software in the hall

Trip quickly wrapped up his work and left Apple in April 1982. Before taking Don up on his offer of free office space, Trip spent several months working from home, refining the business plan. He incorporated the company in May 1982 and funded it initially with $200,000 (£14,000) of his own Apple stock profits.

During this time, Trip worked on learning about the music industry business model he planned to emulate. He flew to Los Angeles after a venture contact introduced him to legendary A&M Records co-founder Jerry Moss. Trip also spoke with a music industry lawyer and got a copy of a recording contract to learn how to structure contracts for his software 'artists'.

While still working from home, Trip employed his first few members of staff. The first was experienced PR man Richard Melmon, whom Trip knew from a stint at Apple. Richard left his job at VisiCorp, maker of the early spreadsheet product VisiCalc, to join the promising company.

'He was by far the most important and highest-ranking guy I hired that year', Trip recalls. 'I hired him because I felt I should have someone older than me around to provide a little adult supervision.'

Richard and Trip would turn out to clash, and their versions of events differ – Richard's biography suggests that he, not Trip, raised the funding money for EA, for instance. In any case, Richard would end up leaving EA after just a few years.

The budding company quickly outgrew its one small room in the back of Don's office suite, with some staff camped at card tables in the hallway.

From Apple, Trip drew product manager Dave Evans, gaming fan Joe Ybarra, and one of the rare women in tech at the time, Pat Marriott. The trio would be Amazin' 'producers', working with talented game designers to create products and bring them to market.

The team was rounded out by an office manager, Stephanie Barrett. In August, the small team took up residence in Don's California offices. The budding company quickly outgrew its one small room in the back of Don's office suite, with some staff camped at card tables in the hallway.

Playing hardball

Trip kept paying the bills: for payroll, equipment, and software development in-house, as well as fees to outside software 'artists'. He had the resources to keep going in this fashion for another year or so but felt he needed to bring in investors to tap their business expertise and accelerate the company's growth.

Several investors were interested, but Trip focused on those he wanted on board, starting with Don, and Ben Rosen from Sevin Rosen Funds, whom he knew from Apple. Others came knocking: Trip recalls picking up the phone at his home in the Portola Valley to find future legend John Doerr, who was then new to Silicon Valley venture capital firm Kleiner Perkins Caufield & Byers.

As he wasn't desperate for the cash, yet, Trip was feeling cocky. Thinking that Don wanted too rich a deal, Trip played the venture capitalists off against each other to get a better valuation for his company, lowering the percentage of Amazin' the venture capitalists' money would buy. In the end, he raised $2 million (£1.25 million) in the first round at the end of 1982, half from Don, with the other half split between Sevin and Kleiner.

Amazin' then moved from Don's office to a small office of their own in October 1982. During the company's short stay there, Trip continued hiring, luring Stanford friend William Bingham ('Bing') Gordon. Other early hires were Tim Mott, David Maynard and Steve Hayes, all from Xerox PARC. Amazin' soon moved to more spacious quarters, still in California, where the company would remain for more than a decade.

Becoming Electronic Arts

Around the time of the move from Don's office, the newly hired team were pushing for a new company name. Some team members disliked the Amazin' moniker. In one early business plan, Trip had used the name SoftArt as an amalgam to convey both software and artistry. But both Trip and Richard Melmon knew Dan Bricklin, founder of VisiCalc maker Software Arts, and thought it best to avoid such a similar name.

Trip wanted to include the word 'Electronic', and suggested it might be called Electronic Artists, in part as a tribute to independent movie studio United Artists, whose model of artist-driven production he sought to emulate. But Hayes reportedly objected, saying that the developers were the artists rather than the staff. Finally, the team settled on Electronic Arts as the new name.

Bad timing

Despite all the years of Trip's planning for his launch, the newly renamed company's timing turned out to be a bit off. The technology needed to play truly full-featured electronic games had arrived, but had not yet been widely adopted by consumers. The dominant game system at the time was an 8-bit Atari console, which offered a puny amount of memory.

Trip knew from the start that he didn't want to create games for the Atari. While waiting for the game console industry to mature, the company would focus on creating games for PCs. This posed its own challenges as the most popular PC of the time, the Commodore 64, did not yet come with an external disk drive. One would be added in late 1983, but at an extra charge that would discourage many home users.

To counter this problem, Trip devised a method that ended up being used in Europe for the company's first game releases: the games were converted to audio signals on a tape cassette. With the help of an A/B adapter cord, the data could then be input to the computer to play the game.

In 1982, EA's producers had released their first games for the Apple II – Hard Hat Mack and Axis Assassin – as well as a few games for the hated Atari 800 console – Pinball Construction Set, Archon, M.U.L.E., and Worms.

In keeping with Trip's recording artist philosophy, each game was packaged like a record album with an eye-catching, graphical cover. This immediately set EA's products apart from competitors, whose packaging was less slick-looking.

Rather than signing a distribution deal with an established company or competitor to get the games into stores, Trip and the entire team set out to meet thousands of independent computer shop owners to sell them, one by one. It was hugely time-consuming, but paid off in new relationships – and enabled a distribution scheme in which there was no middleman so EA kept more of the profits. Of the first group of games, Archon and Pinball Construction Set emerged as the big sellers.

A key game was released in 1984 that would set the course for much of EA's future success. The basketball-themed Dr. J and Larry Bird Go One on One took Trip's recording artist theory one step further, leveraging the name recognition of the two sports stars to sell games. Fans loved the chance to essentially *be* one of their sports idols, and the game went on to be EA's best-selling release for the Apple II.

In keeping with Trip's recording artist philosophy, each game was packaged like a record album with an eye-catching, graphical cover. This immediately set EA's products apart from competitors.

During the scramble of the first few years, Don fulfilled Trip's expectations, offering universally critical feedback and never making a positive comment. In July 1984, he sent Trip an EA budget with two numbers circled: burn rate and cash reserves. 'Two months left!' it said. But Trip knew sales of Dr. J were going to avert a financial crisis.

Trip quickly learned that while he was envisioning the game designers as the prime selling point, gamers were loyal to the game, not the designer – a revelation that would shift the company's marketing focus for good. Sales that first year were $5 million (£3.74 million) – the company was off and running.

Just six months after the first venture capital round, Trip went back and raised $3 million (£2.24 million) more in investor funding, mostly from the same investors. For the second round, with a few products out and several of them shaping up as solid sellers, Trip was able to obtain the funds at a company valuation four times greater than on the first round.

The desert years

As the company was releasing its first games, the hope was that games consoles would soon become a viable platform for EA's games, too. But instead, the games console industry collapsed. Atari's system was dated and the company had failed to plan ahead to release a new, more robust version. Consumers lost interest, causing retailers to stop stocking the games and suspect that electronic games might just be a fad.

Trip remembers the next few years as a time of serious hard work. The company scored successes with more celebrity-driven games, including Jordan vs. Bird: One on One and Earl Weaver Baseball.

By concentrating on games for computers and releasing popular titles, the company was able to bring in $11 million (£8.48 million) in sales in the financial year ending March 1985. EA began to turn a profit in autumn 1984.

'We were profitable', he recalls, 'but we had to be disciplined about how much we spent. We made sure we didn't overstep our bounds.'

In 1988, Trip decided to try international expansion as a means to grow during the gaming industry slump. The company acquired game-creation houses in Australia and France, opened an office in Japan, and in general overspent. Trip remembers the international foray as a 'misadventure' from which the company beat a hasty retreat.

Breakout success

Fortunately, 1988 also saw the release of a game that would prove to be one of the company's biggest franchises. Originally called John Madden Football and later Madden NFL, the game would go on to release annual versions and sell 85 million copies in 2010 alone. Madden would be joined in 1993 by another major sports franchise, FIFA. Together, the brands would drive the success of EA Sports, one of the company's biggest niche brands.

On the heels of the Madden success, EA went public in September 1989, netting $8 million (£4.88 million) for the company and more for its investors. The IPO (initial public offering on the stock market) gave EA a valuation of $84 million (£51.3 million). Sales that year were $63.5 million (£38.8 million), and profits were $4 million (£2.44 million).

Getting Sega on board

As EA was enjoying its successful IPO, a glimmer of hope appeared on the games console horizon. Nintendo had had a successful 8-bit game machine over the previous few years which, like the Atari before it, EA mostly ignored. But now, the more robust 16-bit Sega Genesis console was set for release in America. Trip was determined to turn it into a gold mine.

There was a major problem, though: it wasn't known exactly what machine Sega would bring to the States. EA designers obtained a Japanese Sega console, hoping that the US machine would be identical, and that EA could produce a game that worked on it. One big fear was that Sega might implement a security 'chip' on its games for the US market, a feature Nintendo employed.

In analysing the Sega machine, EA's software designers found that it used the identical 16-bit microprocessor the team was familiar with from its Sun workstations, as well as Apple's Lisa and later models. Taking the gamble that a security chip wouldn't be introduced and torpedo the effort, EA moved forward to reverse-engineer game designs for Sega's console based on the team's knowledge of the microprocessor.

While this was in process, Trip also actively contacted other software design studios to offer EA's help in creating games without Sega's official blessing. At the same time, Sega was calling on Trip to negotiate a licence agreement. But Trip didn't want to pay through the nose for the right to be an official Sega licensee. He put the word out that EA would release its games with or without a licence agreement with Sega.

'I was rope-a-doping them', Trip recalls, 'being really polite, pretending to show some interest – then telling them what I didn't like about their agreement.'

The situation came to a head as May 1990 loomed. EA planned to unveil its Sega games at the Consumer Electronics Show that month. Sega caught wind that EA was setting itself up as an alternative channel for dozens of other Sega game producers. This idea terrified the Japanese firm, and the then-Chairman David Rosen was deployed to get Trip in line.

'Rosen read me the riot act and told me there'd be a big scandal and a lawsuit if we released the games without a licence', Trip says. 'But they were much more willing to make a deal than I realised, because they wanted this problem to go away.'

On the eve of the show, a favourable licensing agreement was finally hammered out after a round-the-clock negotiation session between Trip and Sega's lawyers. Instead of paying the $8 (£4.48) per unit Sega wanted, EA would pay just $0.40 (£0.22). The deal would be a bonanza for both sides – EA's games helped bolster Sega's market share in the USA, and the alliance gave EA a huge market for product at a low fee.

Whereas Nintendo didn't allow any one producer to release more than five games a year, EA was able to introduce 40 games for Sega in the next two years, skyrocketing the company's revenue. Another 23 games would come from independent studios affiliated with EA. Nintendo introduced a 16-bit machine the following year to compete with Sega, and allowed developers to adapt existing games for the new system, opening up another major revenue channel for EA. By the end of 1993, EA's market capitalisation soared to $2 billion (£1.13 billion).

Where are they now?

In 1991, Trip left EA to start a new gaming company, 3DO, but the effort failed. In 2003, Trip founded another multi-platform gaming company, Digital Chocolate, where he is CEO today. The 400-employee company had more than $30 million in 2010 revenue. Its hit games include Millionaire City. The company has had its games downloaded onto mobile devices more than 100 million times, and its online computer games have seen more than 100 million sessions.

EA would continue to dominate its industry for two decades, the only gaming company to enjoy such an unbroken streak of success. The company would go on to introduce many more wildly popular games, including Need for Speed in 1994, and The Sims in 2002, which captivated female gamers and spawned many sequels. The company also grew through many acquisitions, including the 2011 purchase of online game hit studio PopCap Games for $750 million (£486 million).

Towards the end of 2011, EA's history of linking with well-known celebrities and brands continued with the launch of Star Wars: The Old Republic, a MMOG (massively multiplayer online game) in which players engage in battles on planets featured in the Star Wars movies.

zynga

Zynga

Creating internet treasure

Founder: **Mark Pincus (shown)** **(founding team: Eric Schiermeyer, Justin Waldron, Michael Luxton, Steve Schoettler and Andrew Trader)**	
Age of founder: **41**	
Background: **Three previous start-ups: FreeLoader, Support.com and Tribe.net**	
Founded in: **2007, USA**	
Headquarters: **California, USA**	
Business type: **Online social gaming**	

F**ew start-ups are valued at $3 billion** (£1.92 billion) two years after they open the doors. But that's what happened at social gaming company Zynga. The company's seemingly overnight success was possible in part because its founder made his mistakes at earlier start-ups, before coming up with an idea that would transform the gaming industry.

Portrait of a serial entrepreneur

From early on, Mark Pincus set his sights on business success. He graduated in 1988 from the University of Pennsylvania's Wharton Business School, and followed this with a Harvard MBA in 1993. In between, he had a fitful career in finance, going through four jobs in five years.

Employers included investment firm Lazard Freres, consultancy Bain & Company, and Tele-Communications Inc. (now AT&T Capital), where he worked under telecom legend John Malone. Mark recalls that he was asked to leave his Bain internship midway through the summer.

'I realised I didn't have a career working in anyone else's company', Mark recalled at an entrepreneur event in 2009.

In 1995, he started FreeLoader, a push-technology news service that delivered customer-selected feeds. His co-founder was Sunil Paul, a technology developer who left $1 million (£633,000) in unvested stock options on the table at his former employer, America Online. Thanks in part to a media blitz Mark orchestrated, FreeLoader quickly became well known.

Sunil's gamble paid off: in less than a year, the company was acquired for $38 million (£24.3 million). Buyer Individual Inc. had initially offered $25 million (£16 million), but Mark had turned it down.

While the financial windfall was incredible, Mark regretted that his short FreeLoader ownership didn't let him figure out the company's true goals. He also had the unhappy experience of working briefly for Individual after the sale. The new owner quickly lost interest and shut down FreeLoader in 1997.

'I realised I didn't have a career working in anyone else's company', Mark recalled at an entrepreneur event in 2009.

Later the same year, together with Stanford graduates Cadir Lee and Scott Dale, Mark founded Support.com, which offered computer tech support. Support.com went public at the height of the dot-com boom in 2000 and was renamed SupportSoft Inc.

The problem? Mark wasn't interested in tech support. And once again, he had lost control, retaining just 15% ownership after the IPO (initial public offering). He described Support.com's founding as almost accidental: 'Before I knew it, I was the CEO of a large, boring tech-support company.'

Breaking away in early 2003, Mark co-founded Tribe Networks Inc., one of the first social media platforms. Tribe was enabled by a key patent for social network technology, purchased for $700,000 (£428,000) jointly by Mark and Reid Hoffman, founder of LinkedIn. But the platform didn't catch on. In March 2007, Tribe was sold to an unlikely partner: telecom/networking giant Cisco Systems Inc. Mark and co-founder Paul Martino ended up getting fired from their own start-up, recalls Paul, who later became managing partner at investment firm Bullpen Capital.

After Tribe, Mark later recalled, 'I stepped back and was more thoughtful. I was around 40. I realised I wanted to start a consumer internet service that would be around for a long time, and that really mattered. I set my goals high and really wanted to start a company that would be profitable early and not controlled by investors.'

Ironically, both those goals would prove challenging in his next venture. Though Mark had publicly derided other companies that took too much money from investors, his next start-up would raise more venture capital than almost any other – a cool $1 billion (£500 million).

Game on

Searching for the next big consumer internet idea, Mark was drawn to the world of online gaming. People were playing games online in 2006, especially casino games such as poker. But they could play only against the computer or unidentified individuals.

At the time, Facebook had 50 million members. Mark observed that the most common activity on Facebook was viewing friends' photos. Beyond that and writing updates, there wasn't much to *do*. To address the problem, Facebook opened up its site to outside developers in 2007, so that new programs could be designed for the platform.

Mark saw his opportunity. His new start-up's software would let users play against their Facebook friends. While most social networks aimed to help people make new connections online, his would offer a new way to connect with *people you already knew*.

The initial goal was to create and launch one social game. Mark decided that it would be easier and faster to create a socialised version of a poker game than to create a new game from scratch. It would also be easier to get Facebook users to try a variation on a familiar game. This would turn out to be a canny move; while competitors slaved to create custom games, Mark's start-up would be quick out of the blocks.

A non-techie himself, Mark began tapping his extensive professional network to find experienced programmers who could create and operate the game. Paul recalls Mark asking him and another Tribe co-founder, Chris Law, to meet him for lunch at a coffee shop to discuss his start-up plans.

While Paul and Chris awaited Mark's arrival, a horrific car crash took place outside. Paul rushed out to find Mark emerging from a wrecked BMW he'd been test-driving. The salesman screamed at the other vehicle's driver, who had run a red light. But Mark strolled into the restaurant clad in his usual work attire – a hoodie and jeans – and sat down as if nothing had happened.

'He was literally almost killed', Paul recalls. 'I say, "Do you want to go to the hospital?" and he says, "No, I want to tell you about this start-up idea I have. Could you hire me a dude to write a poker app?"'

Paul and Chris loved Mark's social game idea. Chris had done research at Tribe on Korean social network sites that sold virtual 'gifts' users could give to friends. Mark's social games would offer a platform for selling such virtual goods.

Another new aspect: unlike traditional online and console games, where players paid to purchase a game, these games would be free. Only players who chose to purchase upgrades or virtual items would pay.

The initial goal was to create and launch one social game. Mark decided it would be easier and faster to create a socialised version of a poker game than create a new game from scratch. This would turn out to be a canny move.

At first, Mark funded the new venture himself. The founding team consisted of Eric Schiermeyer, Michael Luxton, Steve Schoettler, Andrew Trader and Justin Waldron. Nineteen-year-old Justin was a computer science student at the University of Connecticut, whom Eric recruited to serve as lead engineer.

Michael and Eric came from eUniverse (now Intermix Media). Andrew had been the CEO of Utah Street Networks, which operated Tribe.net. Server engineer Steve had worked with Mark on a short-lived project after Tribe sold. Other key early recruitments were Mark's co-founders from Support. com, Scott Dale and Cadir Lee, as well as Kyle Stewart, another Support. com veteran.

On Skype ... and in a garage

In June 2007, work began on Texas HoldEm Poker (later known as Zynga Poker). The team worked remotely for several months, staying in touch via Skype and AOL Instant Messenger. Justin was on his summer holiday from university and living in Connecticut, while Mark and the rest of the team were scattered in various Californian locations. Steve was working out of a converted-garage home office, and sometimes Michael – who lived in nearby Sunnyvale – would join him there. But for the most part, it was a virtual team.

Zynga's Texas HoldEm was launched on Facebook that autumn. Facebook users took to the game quickly. Paul recalls that within a few months Mark told him Zynga was pulling in $1 million (£630,000) monthly. A key innovative feature of the game platform was a 'social bar' that showed users what other games their friends played.

Seeing encouraging initial results, the team took an office at the Chip Factory, an office building Mark owned in San Francisco. The staff grew quickly to 27, as Zynga hired more game developers and introduced socialised versions of other games, including blackjack, and its own versions of popular tabletop games Risk, Boggle and Battleship.

'For me it wasn't the initial numbers that convinced me [to move to San Francisco]', Justin later wrote, 'but the feeling that what we had created was fundamentally different than what gaming had been, and would therefore be completely disruptive. It felt like the first time you used Facebook or any other product that you now can't imagine living without.'

Going to the dog

As Mark sought investors for the growing business, there was a problem: the start-up had yet to be incorporated and was operating informally as Presidio Media. It was time to solidify the business structure and pick a name to brand the business.

Mark looked no further than his beloved pet American bulldog, Zinga, who accompanied Mark nearly everywhere. The name comes from an African word for a beautiful female warrior. The domain name Zinga.com was already taken, so with a spelling change, the name became Zynga in February 2008. Zinga's profile would also become the company logo.

Zynga's logo features the profile of Mark's beloved pet American bulldog, Zinga.

Ka-ching + a light bulb

The combination of Mark's previous start-up track record and the poker game's early success made pitching to investors easy. In February 2008, Zynga raised $10 million (£5.39 million) in first-round financing, with the round led by Union Square Ventures. Participants included Paul Martino, LinkedIn's Reid Hoffman, MTV founder Bob Pittman, Facebook investor Peter Thiel, and Foundry Group.

One possible investor that didn't get on board was gaming industry leader Electronic Arts. Paul says that Mark was nearly laughed out of the building. The games were all *free*?

'A lot of people didn't believe it – that you could build a company with that as a revenue model', recalls Steve, who's now founder of education start-up Junyo. 'But we knew we were on to something.'

There was an upside to the EA meeting – Mark met EA executive William 'Bing' Gordon, who immediately grasped how social gaming would shake up the industry. William told Mark his goal should be to create an internet treasure – the sort of company that provides something so useful, customers can hardly remember life without it. A Google. A Blackberry. A Facebook. Mark realised that was exactly what he wanted to do with Zynga.

Doubling down on revenue

In those early days, Steve recalls, 'We weren't concerned with revenue. We were still working on trying to reach more users and find out ways to make the game fun, so they'd stay and keep playing.'

One possible investor that didn't get on board was gaming industry leader Electronic Arts. ... The games were all free?

To bring in some income during this initial ramp-up, Mark essentially sold Texas HoldEm's traffic to other developers, who placed ads on the pages where Zynga's Facebook games ran.

If players clicked on the ads, Zynga received a commission. The company collected just under $700,000 (£350,000) in revenue in 2007 this way. As Zynga's traffic grew, this income stream became a rushing river.

By early 2008, Zynga reported that its audience was clicking the ads 50,000 times a day, with Zynga pocketing $0.50 (£0.27) each time. Then, in March 2008, Zynga introduced the ability to buy virtual poker chips. To Mark's surprise, some players spent $20 (£10.80) at a time.

Though fewer than 5% of players would spend real dollars to purchase virtual goods, the small purchases added up. Sales in 2008 leapt to $19.4 million (£10.5 million). The company lost more than $22 million for the year (£11.9 million), though, as it invested in more staff and Facebook ads to lure new players.

In July 2008, Zynga would raise $29 million (£15.6 million) more in venture capital and add $15.8 million (£8.5 million) more in November. The funding would help Zynga make a key purchase: YoVille, a game studio whose eponymous game would prove a major franchise for Zynga.

From the mafia to a farm

That autumn, Zynga had its first big success with an original game. In Mafia Wars, players fought others as they built a mafia crew. Mafia Wars spawned a sequel, grew to eight million monthly users and helped Zynga become the top Facebook app developer in April 2009. The company also moved on to other platforms with its first iPhone release, Live Poker. With business booming, Zynga moved to larger offices just a few streets away from the Chip Factory.

Though fewer than 5% of players would spend real dollars to purchase virtual goods, the small purchases added up.

As the venture capital flowed in, Mark took careful steps to avoid diluting his ownership. He created private stock shares with stronger voting power than the common shares, ultimately retaining nearly 40% ownership of the company.

The next two years would see mind-boggling revenue growth. Sales shot up more than sixfold in 2009 to over $121 million (£77.3 million), and would similarly skyrocket to nearly $600 million (£388 million) in 2010. But it would take until 2010 to achieve Mark's second big goal: profits.

Mafia Wars was Zynga's first original game hit.

Zynga values

Zynga had a clear approach in running the business: measure and analyse everything. Interviewed for an online Wharton journal, Andrew recalled: 'I believe the differentiator between Zynga and a lot of our competitors [was] the ability to test, analyse, optimise [and] repeat that cycle. Everybody at Zynga – developers, product managers, business people, executives, CEO, everybody – had that focus on metrics and transparency, which really did allow us to innovate quickly, test things really, really aggressively and, ultimately, kind of dominate this space ...'

In shaping Zynga's corporate culture, Mark wanted to avoid creating the stifling environment he'd hated at his jobs. He empowered employees with an 'everyone is a CEO' philosophy.

Wanting to pamper his hard-working staff, Mark hired a trainee chef from a nearby culinary school to serve up healthy lunches and dinners. The company offered on-site massage, acupuncture, paid gym memberships and other perks.

Taking their lead from Mark, many employees brought their dogs to work. The company also had no traditional holiday rules. Instead, employees were encouraged to take time off as needed to rejuvenate and avoid burnout.

Doing 'every horrible thing'

The next major game would be a game-changer. In summer 2009, FarmVille was an instant smash, becoming the first Facebook game to reach 10 million daily users. (The ensuing outpouring of status updates from FarmVille players pleading for game items proved so annoying to non-players that Facebook would later change its policy to limit the notices.)

But all was not well. Also in 2009, the pay-per-click advertising revenue model that allowed Zynga to log early revenue became notorious for dodgy ads. Some automatically signed up visitors for monthly charges, for instance, while others had dubious product offers. At one point, the poker game gave users chips if they downloaded an advertiser's toolbar, which then proved difficult to remove.

The scandal was dubbed 'Scamville'. Some players filed a class action lawsuit that would drag on for two years before finally being settled in Zynga's favour.

In a talk given to entrepreneurs at the University of California, Berkeley that year, Mark said, 'I knew that I wanted to control my destiny ... I did every horrible thing in the book to just get revenues right away.'

Coming as it did around the time the Scamville scandal broke, the remark was widely interpreted to mean that Zynga knew and didn't care that some advertisers were shady. But Mark later denied this, saying he simply meant that entrepreneurs should keep their independence and focus on generating

FarmVille was another instant smash for Zynga.

revenue quickly. Whatever he meant, the timing of the comment – filmed and widely circulated on YouTube – couldn't have been worse.

Zynga responded by removing all ads from its platform in November 2009. Ads returned in January 2010, under a more stringent screening process. With the help of a media blitz similar to the one Mark had pulled off at FreeLoader, the company rebuilt its reputation. Mark was a willing promoter, posing dressed up as a farmer to plug FarmVille and playing poker with Zinga.

The company also faced a steady drumbeat of criticism that its games ripped off those of other developers. Disney's Playdom and the independent maker of Mob Wars were among many who sued and settled out of court. For its part, Zynga sued Playdom when seven of its employees defected to the company. Zynga alleged that the ex-workers supplied Playdom with the 'Zynga Playbook', which outlined the company's strategies and plans. This, too, would be quietly settled a year later.

Investors were unconcerned by the legal issues. At the end of 2009, Zynga raised $180 million (£115 million) from a new set of investors including Andreessen Horowitz and Russian mogul Yuri Milner's Digital Sky Technologies. Another investor round from Google and Softbank Capital would pour in $300 million (£194 million) more in June 2010.

As 2010 rolled on, Zynga expanded with new games, new platforms, translations of games into foreign languages, and new geography. The company's first foreign office opened in Bangalore. Zynga launched many new versions of its games, such as FrontierVille and CityVille. The latter, a permutation of the old YoVille game, would become Zynga's most popular game ever.

The company also brought games to Yahoo! and the iPhone. Zynga began allowing corporations to advertise within its games – for instance, convenience store 7-Eleven introduced branded items inside FarmVille, Mafia Wars and YoVille. Branded versions of Zynga games were also unveiled, tied to celebrities such as Lady Gaga and popular movie releases *Rango* and *Megamind*.

As Zynga became more successful, Facebook wanted a bigger cut of the take and wanted Zynga to switch from collecting cash payments to using Facebook Credits. The issue was resolved after a negotiation in May 2010 with the signing of a five-year agreement that saw Zynga switching to Facebook Credits and Facebook gaining a hefty 30% cut of the company's Credits revenue.

Fortunately, Zynga's growth rate was so massive that the effect of the cost hit was almost imperceptible. Sales grew nearly sixfold in 2010 to close to $600 million (£388 million), and Zynga saw its first annual profit of nearly $28 million (£18.1 million).

Where are they now?

In February 2011, Zynga topped $1 billion (£647 billion) in venture capital raised with a massive, $485 million (314 million) investment round that included Morgan Stanley, T. Rowe Price, Fidelity Investments and Kleiner Perkins Caufield & Byers. Five months later, Zynga filed to go public, seeking to raise $1 billion (£647 million). The company's total value was estimated at between $15 billion (£9.71 billion) and $20 billion (£12.9 billion). Revenue in 2011 was close to double the 2010 annual figure.

In late 2011, the company's games had 232 million monthly users, and Zynga owned four of the top five games on Facebook. The company went on an acquisition spree in 2010 and 2011, spending nearly $27 million (£17.5 million) to snap up 14 other game producers including Wonderland Software and Newtoy. To accommodate its growth, the company moved into new offices, expanding to more than 400,000 square feet of office space in San Francisco.

The company also faced down criticism that its business model was too dependent on Facebook. Zynga announced Project Z, a planned stand-alone website where Zynga games could be played. New games were slated, including CastleVille, the company's most lavish game yet, with Hollywood-movie-level graphics and a full orchestral score.

Despite a late-2011 plunge in the US stock markets, Zynga went public in December 2011, raising a cool $1 billion (£647 million) in the biggest tech IPO since Google's back in 2004.

Neon Play

A gaming sensation

Founder: **Oli Christie**	
Age of founder: **39**	
Background: **Copywriter/creative director**	
Founded in: **2010, UK**	
Headquarters: **Cirencester, UK**	
Business type: **Mobile gaming**	

As a student, Oli Christie had a dream: to forge a successful career in the advertising industry. After a slow start in the industry, Oli eventually got his ideal job as a creative director of an online ad agency, where he became increasingly focused on developing simple, addictive Flash games.

When he saw the growing popularity of the iPhone and the opportunities it represented, he took the cue to leave the comfort and prestige of his advertising work and use his knack for creating addictive games to make his fortune on the new platform.

Despite starting with minimal investment and no employees, office or experience, within 20 months Oli had created one of the fastest-growing mobile app developers in the UK, with 60 apps across all platforms and 11 different games that have received more than a million downloads. An example of getting things right in a boom industry, Neon Play's story is one of being in the right place at the right time.

First business

Armed with a degree in psychology and sociology from Exeter University, Oli's aim was to enter the world of advertising as a copywriter, but he found it difficult to break into the industry as a graduate. Instead, he decided to make his own way in the world whilst waiting for an opportunity to come up.

'You should always try and get experience yourself in other people's companies before you start your own. Learn on their behalf rather than making your own expensive mistakes.'

In the early 1990s Oli started his first business, Action Stationery. Action Stationery sold letterheaded paper with 52 different designs featuring famous cartoon characters to various outlets such as Office World. The business really took off, but Oli shut it down after four years as it was not making enough money to survive. 'In hindsight it was a mistake, because I knew nothing about running a business really – I knew nothing about stationery or retail', says Oli. 'But it was a good learning experience in one respect.' Now he believes 'you should always try and get experience yourself in other people's companies before you start your own. Learn on their behalf rather than making your own expensive mistakes.'

Picking himself up after the disappointment of Action Stationery, Oli decided it was time to have another go at entering the advertising industry, starting a job as an account manager at a niche marketing company as a way to get his foot on the rung. However, despite working with increasingly high-profile clients such as Abbey National and the Royal Mail, his desire to write copy remained. He began putting together a portfolio of his own 'stick drawings and headlines' to show to potential employers. Despite the portfolio being 'very shoddy' by Oli's own admission, he managed to land himself a job as a junior copywriter at marketing company Billington Cartmell in 1999.

At Billington Cartmell Oli was responsible for writing the copy on sales promotions, direct mail and advertisements for some major brands and it seemed he had found his dream job at last. 'I absolutely loved it', Oli says of his time there. 'I was writing all the headlines on packs of Hula Hoops and cans of Coke – we were working for some awesome brands. It was an exciting time.'

Despite enjoying the excitement and security of his job as a copywriter, an opportunity soon came along which Oli couldn't refuse. A friend of a friend had started his own online marketing agency, Panlogic, and asked Oli to join the nascent company as Creative Director – a huge promotion. 'The internet was probably responsible for accelerating my career by five to 10 years', says Oli. So, in May 2000, Oli joined the burgeoning company.

Splat the MP

Panlogic started out producing internet banner advertising and website design for its clients, but Oli and his colleagues soon noticed that a new phenomenon – online Flash games – was sweeping the internet, and they saw an opportunity to develop simple, free-to-play games for clients as another form of viral marketing. But before they could offer this service, they needed to learn how to use the technology themselves, so decided to develop a 'test' game to become familiar with the development tools. 'The general election [of 2001] was coming up and we had a brainstorm – and asked "what happens during elections?" One idea was that people chuck eggs at politicians', says Oli. They set about developing a simple game, Splat the MP, set in the Houses of Parliament where the player threw eggs at cut-outs of various MPs and public figures of the time.

'The game went completely and utterly ballistic – I think it ended up being the most viral game of that year.'

The timing of the game's launch was nothing other than serendipitous. On 16 May 2001, hours before they were to release the game, prominent Labour MP John Prescott was involved in an incident in which he punched a protestor who had thrown an egg at him. The Panlogic team spotted an opportunity, and promptly added a John Prescott character to the game, complete with an animated fist punching the screen when the player landed a hit. 'We launched it literally hours after Prescott had punched this guy', remembers Oli. 'The game went completely and utterly ballistic – I ended up being the most viral game of that year.'

By the evening of launch day, Oli and the Panlogic team were appearing on international news outlets around the world, and their game would be played by over 10 million people in the following week. 'It was incredibly fortunate – a case of being in the right place at the right time', says Oli. 'But what it did is it showed us the power of viral.'

The success of Splat the MP gave Panlogic a headline-grabbing platform from which to demonstrate their competence in the world of online games. Soon, they were the leading viral marketing agency in the UK, and Oli was overseeing the development of Flash games for the likes of the BBC and lastminute.com. One of Oli's creations at this time was a game entitled Boring Boring Boring – where the player attempts to throw balls of paper into a bin from varying distances. Later, the iPhone game Paper Toss appeared to liberally 'borrow' nearly all Boring Boring Boring's gameplay elements – something that Oli says he is 'upset but not bitter' about. 'It's good to know that it's become one of the most successful iPhone games of all time', he says of Paper Toss.

Going it alone

During his time at Panlogic, Oli got married and had his first child – and after five years at the company he felt it was time to move closer to home. A fan of the rolling Cotswold hills, Oli was finding it increasingly difficult to juggle a full-time job in London with a wife and child in Gloucestershire. In 2005 he left Panlogic to join locally based email marketing firm Inbox Digital (now renamed 20:20) as their new Creative Director. He brought his nous and expertise in the world of online games into Inbox's repertoire and helped the company usurp his old employers Panlogic as the most successful viral games agency in Europe, overseeing the development of numerous successful 'advergames' for multinational clients such as 3M, Gillette and Panasonic. His growing prestige in the emerging category of viral marketing led to numerous awards, including Best Game in the 2007 NMA Effectiveness awards and Best Viral Campaign in the 2006 YDA awards.

Despite his success and firmly established reputation as an online marketing guru, after six years at Inbox Oli began to spot some deficiencies in the business model. 'When we built a game for a client we were charging them between £20,000 and £50,000', he explains. 'And that was completely capped – whether we got one hit or 10 million hits (and a lot of our games did get 10 million hits), we were never going to earn more than our fee.'

He also saw the rise of a new and exciting platform in the growing smartphone industry – and Apple's offerings in particular. 'When the iPhone came along [in 2007] everyone was reading all these stories about people making a fortune out of very simple, casual games', he recalls. 'I thought to myself "Well, I'm making these simple games – and I'm also working for somebody else, so not getting anything more than my basic salary." So I saw an opportunity to create my own games and sell them myself, and if I sold hundreds or thousands or millions, then I'd get rewarded for that success in the recurring revenue.'

> '*I knew how to make a game and it was just a matter of believing in yourself and going for it.*'

Spurred on by this ambition, Oli took the bold step of leaving his safe post at Inbox in May 2010 to start his own iPhone app development company – a decision he admits was 'absolutely terrifying'. 'My wife had just had our third child, and she obviously wasn't totally over the moon with me quitting a good salary and starting a new company with all the stress that entails', he says. 'But I believed in it – you could see that there was going to be a boom in smartphones and games were going to be a big part of that. I knew how to make a game and it was just a matter of believing in yourself and going for it.'

The first game

Oli founded Neon Play in Spring 2010, with an investment of £40,000 taken from his own savings. It was started in his kitchen, with little more than a book of around 100 ideas for simple, addictive, low-cost mobile games that he had written on holiday. Before the company could get going, however, Oli had to surmount one major obstacle; he had no idea how to actually program a game. 'I'm a complete technophobe, sadly', he admits. 'My skill in games is in the ideas and project management.'

So he put out an advertisement online for a technical director and partner for the young business, describing the job as the 'opportunity of a lifetime'.

Flick Football was the first of many successful games for Neon Play.

He only received one reply, from a developer called Mark Allen, who was working at console giant Midway in the USA but wished, fortuitously, to come back and live in the Cotswolds. Mark had turned down a job at a much larger games company to come and work with Oli, also recognising the huge potential in mobile gaming start-ups. The two got on famously and became business partners. 'I had my small game experience, and he had his big game experience in the console industry, working for Midway and Acclaim and making games such as Crazy Taxi and Mortal Kombat', says Oli. 'It was a perfect mix of skills.'

The pair set out picking an idea for Neon Play's first game from Oli's book. 'It was about April or May 2010, and the World Cup was in June, so we thought "let's do a football game"', he recalls. The idea for the game, Flick Football, was appealing in its simplicity – the user would use their finger to 'flick' a football around a wall of defenders and into a goal.

Soon into development, Oli and Mark realised such a game would require more skills than the pair of them possessed and they recruited a team of five freelancers to work on various aspects – a designer who took care of the look and feel of the game menus, two 3D experts who modelled the stadium and the animations of the footballers, an audio technician who worked on the game sounds and a commentator to provide the in-game voice-overs. 'Mark and I were in my kitchen and all the freelancers were

Oli with his ever-expanding current team at Neon Play.

working remotely, so it was all by phone and email', he explains. 'It was quite tricky to co-ordinate, but we managed it in the end.'

Flick Football was released on the iPhone App Store in June for an initial price of 59p (of which 70% went to the company with the other 30% going to Apple and Google), with a free Lite version also released to entice consumers to buy the full game. Soon after launch, it became apparent that Oli's remarkable knack for being in the right place at the right time would reappear. The world was in the grip of World Cup fever, and Flick Football's simple, addictive gameplay and appealing design aesthetic was perfectly placed to take advantage of this. Straight from release, Flick Football shot up the charts into the top 10 paid apps on the Apple App Store globally, and Neon Play was already in profit within a few weeks. 'It was the perfect storm, really', admits Oli.

The success of Flick Football enabled Neon Play to immediately hire two more staff (another programmer and an artist/3D modeller) and move into their first office, a small rented room in the local town of Cirencester. Neon Play now had a real development team, with Oli overseeing the project management and taking care of the marketing and in-game copy.

Bringing home the bacon

Despite the success of their first app, in the first few months Oli pursued a business model with a healthy dose of realism, not wishing to rely entirely on their own offerings in case the follow-ups to Flick Football were less successful. One additional source of revenue in the early days was client work, making branded apps that the company was paid a flat fee for; similar to what he had been doing at Inbox and Panlogic. 'I didn't really want to do it, because I'd spent 20 years working for clients and I was a bit sick of it, to be honest', he admits. 'But the client and agency work did help pay the bills in the initial months.'

Another opportunity to bring in revenue that Oli spotted was licensed children's games – he saw potential in the children's market, especially on the newly released iPad, and Neon Play set about approaching rights holders to obtain licences for children's shows on a revenue share model. Two franchises have enjoyed particular success – Cartoon Networks' *Ben 10* and Channel 5's *Little Princess*, and Oli says it wasn't hard to convince these relatively big names to partner up with Neon Play. 'I think my viral games experience and our mobile games success and distribution platform made us a logical partner for these big companies', he explains. 'They really seemed to want to work with us.'

The 10 billion dollar question

One of the company's nine offerings at the beginning of 2011 was Paper Glider, another game with a simple but effective premise. The user would swipe the screen to send a paper plane into flight and had to keep it in the air as long as possible.

Paper Glider was a runaway success for Neon Play, charting at number one on the UK app sales chart and number two in the USA at the beginning of 2011. But another piece of astounding good luck helped this success turn stratospheric. On 22 January 2011, Oli received a call from an Apple employee informing him that that morning, Gail Davies of Kent had downloaded Paper Glider – making it Apple's 10 billionth download from the App Store. The lucky downloader received a $10,000 (£6,200) iTunes gift card, and Oli and his company reaped the rewards of the enormous media coverage. 'We'd peaked at the perfect time in the charts anyway', he says, 'but what it did was help put Neon Play on the map – suddenly we were on global news, because obviously it was a big news story for Apple to have reached that milestone.'

Oli received a call from an Apple employee informing him that that morning, Gail Davies of Kent had downloaded Paper Glider – making it Apple's 10 billionth download from the App Store.

The company wasted no time in exploiting this fortune, taking advantage of the press and TV coverage to full effect and expanding the range of Paper Glider games, developing new offerings such as Paper Glider Para Drop, Paper Glider Bomber and Paper Glider Crazy Copter. 'The Paper Glider game series have had 13 million downloads between them; it's been our most successful IP', says Oli. 'We got very lucky.'

In November 2010, Neon Play began experimenting with the latest trend in the industry, beginning to move their offerings from a paid to a 'freemium'

Paper Glider took Neon Play to a new level in the gaming world.

model – where the user downloads the application for free but is given the option of paying for in-game upgrades or new features. 'What [freemium] enables us to do is to break down the barriers to entry for people to play it, and then within the game there's advertising, which helps us to get some revenue, but also in-app purchases to keep people playing', explains Oli.

Neon Play is constantly changing its business model to adapt to the rapidly shifting needs of the industry.

They have recently branched out into releasing games for Android devices, a move which comes with its own unique challenges for the company. 'The classic Android user is not somebody who wants to pay for stuff; they're more freebie merchants, so there's a challenge from a monetisation point of view', Oli says. 'There's also the issue of the fragmentation of the market, because there are so many different handsets and app stores – from a developer's point of view it's a bit of a nightmare really.'

But Neon Play is constantly changing its business model to adapt to the rapidly shifting needs of the industry. Oli says the studio's relatively small size has helped them in this regard. 'If we do a game, and halfway through we think "you know what, this isn't much fun" we can bin it very easily', he explains. 'Because we're smaller, we can change and pivot more quickly as a company – it's like moving a speedboat as opposed to an oil tanker.'

Where are they now?

Neon Play continues to enjoy success, with the company hitting the milestone of 30 million downloads across all their apps in 2012 – a fantastic achievement over just 20 months of existence. They have expanded their operation to 15 employees and have recently moved into a stunning new open-plan studio in Cirencester. The company's success has not gone unnoticed by the industry, and Neon Play won 10 industry awards in its first 20 months. Oli himself picked up the gong of the Chamber of Commerce's Entrepreneur of the Year 2011 and Neon Play became the Start-up of the Year in the Nectar Business Awards.

Neon Play also has plans to eventually become a publishing as well as a development company, using their own exposure and loyal network of users to help developers launch their own games. One such game, Jumbled, has already been released; but Oli admits the process is one in which they are taking 'baby steps'. 'Our main focus is creating our own games', he says. 'Because we retain 100% of the revenue. We're not pushing it too hard until we become a bit bigger.'

One other thing Oli has learned is the value that PR can give to a small company. 'It's been massive', he admits. 'I think we're lucky that we're in a boom industry so people want to know about us; but we've always been very conscious that through PR you can get a lot of cheap and often free exposure and that has really helped us grow.'

Pixar

Doing the impossible

Founders:	**Ed Catmull, John Lasseter and Steve Jobs**
Age of founders:	**41, 29 and 30**
Background:	**Computer graphics PhD, Disney animator and Apple computer founder**
Founded in:	**1986, USA**
Headquarters:	**California, USA**
Business type:	**Computer-animated motion pictures**

At first glance, **Pixar seems an almost magically** successful company. It's turned out an unprecedented, unbroken string of hit animated movies: *Toy Story, A Bug's Life, Toy Story 2, Monsters Inc., Finding Nemo, The Incredibles, Cars* and many more. It's hard to imagine, but the company that is now Hollywood's most reliable mega hit factory faced a gruelling 10-year climb to success.

Pixar's founders faced a daunting obstacle: when the company started, their dream – to create a full-length, animated feature entirely on the computer – was simply impossible. *The technology did not yet exist.* It took a few strokes of luck, a very generous benefactor and the combined talents of two of the founders to keep the company alive and to build the technology needed to make the first computer animated film.

Computer graphics meet animation

Pixar grew out of a division of *Star Wars* creator George Lucas's Lucasfilm production company. An early employee of the Computer Division was Ed Catmull, a computer graphics enthusiast and 1974 PhD graduate of New York Institute of Technology, then the cutting-edge source for advances in the field. Ed was excited by computer graphics' potential for use in animation.

In the early 1980s, the Division worked on solving some of the technical challenges of animating objects on the computer, such as eliminating the jagged edges of computer-mapped objects, making realistic shadows and creating lifelike 'motion blur' as objects pass across the screen. There were hardware problems, too, as computers didn't yet have the power and speed required to quickly process or 'render' images. The Division developed useful tools for conquering these problems, including the software Renderman, which quickly became the industry standard.

Ed was looking for an animator who would bring the new tools to life. At the same time, a Disney animator was looking for a more visionary company where he could explore computer animation.

John Lasseter had wanted to be a Disney animator from childhood, and studied under the studio's top animators at California Institute of the Arts, where he won two student Academy Awards. He was quickly hired by Disney and worked on films including *The Fox and the Hound*, but was frustrated in his efforts to sell the tradition-bound studio on the merits of three-dimensional computer animation. Minutes after pitching to the then-studio head Ron Miller his idea for a 3D animated version of the popular children's book *The Brave Little Toaster*, John was fired.

While John was devastated, this was great news to Ed, who had seen John's short film work at computer graphics conferences. The two ran into each other at a conference aboard the *Queen Mary* in California, and Ed immediately asked John to do a freelance project for Lucasfilm. By 1984 John was working full-time for the Division.

Ed was looking for an animator who would bring the new tools to life. At the same time, a Disney animator was looking for a more visionary company where he could explore computer animation.

At first, John found Lucasfilm an intimidating place. 'I mean, there I was, surrounded by all these PhDs who had basically invented computer animation', John relates in *To Infinity and Beyond! The Story of Pixar Animation Studios*. 'But then I realised they couldn't bring a character to life with personality and emotion through pure movement like I could.'

Though the animators in the Division were considered less important than the main hardware and software teams and were installed in offices down a back hallway, they were kept on because their work helped demonstrate the Division's tools to other animators. At 1984's SIGGRAPH computer graphics conference, John made a big impact with his first work for Lucasfilm, a one-minute computer-animated short featuring a bumblebee, *Andre and Wally B*. The work was made possible by a new high-speed computer the Division had developed that was designed for computer animation and offered more rendering speed.

With the computer's creation, the need for a name arose. In a move emblematic of the company culture Pixar would develop, the name chosen was a collaboration. Division co-head Alvy Ray Smith, who'd grown up in New Mexico and had learned that Spanish infinitive verbs often end in '-er', suggested 'Pixer', as a cool way of saying 'pixel-maker'. Others countered that an '-ar' ending would sound more high-tech, and so it became the Pixar Image Computer. The name would soon serve as the company's moniker as well.

Time to go

While the Division had some small success selling the Pixar computer to customers such as film studios and medical imaging firms, it faced an uncertain future. Two of its best products, EditDroid and SoundDroid, which broke ground in editing film and sound, had been spun off and were no longer generating income for the Division.

A tense two years followed the SIGGRAPH success, during which the Division faced repeated threats of shutdown. Ed fended off many attempts by Lucasfilm to fire key employees. He sensed it was important to keep his team together and maintain the trust he'd built.

But George Lucas was growing increasingly uninterested in overseeing a technology company where the technology was still far from commercially viable. He sensed a large capital investment would be needed for the Division's leaders to achieve their ultimate goals. He also didn't want to run a hardware company. Lucas wanted to sell.

Ed fended off many attempts by Lucasfilm to fire key employees. He sensed it was important to keep his team together and maintain the trust he'd built.

Alvy and Ed realised they needed to learn how to run the Division as a stand-alone business. The pair headed off to a local bookshop, purchased a 'how to start a business' book and wrote a business plan for Pixar, envisioning a 40-person company. Now, all they needed was an investor willing to pay Lucasfilm's asking price: $15 million (£11.6 million) plus another $15 million in funding for the new company.

Enter Steve Jobs

Time dragged on, and no buyer was materialising to buy Pixar. There was one bright spark, though: Apple Computer employee Alan Kay, who had attended the University of Utah with Ed, heard about the Division's sale. He thought his boss, tech-wunderkind Steve Jobs, might find Pixar interesting.

Steve did. Apple was known for its groundbreaking 2D computer graphics. Initially, Steve envisioned that Apple would buy Pixar and apply the team's talents to improving computer graphics. Smith and Ed declined the offer, as they wanted to continue towards their goal of using computer graphics for animated film. Turning down an apparent saviour for their financial woes was a controversial move among Division staff that 'nearly tore us apart', Ed recalled.

As it turned out, Steve was in a power struggle with the then-Apple CEO John Sculley over low sales of the first Macintosh computer – a struggle he would ultimately lose. After Steve got the axe in spring 1985, he reconsidered Pixar's goals. Seeing the animation work the team had done, Steve was converted to their mission of creating computer-animated films.

'I ended up buying into that dream both spiritually and financially', he recalled a bit ruefully in the documentary *The Pixar Story*.

He contacted Lucasfilm again, with a plan to spin Pixar out on its own. While Pixar hung by a thread at Lucasfilm, the negotiations dragged on, leaving the team to agonise over whether Pixar had a future. It took until February 1986 to finally reach a deal.

> After Steve got the axe in spring 1985, he reconsidered Pixar's goals. Seeing the animation work the team had done, Steve was converted to their mission of creating computer-animated films.

With no other buyers on the horizon, Steve snapped up Pixar for a relative steal: $5 million (£3.41 million) to Lucasfilm and another $5 million in guaranteed funding for the new company. At last, Pixar had won independence and fresh funding with which to drive toward its goal of creating feature films.

The long climb

Steve might have hesitated if he had known it would be nearly a decade from the day he signed the deal until Pixar would become financially self-sustaining.

If $5 million sounds like a lot of money, it went fast at the highly technology-reliant new film production studio. Pixar needed to both hire top animators and break new technical ground to develop the ability to create a realistic-looking, feature-length film entirely on the computer. The team was soon scrambling for ways to bring in revenue.

Pixar eventually moved from Lucasfilm's headquarters to their own office nearby. The building quickly acquired a look that was a cross between a college dorm and an acid trip. Animators each decorated their cubicles in themes that suited them – one looked like a wooden clubhouse, another an opium den. Workers rode scooters and see-saws in the halls, and generally let creativity run free.

As at Lucasfilm, there was some success selling the Pixar computer, but the audience was limited. Pixar bundled the computer with software and sold it as CAPS: the Computer Animation Production System. Disney bought the system, which brought breakthrough effects to *Beauty and the Beast*, the first animated feature to be nominated for a regular Best Picture Academy Award.

Pixar continued to grab attention for its breakthroughs. Its next was a computer-animated short film, *Luxo Jr.*, directed by John, in which an amazingly lifelike desk lamp and a smaller 'child' lamp play with a ball. Computing power was so limited that a plain black backdrop was used for the short. Nonetheless, the film played to a standing ovation at SIGGRAPH, and playful Luxo would become the Pixar symbol.

This was great for Pixar's reputation, but still didn't pay many bills. Only 120 computers had been sold by 1988, and Steve was applying pressure to make the company profitable. Budgets were repeatedly trimmed.

'He put us through a lot of pain', Alvy Ray Smith recalled. 'But, at the same time, he was unwilling to let the company go bankrupt.'

Going commercial

While Pixar continued to make successful short films, the company turned to a more lucrative art form to bring in more cash: TV adverts. The first ad, 'Wake Up', was for Tropicana orange juice. The team became known for its skill in creating animated characters for adverts, including a boxing bottle of Listerine. John won a Clio award, the ad industry's Oscar, for 'Conga', an ad that featured gummy Life Savers (a brand of American sweets) dancing in a nightclub.

Recruited for the advertising effort were two animators who would later direct films for Pixar, Andrew Stanton and Pete Docter. When Andrew arrived he had literally never touched a computer before. He was a quick learner though, and soon created a computer-animated Trident chewing gum ad in which a spearmint-leaf singer sang at a cabaret piano.

Goodbye, hardware

The advertising side did well financially, but the huge cost of hardware and software development was crushing the company. The company had grown to 140 employees. At the same time, the CAPS system needed ongoing support to maintain Pixar's good relations with Disney.

The studio was taking note of Pixar's progress, and after each short film John would get a call asking him to quit and come back to work for Disney. That John kept turning Disney down bolstered morale greatly at Pixar. Even though Pixar constantly teetered on the brink of financial collapse, John chose it over the security of the big studio.

When local hardware firm Vicom Systems offered to buy the Pixar Image Computer and CAPS system, Ed knew it was a major turning point. He felt strongly that the costs on the hardware side would prove fatal to the company and that both sides of the business would fare better separately. The sale was made and Pixar shrank back to 50 employees, greatly lessening its overheads.

Most of Pixar's focus was on making short films and commercials. One of those shorts, *Tin Toy*, about a wind-up toy, triggered a fateful comment from Disney animator Joe Ranft, who had worked on *Beauty and the Beast*.

Seeing the film with John at a 1988 Dutch animation festival, John recalls Joe's enthusiasm for the concept: that toys could be alive. Joe thought that many more stories could be told this way. And the wheels started to turn in John's head about doing just that – telling a new, bigger story about toys.

'I'll always be grateful to Joe for seeing the larger potential in *Tin Toy*', John says in *To Infinity*. 'Who knows if I would have looked at it as a door to a bigger world if it hadn't been for him?'

Shortly afterward, Disney upped the ante with John. After a shareholder revolt, Disney's leadership changed and Walt Disney's nephew Roy Disney was now in charge. If the studio couldn't hire John back, Roy reasoned, they would partner with Pixar to produce a computer-animated film.

Steve served as Pixar's negotiator, hammering out a three-picture deal in 1991 with Disney chairman Jeffrey Katzenberg. Pixar would produce, while Disney would promote and distribute. The terms were less than stellar, but

Pixar had the machinery in place at last to make and distribute their first feature.

It would take four long years for that first picture to make it to the screen.

'It took us a long time to build the technical foundation', Steve commented in an interview shortly after the release of *Toy Story*. 'We were pioneering every step of the way.'

The making, and remaking, of *Toy Story*

The task facing Pixar's animation staff was a daunting one. The team estimated it would take 100 early '90s supercomputers two years to render all the animation needed for a computer-generated feature film. As it turned out, the production took so long that more powerful computers became available – but rendering the film still took a full year.

'It took us a long time to build the technical foundation', Steve commented in an interview shortly after the release of Toy Story. 'We were pioneering every step of the way.'

John soon discarded the idea of building the feature around the star of *Tin Toy*, and he developed an entirely new storyline featuring a cowboy, Woody Pride and a modern spaceman, Buzz Lightyear. Later, Woody and Buzz both became 12-inch dolls so that they fit together better onscreen. The jealousy between old and new toys was at the heart of the film.

But as production proceeded, Disney's Jeffrey Katzenberg carefully watched its progress and issued copious notes. The story went through rafts of revisions as Jeffrey pushed to make the characters more 'edgy', more adult. In particular, Woody became an increasingly nasty character. John knew he was going down the wrong road when actor Tom Hanks, who was voicing Woody, noted that he rarely got to play baddies.

Finally, a year into production, Pixar brought its assembled reels to Disney for a screening. The event became known at Pixar as 'the black day'.

The film was a disaster. It wasn't funny. It didn't have the heart that had won renown for John's short films.

Disney wanted to halt production, lay off most of the Pixar team, and move a few key Pixar animators to its own California headquarters to rework the film under close supervision. In John's view, this was to be avoided at all costs. John begged Disney for two weeks in which to write a new storyline and prove they could complete a winning film.

Energised by the reprieve, Pixar employees worked around the clock to recapture the fun and joy they originally saw in the *Toy Story* idea. Woody became a far more likeable character, and the interplay between the toys crackled with jokes again.

Incredibly, within the scant two weeks granted them, Pixar completely remade the entire first third of the movie. Impressed with the new version, Disney reversed its decision: production was back on.

As the story continued to be animated, Ed's technical team faced the daunting task of fully animating 80 minutes of film. Previously, the most computer animation in a film had been 10 minutes of dinosaurs in *Jurassic Park*. Rapidly, the team constructed programs that would allow networked computers to work together to speed up the rendering process.

In all, Steve would invest a staggering $55 million (£36.6 million) in Pixar prior to *Toy Story*'s release. The company would probably have faced extinction without his commitment, John recalled in a Facebook page tribute the week of Steve's death in October 2011: 'He saw the potential of what Pixar could be before the rest of us, and beyond what anyone ever imagined … Steve took a chance on us and believed in our crazy dream of making computer-animated films.'

As Pixar readied *Toy Story* for release, there was a huge question mark hanging over the project: what would audiences used to 2D animation think? Would they take to Pixar's computer-generated toys? The first preview Disney held for the film while it was still in process got the lowest scores in the company's history. However, a later screening of the nearly completed film received high marks.

'He saw the potential of what Pixar could be before the rest of us, and beyond what anyone ever imagined', John wrote. 'Steve took a chance on us and believed in our crazy dream of making computer-animated films.'

The fears proved unfounded. *Toy Story* opened in November 1995 and was an instant smash. It would go on to gross more than $360 million (£228 million) and spawn two sequels that would each gross even more. The movie won a Special Achievement Oscar as the first ever computer-animated film.

Unfortunately, Pixar didn't benefit much from *Toy Story*'s success. In particular, its agreement with Disney left Pixar with little participation in the lucrative merchandising associated with *Toy Story*. So the millions of Woody and Buzz toys sold did not enrich Pixar's coffers. But Steve was thinking ahead about this, and had a plan to prevent Pixar from missing out on this revenue in future.

The IPO

Confident that *Toy Story* would be a success, Steve began pushing during late production for the company to do a public offering. John thought the idea crazy, thinking it would be better to wait until Pixar had two successful films under its belt. But Steve's logic was that to better their deal with Disney, the company would have to put up half the production money for future films.

To do that would take big money. Steve was at the limit of what he could contribute. Pixar needed to go public to get more capital.

In a high-risk strategy, Steve timed the IPO (initial public offering on the stock market) to debut the same week as *Toy Story*'s release. But with the film's success, Pixar's IPO was the largest of 1995, raising $140 million (£88.7 million). With the IPO, Pixar changed its name to Pixar Animation Studios, signaling that its entire focus would be on animation going forward. With the IPO cash in hand, Pixar renegotiated its Disney deal, obtaining a 50% share of merchandising on future films.

Where are they now?

With each successive film, Pixar broke new ground in animation and it became known for developing moving, unique storylines that enthralled audiences. From animating hundreds of insects in huge crowd scenes for A Bug's Life *to creating animated fur in* Monsters Inc., *and realistic fabric and human hair for* The Incredibles, *Pixar's* team kept breaking the mould. Pixar films have won six Best Animated Feature Oscars.

Pixar's deal with Disney had been extended through the years but was coming to an end in 2005, prompting a re-evaluation of whether the studio was the right partner going forward. A rift had emerged between the two: Disney wasn't willing to accept Toy Story 3 as one of the movies Pixar owed under their contract, preferring an original feature rather than a sequel. Disney also announced that it would make sequels of all Pixar films, with or without Pixar's participation. In 2004, the two broke off renegotiation talks.

The stalemate played a role in another management upheaval at Disney. The then-CEO Michael Eisner was ousted in favour of Bob Iger. Bob wanted Pixar back in the fold, and made a new offer: to buy Pixar outright.

In 2006, Disney acquired Pixar for $7.5 billion (£4 billion) in stock. The move returned John to Disney at last as Chief Creative Officer for both Walt Disney and Pixar Animation Studios, and Ed now serves as President of both Walt Disney and Pixar Animation Studios.

Since uniting with its former production partner, Pixar has continued cranking out the hits, including Ratatouille, Wall-E and Up. Ironically, when Toy Story 3 finally came out in 2010, it became the highest-grossing animated film by any studio to that date, earning over $1 billion (£647 million).

Twitter

How 140 characters changed the world

Founders:	**Jack Dorsey, Christopher Isaac 'Biz' Stone and Evan Williams**
Age of founders:	**29, 31 and 33**
Background:	**Software developers/Google employees/serial entrepreneurs**
Founded in:	**2006, USA**
Headquarters:	**California, USA**
Business type:	**Social media/microblogging**

I n five short years, Twitter grew – and *grew* – into a tool that revolutionised global communications. It became so ubiquitous that using it became a verb: to tweet. The brief status updates of Twitter would change the way news is reported, governments are toppled, and charitable donations are solicited.

But Twitter is almost as famous for what it hasn't done: turn a profit. Despite attracting a huge audience and raising over $1 billion (£647 million) in venture capital, Twitter continues to struggle to find a business model that will let it cash in on its popularity.

Three geek dropouts and how they grew

As a teenager growing up in Missouri, Jack Dorsey created software that helped taxi and ambulance dispatchers locate their vehicles. Jack briefly attended two different universities before dropping out altogether in 1999.

He moved west, to California, and began working on a web-based dispatch start-up idea. In July 2000, inspired by the web-posting service LiveJournal, he got an idea for a simple, real-time update service – a more 'live' LiveJournal.

He sketched the idea on a sheet of wide-ruled notebook paper. There would be a small box for writing what you were doing, room for a bit of contact information, and a search bar for finding others on the service.

That was it. Jack wanted to call it Stat.us.

Evan Williams grew up on a farm in Nebraska. He lasted a year and a half at the University of Nebraska before dropping out in favour of a string of tech jobs. In 1996 he moved to California to work for technology publisher Tim O'Reilly and his O'Reilly Media. He began in marketing but quickly switched to writing code as an independent contractor. 'I was bad at working for people', Evan would later say.

In 1999 he co-founded Pyra Labs with ex-girlfriend Meg Hourihan. Pyra's hit product was a simple, early web-logging platform called Blogger, a term Evan coined.

Blogger lacked a business model – the platform was free. Evan wanted to focus first on improving the user experience and building the audience, and figure out how to make money afterwards.

Unsurprisingly, funds soon ran out. The small staff continued without pay for weeks but eventually staged a mass walkout that included Hourihan. Evan ran the company solo until securing an investment from VisiCalc creator

Dan Bricklin in April 2001, after Bricklin learned of Blogger's woes from a post on Evan's blog, Evhead. The staff was rehired, and Blogger's software was rewritten so that it could be licensed to other companies.

In 2002, Evan's next-door neighbour Noah Glass introduced himself after spotting the Blogger logo on Evan's computer monitor. Noah's start-up, Listen Lab, was working on a way to post audio recordings on Blogger, a feature Evan added as Audioblogger.

Google acquired Blogger for an undisclosed sum in 2003. Evan spent about a year overseeing Blogger at Google before leaving in 2004 to create a new start-up with Noah.

Biz Stone studied writing at one university and the arts at a second, but he lasted just a year at each institution before dropping out. He worked as a designer for publisher Little, Brown and Company for three years before getting the entrepreneurial urge.

He launched the free journalling service Xanga in 1999. When Blogger's paid version came out, Xanga licensed it and Evan and Biz formed a long-distance friendship. In 2001, Biz left Xanga (which continues to operate today), and when Google purchased Blogger, he was recruited by Evan.

Hello, Odeo, goodbye

Both Evan and Noah saw how difficult it was to find and organise podcasts. In early 2005, they launched a start-up designed to solve this problem. They called it Odeo.

Evan's Blogger success made it easy to find investors. Odeo quickly raised $5 million (£2.75 million) from Charles River Ventures and an A-list of angel investors including Evan's former boss Tim O'Reilly and Google investor Ron Conway.

Two early Odeo recruits were Biz and Jack. Unfortunately, there was soon a rather big issue with Odeo's formula: in March 2006, Apple's iTunes podcasting service launched and appeared certain to dominate the market. Moreover, Odeo's technology proved difficult to execute. The 14-member team became demoralised.

Meetings were needed to discuss Odeo's next move. Since software developers tend to work remotely and keep odd hours, getting together wasn't always easy. Staffers were constantly being messaged or emailed to ask: 'What are you doing?'

This problem rang a bell with Jack. He dug out his old sketch of Stat.us.

The birth of twttr

At a playground near Odeo's offices in San Francisco, Jack pitched the Odeo execs. They debated the merits of a web-based communication platform that would bring together email, instant messaging, and mobile-phone texting.

'He came to us with this idea: "What if you could share your status with your friends really easily, so that they know what you're doing?"' Biz later recalled.

Giving himself the username @jack, Jack created the first post on 21 March 2006: 'just setting up my twttr'.

A team of four got the go-ahead to work on Jack's idea. Jack, Noah, Biz and Florian Weber – a Berlin-based expert in the emerging, open source web-development framework Ruby on Rails – worked for two weeks to create a prototype. To enable the service to work with text messaging's 160-character limit, they set a 140-character update limit. At first, it ran on Noah's IBM Thinkpad laptop.

The first ever tweet.

The team brainstormed for a name, as Stat.us was taken. 'Jitter' and 'Twitch' were nominees. Noah finally came up with the name Twitter, which was originally written 'twttr'. Giving himself the handle @jack, Jack created the first post on 21 March 2006: 'just setting up my twttr'.

Odeo's meeting-schedule problem was solved. More significantly, everyone found twttr fascinating and couldn't resist sharing it with friends. By the end of the first day, there were 20 users.

Shortly afterward, Biz got an insight about twttr's value after a hot August day spent ripping up carpeting in his stuffy flat with his wife, Livia. Exhausted, Biz took a break and checked his twttr feed. He found Evan had posted a link to a photo of himself.

'Sipping pinot noir after a massage in Napa Valley', was Evan's tweet.

The sharp contrast between their weekend activities gave Biz a laugh – and he realised twttr offered a uniquely engaging way to communicate.

In no time at all, everyone at Odeo spent more time working on and using twttr than they spent on Odeo. A change was clearly in order. But Odeo had raised money for a podcasting product, and twttr was a text-based service. Also, twttr was an unknown quantity: 'It's too early to tell what's there', Evan wrote on his blog.

Evan took a highly unusual step: he gave all of the Odeo investors their money back in late 2006.

After the buyout, Evan and Biz founded a new company, Obvious Corp., which would develop twttr and find a buyer for Odeo. A key hire was former Blogger product manager Jason Goldman, who would become Twitter's Product Vice President. (Odeo was purchased by start-up SonicMountain for over $1 million (£500,000) in mid-2007.)

One of the first things Evan did after buying out the investors was to fire Noah Glass. It was the Golden Rule of business in action – Evan had the Blogger gold, and though Noah had played a key role in Twitter's creation, the two clashed, and Evan made the rules.

Being a punchline

Two months after launch, Twitter had just 5,000 monthly users. While a few techies were instantly hooked, others didn't understand how it worked, or chafed at the 140-character limit. It was difficult to describe: was it microblogging? a device-agnostic message-routing system?

'For the first nine months, everyone thought we were fools', Biz explained. 'People would say, "That's the most ridiculous thing we've ever heard of." The criticism at the time was Twitter is not useful. To which Ev would say, "Neither is ice cream – should we ban ice cream and all joy?" We were having fun building it.'

Besides the fun factor, what kept the team going? 'From the very beginning, Ev described it as a communications platform that had revolutionary potential', says early employee Jason Stirman, who was Twitter's Engineering Manager. 'It was this simple little website that kept breaking, and people were posting what they had for breakfast, but he had a vision for this thing, even in its infancy.'

The original twttr site – which boasted a green and white colour scheme – was replaced in the autumn with a blue colour scheme and revamped name: Twitter. A year after it was created, in March 2007, Twitter had 20,000 users.

'For the first nine months, everyone thought we were fools. People would say, "That's the most ridiculous thing we've ever heard of."'

Twitter's iconic bird logo.

Following Evan's Blogger model, Twitter was free for users. The company philosophy: build value before seeking profit. All energy went on keeping the site running and users happy. The company supported two important features created by Twitter users: the hashtag (#), enabling users to track popular or 'trending' topics, and the forwarding 'retweet' button.

Rocking Texas

To grow its subscriber base, the Twitter team made plans to attend the Texas music and technology conference South by Southwest (better known as SXSW) in Austin. The previous year, a competing mobile-texting service – Google-owned Dodgeball – had won Best Product at SXSW. In a risky move, Evan and Biz would face down their better-funded competitor before SXSW's tech-savvy audience of more than 100,000.

Twitter's marketing plan was to install two large, high-definition plasma-screen monitors in the Austin Convention Center hallways and display attendees' Twitter updates. There would also be t-shirts emblazoned with the faux status update 'wearing my twitter shirt'.

Initially, the monitors didn't work, and Biz and Evan sweated through much of Friday night fixing them. On Saturday morning, Twitter's server in San Francisco crashed. Then, finally, the screens worked. Attendees stopped to stare at the message scroll – then chose which sessions to attend based on what they read. Many presenters began their sessions by announcing their Twitter usernames. Attendees live-tweeted about what they heard.

In a risky move, Evan and Biz would face down their better-funded competitor in front of SXSW's tech-savvy audience of more than 100,000.

But Twitter made its biggest impact at night. Crowds turned like a flock of birds in the Austin streets as mobile phone users read tweets directing them to the hottest venues and away from dull events.

Twitter was doing exactly what Evan envisioned. 'It was the first time people were able to coordinate in real time', Biz recalled later. 'This was spine-tingling stuff for us.'

Stirman recalls, 'SXSW was fertile ground for this product. You had all these tech people in the city without good ways to communicate with each other, especially at night. They had this "aha" moment – Twitter *is* useful.'

Twitter won Best New Product of SXSW 2007 and the number of users trebled to 60,000. The team returned home to spin Twitter out of Obvious and incorporate it as Twitter Inc. By year-end, Twitter had 200,000 users. Twitter also captured the attention of the media and influential tech bloggers. It quickly permeated pop culture: in the autumn, the forensic techs of *CSI* would solve a crime after following a tweeted clue.

Investors took note. In July 2007, Twitter landed $5 million (£2.5 million) in venture capital investment led by former Odeo investor Charles River Ventures. Other investors included Union Square Ventures, Netscape co-founder Marc Andreessen, Ron Conway and Feedburner creator Dick Costolo, who'd worked at Google with Evan.

A whale is born

After SXSW, Twitter would experience the hockey stick-shaped, straight-up growth curve that is the dream of every start-up entrepreneur. In March 2008, when Twitter hit 400,000 users, the company set out to completely rebuild Twitter's technology to support the skyrocketing user base.

It didn't work. Twitter would be down, sometimes for three days straight. The company still had only two dozen employees. Any big pop culture or technology event – say, Apple's Steve Jobs speaking at a conference – could cause a huge traffic spike and crash the system. Jack, Twitter's first CEO, ceded the post to Evan.

'We weren't ready for the number of people around the globe who would find Twitter so useful and so relevant to their daily lives', Biz recalled in a an interview.

Why couldn't Twitter fix its technical problems? It had money to hire more staff, but few engineers had both the necessary expertise in Ruby on Rails and the willingness to work in Twitter's frantic start-up environment, Stirman recalls. To top it off, the founders were picky about whom they hired. As a result, Twitter's hiring lagged far behind its staffing needs. And by June 2008, QuantCast estimated that Twitter had 700,000 monthly users.

At first, visitors attempting to access Twitter during outages saw the Twitter bird gazing sadly at a damaged robot. Biz wanted something more reassuring and purchased a graphic by Shanghai artist Yiying Lu of a whale being lifted out of the water by many birds, each pulling a rope.

Quickly dubbed the 'fail whale', the image became both an object of derision and a cult hit. The fail whale inspired a fan club, t-shirts, and at least one tattoo. The chronic technical breakdowns did not discourage potential investors, either.

'When your product is so popular that your servers are crashing every day', Stirman says, 'that's the sort of thing venture capitalists salivate over.'

In May 2008, Twitter would raise another $15 million (£8 million) from Union Square, Amazon founder Jeff Bezos's Bezos Expeditions, Spark Capital, Digg founder Kevin Rose, and social media author Timothy Ferriss.

Businesses@Twitter

Twitter's lack of a business plan made it the subject of many jokes around Silicon Valley. Entrepreneurs created and compared lists of possible Twitter monetisation schemes.

Despite this, the founders resisted the idea of simply slapping ads on the site and searched for less obnoxious revenue ideas. Meanwhile, big companies began experimenting with Twitter. In 2008, Dell reported that it had made $1 million (£539,000) selling reconditioned computers from its outlet store by offering discount vouchers on Twitter. Train provider South West Trains has attempted to improve customer service through its account, @SW_Trains, which responds quickly to customer complaints.

At the same time, other entrepreneurs were building businesses on Twitter's back. The company's open source platform let developers use Twitter's code to create related services. Hundreds of thousands of Twitter apps would be built, including the Twitter scheduler Tweetdeck, which became so popular that Twitter would later acquire it for $40 million (£21.6 million).

Some users tried out new personas on Twitter. A few were so popular they ended up with publishing and public speaking deals. Two standouts were Fake Steve Jobs and Fake AP Stylebook (style tips for 'proper writing').

Train provider South West Trains has attempted to improve customer service through its account, @SW_Trains, which responds quickly to customer complaints.

Rise of the Twitterati

Aside from the obvious fakery of Fake Steve Jobs, however, Twitter had a big problem with covert imitators. As celebrities and prominent politicians began to show an interest in Twitter, other users were setting up accounts, pretending to be a popular film actor or pop star, and sending out messages that embarrassed the real star. To encourage celebrity participation and eliminate these spoofers, Twitter created a Verified Accounts program.

One late-2007 adopter was then-presidential hopeful Barack Obama, who cannily used social media to rally voters. In 2009, Oprah Winfrey, Lady Gaga and Ashton Kutcher joined, with Ashton becoming the first person to gain a million Twitter followers. The celebrities were a promotional bonanza for Twitter – each drawing press coverage and masses of followers, many of whom joined to connect with their idol. Oprah created a 43% traffic spike when she joined live on her talk show in April 2009.

The celebrity sparkle helped skyrocket Twitter's audience to five million users by the end of 2008, and to over 71 million in 2009. With just 50 employees in 2008, Twitter struggled to keep up.

'It's like we're on a rocket ship that we're just painting and suddenly it took off and we're holding on to the ship with our fingernails', Biz told the *New York Times*.

Institutional investors including T. Rowe Price and Morgan Stanley put another $135 million (£86.2 million) into the company in 2009, at a reported valuation of $1 billion (£639 million). The financial support bought Twitter more time to explore non-intrusive ways of earning revenue from the growing audience.

The new emergency broadcast system

Users delighted in announcing their trivial activities on Twitter. But the founders always imagined that Twitter would have a higher purpose of connecting people around the world to promote good causes.

In April 2008, Twitter fulfilled that purpose. When American student James Buckley was arrested while photographing protests in Egypt, his call for help was a single-word tweet: 'Arrested'. His 48 followers quickly contacted the US Embassy and the press. Buckley was soon able to tweet, 'Free'.

In natural disasters, too, Twitter proved invaluable. When an earthquake hit China in May 2008, Twitter became the go-to news source for early disaster reports, as users on the scene tweeted information from mobile phones. Reporters used the tweets in their stories, and charities joined in with Twitter-based fundraising appeals.

Twitter became an essential tool for political activists. This became clear during Iranian protests in June 2009, when the US State Department asked Twitter to postpone scheduled maintenance that might take the service offline.

HOW THEY STARTED

In late 2010, the Middle East began to erupt in anti-government protests that became known as the 'Arab Spring', and as oppressive regimes in Tunisia and Egypt toppled, political observers credited Twitter with playing a supporting role. In perhaps the ultimate demonstration of Twitter's importance, Egypt shut down internet access in January 2011 to prevent protesters from using Twitter.

In August 2011, when riots swept across London, Twitter's instant updates provided users with news of the attacks faster than news channels could even report. Twitter was also used as a tool to arrange clean-up parties in the aftermath, bringing Londoners together in a time of chaos.

A screenshot of a Twitter news feed.

A business model is born

As Twitter struggled to find a way to earn revenue, its leadership changed repeatedly. Evan had taken the reins from Jack in 2008, while Jack left to found the mobile payments start-up Square.

In autumn 2009 Evan brought on investor and friend Dick Costolo as Chief Operating Officer. When Evan stepped down as CEO in October 2010, Dick became the new CEO. In January 2010, Kleiner Perkins Caufield & Byers added a $200 million (£129 million) investment to Twitter's pot.

After some testing in late 2009 with half a dozen corporate advertisers, several revenue-generating programs officially debuted in summer 2010. Companies could buy 'promoted' tweets – at $100,000 a day – and hashtagged 'trending' topics. (If a promoted tweet isn't clicked on, a 'resonance algorithm' detects this and removes it from view.) Local ads were announced as a coming option, but at the end of 2011 had yet to materialise.

Twitter reports that its promoted tweets get click rates of 3–5%, which is roughly 100 times better than typical click-through rates for online ads. In 2011, promoted tweets began appearing at the top of users' search results.

Where are they now?

In early 2011, Jack returned to Twitter as Executive Chairman while continuing as CEO at Square. Evan left Twitter, and Biz would follow Evan out of the door to the re-formed Obvious Corp. For his part, Noah Glass's Twitter bio reads, 'i started this'.

In November 2011, Twitter had more than 100 million monthly users and 250 million tweets were posted daily. The company's valuation was estimated at up to $10 billion (£6.5 billion). Hiring finally sped up in 2011, with 500 staff recruited, making 800 employees in total (100 of them in ad sales). Most notably, 2,400 companies were advertising on Twitter. One success story: Paramount Pictures estimated that in a couple of hours on Twitter it sold $1.5 million (£975,000) in tickets for the opening day of its film Super 8.

Internet research firm eMarketer estimated that Twitter would see $50 million (£32 million) in 2011 revenue and $250 million (£162 million) in 2012 – substantial income to be sure, but not yet a figure that justifies the level of investment Twitter has accepted. Is there more potential ahead?

'We've only achieved 1% of what Twitter can be', Dick says.

Will Twitter go public or be sold? The huge amount of venture capital invested – including a mammoth $800 million (£518 million) funding round in 2011 – means a cash-generating event will likely come soon. Both Facebook and Google are rumoured to have made offers.

Linked in.

LinkedIn

Connections are key

Founder:	**Reid Hoffman**
Age of founder:	**35**
Background:	**Technology and product development**
Founded in:	**2003, USA**
Headquarters:	**California, USA**
Business type:	**Professional networking site**

There's an old saying in business: it's not *what* you know but *who* you know. LinkedIn set out to make this a reality in the online world, creating a site aimed at helping professionals connect with each other. Set up in 2003 in the wake of the dot-com crash, the business survived a harsh economic climate and became profitable four years after launch. Today the company has more than 51 million members in over 200 countries and it is reported that someone joins LinkedIn every second.

Technology guru

Reid Hoffman grew up in California, and it seems ironic now that during his childhood his father never let him have a computer, thinking it was irrelevant. It wasn't until Reid went to college, where he studied artificial intelligence and cognitive science, that he got one. In the early 1990s, he won a scholarship to study philosophy at Oxford University, but after a year he realised that the world of academia was not for him. Instead, he had a few ideas for technology-based businesses, one of which was a personal information manager for a hand-held device. Convinced his idea had potential, he networked his way to meeting two venture capitalists. They didn't turn him down flat but advised him to get some experience producing and selling products, and then come back.

Following their advice, Reid sought a job at a high-profile technology company. He landed his first job at Apple in 1994, again using his networking skills (he had heard about an opening in software development through the flatmate of a university friend and applied to the company direct). Nearly two years later, he left Apple for a job at Fujitsu, this time in product management and business development.

During this time, Reid always planned to work for himself one day. His aim was to develop his experience, skills and confidence and prove to the venture capitalists that he was taking them at their word. At both companies, he set himself a strict timeline and mapped out the areas he needed to master before he could strike out on his own, including design and product management, building a team, and producing and selling products successfully.

Reid always planned to work for himself one day. His aim was to build up experience, skills and confidence and prove to the venture capitalists that he was taking them at their word.

In July 1997, Reid quit his job at Fujitsu to set up Socialnet, one of the earliest versions of a social networking site. He'd thought up the concept of social networking long before most people had started using the internet at all. The aim of Socialnet was to build on the kinds of relationships that people have, as a way to identify potential dates, flatmates or even tennis partners. The idea was to put users 'near' the people they'd be interested in, but online. The right person for you could be in the next building, but you'd never know it: everyone would be connected online, so physical locations did not matter.

Reid realised that the only way he would get the business off the ground was to bite the bullet and go for it. He looked at financing opportunities and went back to the original venture capitalists he had contacted years before. This time, they were impressed by his background and his ambitions for Socialnet, and he raised $5 million (£3.05 million) at the end of 1997.

PayPal and beyond

Just over two years later, however, Reid resigned from Socialnet because he wasn't convinced that the company was going in the right direction. The business's strategy had been to partner with newspapers and magazines to encourage subscriptions to the site, but it soon became clear that this was not viable and would not give them the user numbers they needed. Reid had a difference of opinion with the board and left soon after. He had learned a valuable lesson: you can have a brilliant product, but unless you know how to reach tens of millions of people, the product will count for nothing.

'There are three words people use for retail: location, location, location. For the internet, it's distribution, distribution, distribution', Reid said. 'If you don't get this, the value of your site is zero. I hadn't realised this when working at Apple and Fujitsu as they worked with big channels of established customers.'

He told a friend, Peter Thiel, who had studied with him at Stanford University, of his intentions to start another company. Peter was one of the founders of internet payment system PayPal, and at the time was its Chief Executive. Reid had been one of its board members since its launch in 1998, and Peter persuaded him to join the company as Executive Vice President in charge of business development instead of starting another business.

At PayPal, Reid was responsible for external relations including corporate development, banking and international development. All the while, he continued to be fascinated by how the internet (then in the early stages of its commercialisation) accelerated the rate at which people did business. He was particularly interested in how individuals could use the internet to promote their business profile and skills and what influence this would have on their careers.

'There are three words people use for retail: location, location, location. For the internet, it's distribution, distribution, distribution.'

It wasn't until a few years later that Reid capitalised on his online networking ideas, since he believed that it wasn't possible to perfect his business plan while still in another job. In 2002, PayPal was acquired by internet auction site eBay for $1.5 billion (£999 million), and Reid received $10 million(£6.7 million) for his share in the business. He planned to take a year's sabbatical, but just three months later was back on the business trail, too tempted by his desire to start another online business. Even after the dot-com bubble burst, Reid was adamant that there was still potential for online success.

Thriving in a harsh climate

Reid saw nothing but advantages in the harsh economic climate of the early 2000s. He wanted to create a business that would only be possible via the internet and that would change people's lives. He reasoned that in the current climate there would be less competition and therefore a greater chance that his venture would succeed. Reid had several ideas, including a worldwide online computer game, but rejected them in favour of revisiting his passion for how people could be brought together online. He wanted to start a business that would let professional people establish profiles online so that other people could find them, effectively creating a network to enhance and further their careers.

Even after the dot-com bubble burst, Reid was adamant that there was still potential for online success.

In these years, it was harder than before to raise money for an internet venture. Not wishing to waste any time before launching his idea – after all, it had effectively been brewing for several years – he decided to use the money from the sale of PayPal to start the business.

For Reid, having enough capital wasn't the big issue at the start – his main concern was making sure that he had the right team. He gathered a team of people he had previously worked with and known from his university years, whose experience and opinions he valued. The group included Allen Blue, Jean-Luc Vaillant, Eric Ly and Konstantin Guericke. Konstantin had been a fellow student at Stanford; Jean-Luc had worked for Matchnet, an online dating business that had acquired Socialnet; Allen and Eric had worked at PayPal. Over several months they met in Reid's living room and hatched the plan that was to become LinkedIn.

Preparing for launch

As the USA officially entered a recession, the founders worked on the business plan for LinkedIn for several months before launch. Having witnessed the collapse of the dot-com bubble, they knew they needed to prove that the business could grow at a low cost, make money and be sustainable.

In the face of a gloomy economy, Reid continued to believe that starting in a time of recession gave LinkedIn a competitive advantage. Even as consumer internet ventures were no longer the next best thing, LinkedIn now had the opportunity to stand out with a fantastic idea. Investors were interested only in start-ups that could offer a solid, long-term business strategy, something that LinkedIn was determined to prove it possessed. The team wanted to show that it had a sustainable business model based on a number of revenue streams, such as subscriptions, and at its core, a valuable proposition for prospective members.

Reid continued to believe that starting in a time of recession gave LinkedIn a competitive advantage. Even as consumer internet ventures were no longer the next best thing, LinkedIn now had the opportunity to stand out with a fantastic idea.

The business continued to be funded by the proceeds of Reid's PayPal shares, as the founders held off seeking additional investment until they were sure they could prove the value of LinkedIn's business model. By early May 2003, the founders felt confident enough to launch the site. But it was to take several months of hard work for the idea to catch on.

Word of mouth

Reid set himself the challenge of getting a million people to register for the site. LinkedIn's premise – that people could search for other members and share information – meant the site had to have enough people signed up in order for it to be valuable. Right from the start, Reid planned to grow LinkedIn organically by word of mouth – it seemed the most cost-effective and efficient way to attract members. The speed of uptake would also help to demonstrate the site's value to potential investors.

The founders planned to look for a first round of investment to support the business's growth plans once they had recruited a sizeable number of members. The LinkedIn founders began by inviting 350 of their most important, well-connected and trusted contacts to join, encouraging them to get their friends and contacts to join, too.

This worked well. At the end of its first month in operation, LinkedIn had a total of 4,500 members in the network, and the business (using more of Reid's money) set up offices in Mountain View, California, not far from Google's company headquarters. Reid also recruited new staff members to work on the technical side, bringing the total number of employees to 13.

The site wanted to emphasise the strength of the connections between members, so it dissuaded members from randomly adding people to their network. Instead, LinkedIn encouraged members to connect with colleagues, clients and people they had worked with in the past. Connections were therefore based on the trust and experience of those individuals. Reid believed that this increased the value of people's networks by focusing on existing connections in the real world, as opposed to the random connections that are common in some social networks.

On the up

Member numbers were increasing, and timing now seemed to be on LinkedIn's side. When it launched, there were no similar businesses in operation, enabling LinkedIn to develop its concept of online professional networking without worrying about competitors. It didn't take long, however, for other professional networks to spring up, including Tribe

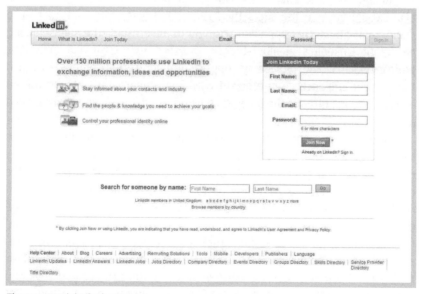

The current LinkedIn homepage.

and Friendster. With a growing interest in the sector, it was not surprising that investor appetite was waking up to the potential of social networking sites, particularly since the US economy was showing signs of a recovery. In December 2003, the stock markets were up for the first time since the internet bubble had burst back in early 2000.

LinkedIn was now ready to seek venture capital funds. Reid recalls how he was besieged by at least a dozen unsolicited visits from venture capitalists. At the end of October 2003, he signed a deal for $4.7 million (£2.87 million) from Sequoia Capital, a leading venture capital firm whose support he'd targeted in the first place. By this time, the site was doubling in size every six weeks and had gained users in more than 80 countries and 120 industries. Several months later, Reid says, he was still hearing from venture capitalists he'd never met, begging to be allowed to buy a piece of his company even though they'd heard about it second- or third-hand.

Although it was common for online businesses to use advertising as their main revenue stream, LinkedIn was determined to be different, having learned lessons from the dot-com fallout. In 2005, two years after launch, LinkedIn introduced two income streams: paid job listings and a subscription-based service, which offered users an enhanced search service allowing them to connect to people they didn't already know.

Reid decided that advertising, while not part of the original business plan, would become the site's third revenue stream, as it had built up a demographic base that appealed strongly to advertisers. The self-selecting nature of LinkedIn's membership (it targeted successful and ambitious professionals) would provide an opportunity for certain brands to reach their target audience in an efficient way. Just a year later LinkedIn turned a profit, the majority of the income coming from its premium services, such as job listings.

LinkedIn became one of the few companies that thrived in the recession that hit during the late 2000s, benefiting from the increased number of people on the hunt for jobs. In March 2008, the site saw its traffic double to just under seven million users, up from 3.3 million a year earlier. Furthermore, the site continued to develop features to increase the value of its services for users.

In September 2008, LinkedIn struck a partnership with financial news channel CNBC, enabling users to share and discuss news with their professional contacts. Community-generated content such as surveys and polls from LinkedIn are broadcast on CNBC, and in return the broadcaster provides the site with its programming, articles and blogs. The networking site sealed similar partnerships with other media owners, including the *New York Times*. Then in 2008, original investor Sequoia Capital, together with Greylock Partners and other venture capital firms, acquired a 5% stake in the company for $53 million (£28.6 million), giving the company a valuation of nearly $1 billion (£539 million), a remarkable achievement for a business that was just five years old.

Where are they now?

In 2010 the company's value rose to new levels, with hedge fund Tiger Global Management purchasing a 1% stake for $20 million (£12.9 million), doubling LinkedIn's estimated value to $2 billion (£1.3 billion).

Now LinkedIn can count itself as one of the largest presences on the web, with more than 135 million members across 200 countries and territories. In June 2011 the number of unique visitors to the site reached 33.9 million, up 63% from the previous year and surpassing that of early social media giant MySpace for the first time. The company went public in May that year and saw its share price more than double in just a few months, making it the most successful tech IPO of the year. But for founder Reid, who is often dubbed 'the most connected man in Silicon Valley', LinkedIn's success to date may be only the beginning.

Match.com

Love online

Founder:	**Gary Kremen**
Age of founder:	**30**
Background:	**MBA, founder of Full Source Software and Los Altos Technologies**
Founded in:	**1993, USA**
Headquarters:	**Texas (originally California), USA**
Business type:	**Online dating**

Some say that the best business ideas come from trying to solve a problem that you understand. That's certainly a view shared by Gary Kremen, founder and ex-CEO of Match.com, the world's first major dating site and one that set the standard for much of the web as it developed.

'I actually started Match.com trying to find love for myself', Gary admits. 'I had this idea that if I could put all the women in the world on a database, and I could sort it, then I'd just marry number one.'

It is not every day, of course, that a yearning for companionship gives rise to a multi-billion dollar global industry, but Gary is not an everyday person. Already a successful digital entrepreneur before he started Match. com, Gary's tale is one of sharp business acumen combined with an understanding of what makes people tick.

Early forays

Gary was born in Illinois in 1963 to two teachers. From an early age it was clear that he had a formidable intellect. As a child he spent hours looking through his telescope and was one of the first among his peers to purchase a home computer (when he was just 12 years old). However, early disciplinary problems at school held him back. He describes himself as a 'behaviourally challenged student' and was frequently in trouble for minor vandalism and computer hacking.

Despite not having the best grades, Gary used his entrepreneurial instinct to 'pitch' his qualities to Northwestern University, a strategy that worked. Graduating with a degree in business and computer science in 1985, Gary worked as an engineer at the Aerospace Corporation for two years. It was while working here that he was first introduced to ARPANET, the US Department of Defense's early precursor to the World Wide Web. Although it was a secure job, it was dull, and Gary's mind soon drifted to grander things. After taking night classes in accounting, he decided the time was right to go to Silicon Valley to earn his millions in the technology industry, and he turned down a prestigious scholarship at the University of Chicago to seek an MBA in California at Stanford Graduate School of Business.

At Stanford, Gary was part of a gifted generation of digital entrepreneurs, with classmates going on to become driving forces in household-name companies such as Microsoft. After graduating, he found a job in a biotechnology company – nothing too exciting, but the company's CEO allowed him to sit in on board meetings, something Gary says gave him the confidence to start his own venture.

When the time came for Gary to start his own business, there was one area in which he boasted almost unparalleled expertise – the online world. 'I was a nerd, okay!' says Gary. 'I was online as early as 1985. How many people can say that?'

This proficiency, combined with the skills he had learned while completing his degrees, gave him an advantage over the many would-be digital entrepreneurs in Silicon Valley in the early 1990s.

Gary's first venture was Full Source Software, co-founded in 1991 with partner Ben Dubin. Full Source would download software from Usenet (an early internet community that preceded today's commercial internet), putting it onto physical media for sale in bulk to large companies. The company was a moderate success, eventually making up to $2,000 (£1,130) a day, but it gave Gary an early glimpse of the enormous commercial potential the World Wide Web had to offer.

A female genesis

In 1989, Gary co-founded his second venture, Los Altos Technologies (LAT), a company that cleaned sensitive data off hard drives for the military and other businesses. (The company was sold to an employee in late 1992 and is still going strong.) While working at LAT, Gary noticed something important: large purchasers were beginning to use systems like IBM's Lotus Notes, enabling administrative staff to send electronic purchase orders without the help of IT staff. It may sound insignificant now, but Gary saw what it meant: an increasing number of women were using these tools to go online for the first time.

'It was the first time I noticed women using the internet', Gary explains. He was an avid user of what were known as '900 number' services: telephone-based dating agencies that enabled people to meet potential partners in exchange for a fee. He realised that the crux of these services' success was their network of users, and he saw similar potential in the small but growing presence of women online. 'It got me thinking, "I wonder if I could do what they do – and charge access to these women?"', he says.

'I was a nerd, okay!' says Gary. 'I was online as early as 1985. How many people can say that?'

The relatively tiny female population online at the time (around 10% of users) did little to faze Gary – in fact, it encouraged him. 'Because there were so few women, I realised that this was the key', he says. 'If you control the few women, you can charge a lot of money to the men.'

Gary saw the huge revenues that print media made from classified advertising, and from dating ads in particular. At the time, newspapers such as the *Los Angeles Times* and *Chicago Tribune* made 10% of their total revenue from personal dating services and 40% overall from classifieds. But he also saw that the industry was slow to react to change and had some key flaws, such as slow turnaround time, lack of anonymity and potential for embarrassment. These were all problems that could potentially be solved by a secure, anonymous and instant online classifieds business. Out of these insights came the idea that would change Gary's life and set him on the path to becoming one of Silicon Valley's best-known entrepreneurs.

First steps

In 1993 Gary set out to realise his vision and founded Electric Classifieds, Inc. (ECI), under which Match.com was developed. The original name of the company was a reflection of the wider vision Gary had for the business: ECI was to be a billion-dollar online classifieds empire with dating being a headline-grabbing way of getting people to look at the internet in a new way.

Gary took out a $2,500 (£1,660) advance on his credit card to pay for the domain name Match.com, as well as a host of others, including Autos.com, Housing.com, Jobs.com, and (famously) Sex.com. The bill continued to increase as he bought a $10,000 (£6,660) SUN workstation to host the site and hired Kevin Kunzelmann as his first employee, finding him on Usenet. Early on, Gary was also assisted by experienced software engineer Peng Tsin Ong, who helped with the construction of the site, provided 10% of the initial start-up funding and acted as Gary's brainstorming partner. Gary also hired Scott Fraize, a software developer.

ECI started operating out of a small room located in a rough area of San Francisco. Gary recalls it as a 'horrible' place: 'I was the starving entrepreneur, living on two meals a day', he recalls. 'But it was really exciting having this small team working out of a little room, watching the business grow so fast – now it's a cliché, but back then it was so powerful.'

At this point, Match.com was barely more than a proof of concept; the site would not be built until 1994. Users would send a picture and personal details to ECI's email address, which would then send profiles of other local users in reply (in exchange for a fee). Despite this rather clunky system, the enormous potential of online dating was soon becoming apparent, with the company seeing explosive growth almost from launch.

'It was insanely fast', Gary recalls. 'We were growing 2–3% a day just from new sign-ups and traffic was growing even faster than that.' What made this growth even more impressive was that initially there was no money set aside for advertising, with the service relying solely on word of mouth.

'I was the starving entrepreneur, living on two meals a day', he recalls. 'But it was really exciting having this small team working out of a little room, watching the business grow so fast – now it's a cliché but back then it was so powerful.'

It wasn't long before this growth attracted the attention of angel investors such as serial Silicon Valley entrepreneur Ron Posner, and just a few months after launch Electric Classifieds had raised $200,000 (£131,000) in funding, giving the project a much-needed cash injection after Gary maxed out his credit card.

Selling the concept

Although online personals were an attractive concept for consumers and investors alike, the problem remained of marketing the business to the wider world, and early on, ECI made a bold decision: to focus the marketing entirely on women who were already online. In the mid-1990s, as the internet was growing in popularity, women made up a large proportion of chat room users, through the likes of AOL and Compuserve.

'I had the vision that one well-connected woman could get 50 other women – who could get 5,000 guys', Gary explains. The company began to

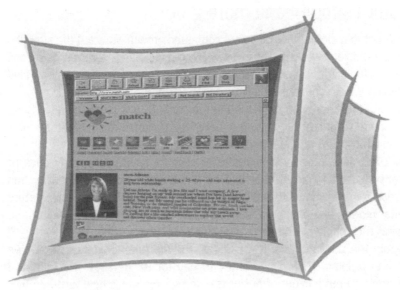

An early version of Match.com.

target the small proportion of women who were already online, advertising on female-focused chat sites such as Compuserve's Women's Wire. The marketing emphasised the safety and anonymity of the Match.com model; online security was still a concern for many women and ECI promised a risk-free service where phone numbers and home addresses were not needed. Initially, Match.com was a free service, but ECI began charging users a monthly fee shortly before the site was finished.

Early on, ECI made a bold decision: to focus the marketing entirely on women who were already online.

Later on, the company widened its reach and began a multifaceted campaign through traditional print and television media, targeting the 25 million Americans who already used dating services but did not have a compelling enough reason to go online.

Growth, growth and more growth

It was not long before the company's continued growth attracted the attention of more outside investors, and in 1994 Electric Classifieds received its second round of funding from venture capitalists, raising $1.7 million (£1.1 million) led by Silicon Valley venture capital firm Canaan Partners.

'It was pretty easy to raise funding because it was pretty novel – there was some scepticism at first, but once we became the market for new relationships, that disappeared', Gary says.

In 1995, just after the first round of venture capital, the early pace of expansion forced Gary to buy one of the largest servers offered by Sun Microsystems, costing $300,000 (£190,000). The problem was, the venture capital money had already been tied up in other parts of the expansion, leaving the company with no money to pay for the server.

'I told the sales guy that it was great, the machine looked good, but we had one problem – I had no money to pay for it!' he says. 'He told me I was going to put him out of business – so I gave him my new venture guy's home phone number and told him to call him up and get the money from him. I made it his problem!' Needless to say, Gary recalls that particular venture capitalist being less than impressed. Despite these early hurdles, the

Gary shows how Match.com sorts ads according to the user's location and preferences.

Match.com website finally went live in April 1995, marking the birth of the site as we know it today.

The combination of Electric Classified's innovative business plan and its huge growth soon proved irresistible to the mass media and Match.com was catapulted out of obscurity to become the darling of the business world. It was the subject of articles in *Wired* and *Forbes*, with Gary being named 36th on a list of the 100 most influential people on the internet. His quirky persona as CEO also proved appealing, with a notable example being an early television interview in 1995 in which he proclaimed that Match.com would 'bring more love to the planet than anything since Jesus Christ'.

Electric Classifieds also saw Match.com's appeal spread to some unexpected sectors. The site quickly proved popular among older women, for example. Gary had thought that this group would be the most resistant to an online dating service, but their troubles finding men in real life led them to embrace the connectivity and global appeal that Match.com offered.

Investor troubles

Despite this success, troubles were beginning to grow between Gary and his investors. The board had doubts about Gary's ability as CEO, aggravated by what he admits was his early immaturity. A major crisis developed when investors found out that Match.com was beginning to target the gay and lesbian sector. Gary saw this group as a loyal market that deserved to be served – but certain investors perceived it differently. 'They went ballistic', says Gary. 'We had some towering arguments about it.'

Another fundamental disagreement soon arose between Gary and the board over the wider direction that ECI was to take. The board was increasingly at odds with Gary over strategy: they wanted to use ECI as a vehicle to sell classifieds technology to newspapers, a process that Gary fundamentally disagreed with.

'[Newspapers] were slow moving and I could see how long it took them to do anything at all. Even though some of them were a hundred thousand times bigger than us, I always knew we could take them on ourselves. I always knew working with the newspapers would turn out to be a dumb idea.'

These incidents and disagreements over strategy led to Gary leaving his post as Match.com CEO in mid-1995. 'We had a big fight. I left', says Gary, simply. 'It was a great time to be starting other things, so I moved on to new ventures.'

'It's the exception rather than the rule that the founder is a good CEO', Gary says. 'The guy that has the idea is not normally the guy with the skills to manage 300 people.'

Gary remained on the ECI board as the chairman, helping with the overall strategy and vision until the Match.com business was sold off to American firm Cendant in 1998 for $7 million (£4.2 million). Again, it was a decision that Gary strongly resisted, believing the brand to be vastly undervalued. From the investors' point of view at the time, it was a canny piece of business, selling a brand for over three times what they bought it for just a few years after investing. But Gary's estimation of the true worth of the business proved to be much closer to the mark, as Cendant sold the site on to US giant Ticketmaster for the eye-watering sum of $50 million (£30.2 million) just one year later. Gary resigned from the ECI board after the sale to Cendant, pocketing just $50,000 (£30,000) – as well as a lifetime account on Match.com.

Despite the acrimonious split, Gary believes his experience at Match.com was an instructive one. He learned that despite having a knack for good ideas and keen business insight, he was not born to be a CEO – a lesson he says can serve as a cautionary tale for other would-be entrepreneurs.

'It's the exception rather than the rule that the founder is a good CEO', Gary says. 'These cases of Amazon, with Jeff Bezos being the founder and CEO, or Mark Zuckerberg – these aren't normal. The guy that has the idea is not normally the guy with the skills to manage 300 people.'

Gary also learned to take a more inclusive approach with investors rather than the combative style he adopted while at the company. He advises: 'When the process begins of building and getting a CEO in, you may as well be part of the process as opposed to fighting it.' He adds that you have to 'kiss lots of frogs' to get the 'right' investors and only regrets his choice in hindsight, if not the investment itself.

Gary's life after Match proved to be very eventful. After leaving the company, he started NetAngels, a venture that offered early collaborative filtering technology – 'kind of like early spyware' – that was merged with another company, Firefly, and was eventually sold to Microsoft.

In the late 1990s Gary became embroiled in one of the longest-running and most notorious disputes in internet history when fraudster Stephen Cohen stole the sex.com domain – which Gary had registered for free when starting Electric Classifieds – and used it to form the basis of a multi-million pornography empire. This battle to save what was rightfully his would take him many painful years, with Cohen's evasiveness almost leading to his ruin, but eventually Gary obtained some of what was owed to him, receiving a $65 million (£42.9 million) judgement, which included Cohen's mansion. Gary now lives in the mansion, and Cohen bought himself a lengthy prison sentence.

Where are they now?

Electric Classified's sale of the Match.com brand proved to be the beginning of the end for the business. Changing its name to Instant Objects, the company persisted with the doomed goal of selling back-end technology to newspapers, and despite raising an additional $25 million (£16.5 million) in venture capital finally shut its doors in 2001.

However, this wasn't quite the end of the ECI saga. In 2004, the defunct company's outstanding debt was bought by none other than Gary himself, who then sold off some patents he had filed while at the company for a handsome profit. 'I bought the debts for maybe $300,000 (£164,000) and made a couple of million dollars from the sale', he says. 'It's a nice story.'

As for Match.com, it competes with PlentyOfFish.com as the world's leading dating site and established the template for many other imitations, fulfilling the potential that Gary always knew it had. It claims to have over 20 million members (1.3 million of whom are paying subscribers) with a 49:51 male:female ratio. It's also a truly global affair, with sites in 25 different countries in eight languages. The company is still under the control of IAC (formerly Ticketmaster) and would comfortably be valued at a multiple of hundreds of millions of dollars. 'I'm happy it's done so well', Gary says. 'I knew as soon as I had the idea it was going to be huge – I've got my vision wrong many times but I got this one right.'

Today Gary devotes his time to investing in ethical and sustainable businesses, in which he sees a lot of potential ('I think the sector's *going to be around for a long time'), and estimates he is an investor in 15 such ventures. A notable recent investment success has been Clean Power Finance, founded in 2007 as an online service that enables solar buyers and sellers to connect with financial products. Kleiner Perkins and Google were some of the other investors and the company reportedly channels $1 million (£500,000) into the solar industry every day.*

But did Gary ever achieve his original goal of finding love? 'I finally got married about four years ago – but it wasn't through Match.com!' Gary explains. 'It was a hybrid model – I offered a reward on the internet of a trip to Hawaii for two if you set me up with my future wife. This guy I know set me up with my wife, and he got his holiday, so everyone was happy.'

◎◎ tripadvisor®

TripAdvisor

Discouering treasure on its trauels

Founder: **Stephen Kaufer**	
Age of founder: **38**	
Background: **Degree in computer science from Harvard University**	
Founded in: **2000, USA**	
Headquarters: **Massachusetts, USA**	
Business type: **Travel reviews website**	

TripAdvisor's 60 million-plus user reviews are some of the most widely read hotel and restaurant assessments in the world. The site draws more than 50 million unique visitors each month and ranks among the world's most trafficked websites. Just over a decade ago, however, TripAdvisor was on the verge of going bust.

A true innovator, the company rode out the storm and led where others tried and failed, building a 'movement' – a thriving community that has nearly eclipsed the company itself. Waving the banner of 'citizen tourism', the company attracts millions daily to its more than 60 million travel reviews. It boasts eight million photos from its members' travels, and a staggering 98% of new topics in its lively forums are replied to within 24 hours. People cannot stay away.

Going on holiday

In 1999, Stephen Kaufer just wanted to go on holiday. He and his wife were trying to plan a trip to Mexico and, on the recommendation of a local travel agency, they went online to check out a few resorts. It was easy enough to find the glossy brochures and guidebooks, he says, but what he really wanted were first-hand opinions from those who had been there. Instead, at every website they visited, they found that the photos and descriptions of each resort were the same.

Stephen was frustrated. It was the height of the dot-com boom, but the principles of Web 2.0 had yet to take hold. Stephen just wanted an honest opinion of each resort, but all he could find in his fruitless web searching was an endless loop of the same recycled promotional material. Eventually he found someone's personal home page that featured a few candid photos from one of the resorts and a paragraph about its facilities. He then realised that if the reality of this resort was quite different from its brochure, then it was probably the same for many more.

'Each time we were recommended a destination and hotel, I'd go online and search high and low to find more information, and each time, we'd find a problem – the hotel wasn't up to par, the destination was unsafe, etc', he says. 'It took an enormous amount of time to research these places properly, and it was through these endless searches that the TripAdvisor concept was born – I wanted a single place where I could get the real scoop on a hotel, not just the official blurb from the property or a travel agent.'

Stephen has always been an entrepreneur at heart. He co-founded his first business, a software development tool company, in 1984 while pursuing his computer science degree at Harvard. That company was eventually sold off in 1998, but, just a year later, Stephen's experience trying to book a hotel had him again thinking entrepreneurially. He said to himself that there had to be a better way to plan a holiday online. Soon after, in February 2000, TripAdvisor appeared.

'I was employed at the time, so I put the idea on hold for about a year and then started gathering a group of people who I thought would be interested in creating what would become TripAdvisor', Stephen says. 'In 2000 we were up and running, albeit in a different way than we do now.'

Life, and near-death, as a search engine

The company actually began life as a search engine. These were the days when sites like Lycos, Go and Excite were the most visited pages on the web, and an upstart Google was fast making a name for itself with its authoritative search results. These were Stephen's models, but approached from the opposite angle. Rather than trying to rank results based on their perceived worth, TripAdvisor simply provided unfiltered links to any travel reviews on the web. Stephen's aim was to unearth the raw, candid opinions about services and popular destinations in the travel industry – the opinions that lurked on personal web pages in the furthest reaches of the internet. Except it didn't work.

'I wanted a single place where I could get the real scoop on a hotel, not just the official blurb from the property or a travel agent.'

Stephen says he had a site he liked, but he wasn't able to figure out how it could make money. 'When we first started out, our business model was entirely different to what it is today', he says. 'We'd planned to sell TripAdvisor as a rich database to travel portals, online travel businesses, etc. We'd hoped to offer such high-quality content that simply being in the travel business necessitated access to the TripAdvisor database, which we would then license out and/or get a share of the revenue generated on the page views from that. All the major players would have it, and no one would try to build it themselves because we'd be so far ahead of the game – that was our planned business model.'

But after a year, he had only one licensing deal, and Stephen says he often joked that the quarterly revenue cheque he received from this wouldn't even cover the weekly free lunch he offered to his employees. 'We found ourselves in the midst of a pretty fundamental problem – we wanted to be paid to have our content featured, but everyone else wanted *us* to pay *them* to have our content featured', Stephen says.

'We came across more trouble when 9/11 hit', he adds. 'It was a hugely traumatic time, particularly for the travel industry. Everything we had in the pipeline was stalled and we were struggling to move ahead and looking at going out of business within the year.'

In the post-9/11 days, TripAdvisor wasn't making any money at all, and Stephen was running through cash quickly. To avoid going bust, he slimmed down the team, took a pay cut and carried on as best he could in the difficult conditions.

'Getting further investment was a tough sell – we were asking for more money, but couldn't show how we'd ever make any', Stephen explains. 'We did manage to get a bit more funding, and it was about this time that we took on Expedia as a client and changed our game plan – we started targeting our content at the end user, rather than travel businesses, and making money through cost-per-click (CPC) advertising.'

Voyage of discovery

Discovering a new business model was quite serendipitous for him, as Stephen admits that by autumn 2001 the company was just months away from folding. Luckily, around this time Stephen noticed something interesting in his traffic figures: when TripAdvisor placed more relevant ads next to its search results, click rates on the ads soared to 15% – way more than the industry average of 0.2%. As this trend continued, Stephen found his elusive money-making potential and adopted a strategy of providing other companies within the travel industry access to its growing number of members via these targeted ads.

When users searched for localised travel information, TripAdvisor began selling keyword-based text ads for companies that offered services within those markets. In essence, the company used the gravitas of its user-generated reviews as a lead through to feed readers on to other industry sites to complete their transactions.

'It proved very effective – we abandoned some of our original ideas and saw great success starting with Expedia, and then moving on to other big players and maintaining our growth to become what we are today', he says. 'Finding a way to make this content profitable wasn't the easiest ride, though, and our business model underwent a few changes, with our biggest early success coming when we discovered TripAdvisor's unique capabilities in CPC advertising.'

When he first started out, Stephen never intended to appeal to the end user, but instead planned on selling TripAdvisor's content to travel companies. When he realised the test site was getting 5,000 hits a day without any effort, he started looking for ways of monetising this traffic. When banner ads didn't prove too successful, he focused on sending extremely qualified traffic to hotels and online travel agents, and then charging them for this traffic.

With users searching for specific destinations on the website, they qualified themselves as interested in those specific destinations, and subsequently hotels in those places. Stephen saw there was huge potential here – if a user was looking at a hotel in Paris, and TripAdvisor surfaced a deep link that took that user straight into an online travel agent's booking pages for that hotel, the company could make some money.

'We approached Expedia and told them we'd like to advertise their hotels on our website in front of a highly targeted audience', Stephen recalls. 'We'd only charge them for the traffic we sent them, and we explained how highly qualified our traffic was. At the time, Expedia had no idea who we were, but we'd piqued their interest and they granted us a trial period.

'After the first month they were sold – 10% of the people who saw the Expedia links advertised were clicking through, when at the time click-through rates averaged about a quarter of a per cent to half a per cent. They started off paying us $10,000 (£6,940) a month, then $20,000 (£13,000), and soon enough we were into hundreds of thousands each month. We'd found ourselves a profitable business model and went from no revenue to breakeven within four months.'

When he first started out, Stephen never intended to appeal to the end user, but instead planned on

selling TripAdvisor's content to travel companies.
When he realised the test site was getting 5,000
hits a day without any effort, he started looking
for ways of monetising this traffic.

It was perfect. But as even Stephen admits, while the company was now on the right course, it didn't yet appreciate how valuable its user reviews really were. 'People told us that they loved the information they found on TripAdvisor and that they'd like to post their own comments. So we added a "write a review" button', he says.

As this functionality was introduced, the number of reviews grew tenfold. But in what he now admits was an error, Stephen didn't foresee the full potential of these 'user reviews' and TripAdvisor buried its user-generated content at the bottom of its pages, beneath links to reviews by outside organisations.

Banking on users

Luckily someone noticed the traffic patterns among the site's visitors, and the trend was clear: the majority were ignoring the outside links and going straight to the database of user reviews.

In March 2002, TripAdvisor turned a $70,000 profit (£46,600), and from that point Stephen began thinking about the company with a view to global expansion, he says. TripAdvisor began expanding its existing content into Spanish, German and Italian to find new audiences – and today it offers content for users in 21 different languages.

But as TripAdvisor grew into a top online destination for honest user reviews, it also experienced the first significant challenges to its commercial growth. As greater numbers of disappointed travelers felt free to post their comments, a number of hotel and restaurant owners became annoyed by the open forum TripAdvisor was providing.

'We'd found ourselves a profitable business model
and went from no revenue to breakeven within four
months.'

Again, this was still in the pre-Web 2.0 days of the early 2000s, and the blogs and social media we now take for granted weren't yet around. A site like TripAdvisor, which was one of the first truly global forums for sharing opinions, was liberating for its users, but a cold shower for those in the hospitality industry.

Stephen's belief in sharing honest opinions works both ways, however: 'Our policy is, the customer stayed there, so they get a chance to voice their opinion. But that's why we have always offered the management a response capability, so they can tell their side of the story.'

What's more, the company claims that reviews are systematically screened by TripAdvisor's proprietary site tools, which are regularly upgraded. And the site's community of (now) more than 60 million monthly visitors also helps report any suspicious content, while a team of quality assurance specialists investigates suspicious reviews.

What's happened, Stephen says, is that the growth of TripAdvisor's user reviews and online visibility has motivated the travel industry to up its game. Hotels, restaurants and other services have increased their quality, and in a Darwinian sense, the best businesses in the hospitality industry have thrived.

'I still meet hotel owners who don't like to shake hands with me because I've hurt their business, but far more often I get people thanking me for helping their brand shine', Stephen has said.

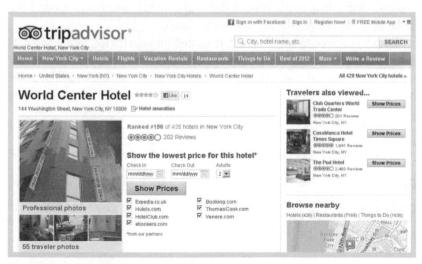

A screenshot of TripAdvisor's website today.

Though he knew he had an innovative idea, Stephen admits that the timing of TripAdvisor's launch proved to be another significant obstacle. By the time TripAdvisor arrived in 2000, the dot-com bubble was bursting and plenty of free-spending internet firms had either gone bust or were well on their way. What's more, investors were growing cautious of handing money over to yet another start-up.

'In our early days, we cut costs wherever we could – my wife owned a small software company that gave TripAdvisor free rent, equipment and supplies in our first year', Stephen says. 'Our office was little more than an attic over a pizza shop, but it was free and it worked. We eventually got too big for this space – it comfortably fit eight people and we moved out when we hit 15 – but even then we were careful to keep our overheads low. This was in the dot-com days, and even though it was commonplace to spend freely, we never did anything lavish.'

making friends the world over

'The company I started out of university was originally self-funded, and although this worked out well, I only briefly considered replicating that strategy with TripAdvisor', Stephen says. 'By this time I had more responsibilities and a family to support, so we chose to raise money rather than self-fund. We went through three rounds of investment, raising $1.2 million (£792,000) in February 2000, another $2 million (£1.32 million) that summer, and a final round toward the end of 2001, which was around the same time the business really started to take off.'

And when the company took off, it soared into uncharted territory for its time. There has always been a wealth of travel information out there, but before TripAdvisor it was difficult to find the most relevant information for one's needs. What Stephen had done was set a successful model for many other industries beyond travel and hospitality.

'I still meet hotel owners who don't like to shake hands with me because I've hurt their business, but far more often I get people thanking me for helping their brand shine.'

'We looked at all kinds of published travel information in newspapers, guidebooks and magazines', Stephen recalls. 'We had staff members who read every single one of these articles, then tagged and indexed them in a way that was easily searchable, providing an incredibly relevant and thorough database that allowed users to search for, and immediately find, only what they were looking for.

'Over time, the focus of our content changed – eventually our travel editorial content was dwarfed by our user review content and users discovered how useful the "wisdom of the crowds" could be in their holiday planning. Instead of listening to one source – a guidebook or an article that may be two years old – they could read 20 reviews, all posted in the last three weeks. It's fresher information that tends to be more detailed and, for many people, more reliable.'

It's this combination of fresh content and targeted advertising that has given the company its incredible run over the past 10 years. TripAdvisor's traffic grew steadily and the company expanded its client set beyond Expedia.com to Hotels.com, Travelocity.com, Orbitz.com and many others.

What's more, as TripAdvisor expanded into new markets, the company that was once just weeks from going bust was suddenly attractive to potential buyers. In 2004, InterActive Corporation acquired the company and made it a unit of Seattle-based Expedia, which was TripAdvisor's first client. Under terms of the deal, TripAdvisor was allowed to operate almost autonomously, with Stephen still at the helm.

Where are they now?

TripAdvisor grew from a tiny start-up in a cramped office with a test site that saw 5,000 visitors a day into the world's largest travel website in over 30 countries with over 60 million visitors a month reading reviews in 21 languages. What's more, its founder still guides the ship as CEO, which is something of a rarity in these days when CEOs leave a year or two after a company has been acquired.

As the 2000s advanced, TripAdvisor itself embarked on an ambitious plan of acquisition. In May 2007 it acquired Smarter Travel Media, operator of SmarterTravel.com, as well as BookingBuddy.com, SeatGuru. com, TravelPod.com, Travel-Library.com and The Independent Traveler

Inc., publisher of Cruise Critic and IndependentTraveler.com. The next year TripAdvisor acquired UK-based user-generated travel site Holiday Watchdog.com, along with Virtualtourist.com, travel comparison site OneTime.com and a majority stake in vacation rental site FlipKey.com.

In 2009, the company purchased Kuxun.cn, China's second-largest consumer travel site and hotel and flight search engine. Finally, in 2010, TripAdvisor acquired the UK's largest independent vacation rental website, Holidaylettings.co.uk.

In recent years, Stephen says, the company has expanded its focus to providing new mobile products, and travellers can now access TripAdvisor's more than 60 million reviews and opinions via smartphones and tablets. The company's apps now have over 10 million downloads and are available in 20 languages, and its iPad app has reached number one among Apple's free travel apps in 85 countries.

In April 2011, it was announced that TripAdvisor would be spun off from Expedia as an independent company operating its brand of travel sites. Finally, later in 2011, it was revealed that TripAdvisor would go public, with the IPO valued at approximately $4 billion (£2.59 billion). On 21 December 2011, the company officially went public and became an independent company listed on the NASDAQ and a member of the S&P 500.

These days the company boasts 530 employees, around 300 of whom are based in Massachusetts, where the company was founded, with 70 more employees based in its London office, its second largest, and others in scattered locations. Its portfolio of websites contains listings and reviews of 400,000 hotels and 500,000 restaurants across 70,000 cities worldwide, and in the travel sector its web traffic is rivaled only by Expedia.

At the time of writing, more than 250 companies have entered into an agreement to feature TripAdvisor content, says Stephen, including destination-marketing organisations, airlines, hotel chains and online travel agencies. More than 150 million people view TripAdvisor ratings, reviews and opinions on sites other than TripAdvisor each month.

Flickr

Capturing the moment

Founders:	**Stewart Butterfield and Caterina Fake**
Age of founders:	**30 and 34**
Background:	**Web programming; blogging and online community development**
Founded in:	**2004, Canada**
Headquarters:	**San Francisco, California**
Business type:	**Image sharing**

t's easy to take your digital camera for granted, or never think about how easy it is to share photos with friends and family from anywhere across the globe. We're now so used to being able to view other people's images online, as well as commenting, tagging or liking them. However, the access to images we are so accustomed to now had very humble beginnings: when, in 2004, a start-up from Canada paved the way for today's social networking phenomenon.

Flickr, founded by then-husband and wife team Stewart Butterfield and Caterina Fake, didn't invent photography, or the idea of posting images online. But they did create the world's first global social network, built around sharing photos. And they pioneered many of the features now associated with Web 2.0 – the new generation of websites based on sharing information and forming online communities.

Every time you tag a picture of your holiday on Facebook, or comment on someone else's images, you are paying homage to the technology Flickr created. There's no denying it: Flickr changed for ever the way most people use, access and respond to images.

A business marriage

Born and raised in British Columbia, Canada, Stewart Butterfield became interested in programming during his teens. After graduating from college in the mid-1990s, he began rising through the ranks at online media company Communicate.com, eventually managing development projects for global giants such as HSBC.

Meanwhile Caterina Fake, born in Pennsylvania, USA, was enjoying an equally meteoric rise. After settling in California in 1994, she began a career as a designer and web developer, before taking the role of Art Director at Salon.com, a news and entertainment website, in 1997. At Salon she played a key role in developing an online community, and harnessing early social software.

This experience gave Caterina a glimpse of an emerging phenomenon, 'web logging', that would come to be known as 'blogging', which allowed people to post their rants, musings and life stories online. She soon became a fanatical blogger, publishing her thoughts on all manner of subjects. It was these blog entries that got Stewart hooked; he became an avid follower of her random musings, and loved her take on technology.

In 2000 the pair met for the first time, randomly bumping into each other at a party. Stewart recalls he made his admiration (and affection) clear, but was rebuffed; Fake had a boyfriend at the time.

However, as he was to prove time and again in business, Stewart persevered. Six months after their first meeting, he found out from her blog that she had broken up with her boyfriend, and travelled to San Francisco to try his luck again. This time she accepted, and shortly afterwards he proposed on the ski slopes of British Columbia.

But Stewart didn't just want Caterina to be his partner in marriage – he wanted to start a business with her too. In his eyes, the business would fuse Caterina's affinity with online communities and his own knowledge of programming. While they were dating he broached his business idea, and Caterina loved it.

Two weeks after returning from their honeymoon in 2002, the duo launched their company, Ludicorp, inspired by the Latin word *ludus*, meaning play. The cornerstone of the new business, based in Vancouver, would be a multi-player online game that they named Game Neverending. The game, inspired by Stewart's love of children's online game Neopets, relied on and encouraged interaction between players. You could meet your friends in this virtual world, swap and trade objects, cook, dance – even stab people with marshmallow daggers.

However, the new game soon ran into difficulties. Looking back, Stewart says that 2002 was the worst time to launch an online company; in the wake of the dot-com crash, securing any venture capital investment to launch a complex game such as Game Neverending was impossible. Furthermore, back-end development soon fell behind schedule. Problems soon began to mount – at one stage, the founders even talked about selling their furniture to pay Ludicorp's bills.

Then, in November 2003, Stewart had a eureka moment. During a conference in New York, he suggested to Caterina that they turn Game Neverending into a photo-sharing service. The game's core technology – a real-time messaging server – would remain the same, but its key objects would be converted to photos; in the new venture, images could be dragged into conversations, creating a distinct reason for people to use the site.

Caterina instantly warmed to the idea. Like her husband, she recognised that photography was a social experience; people took photos for other people as much for themselves, and the internet was opening up endless possibilities for sharing and commenting on images.

But the husband and wife team weren't working alone; they had a handful of employees at Ludicorp, and both founders felt it important to consult their staff before any change in tack was attempted. On 8 December 2003, Caterina and Stewart put their idea to a vote. Ludicorp's employees were asked whether they wanted to keep Game Neverending in its existing form, or move to the photo-sharing alternative. The vote was a tie, but Stewart managed to convince a key team member, programmer Eric Costello, to side with the new venture, which swung it for the founders.

The birth of Flickr

Even after deciding on the change of strategy, the problem of money remained. Ludicorp was still scraping by on a minuscule budget – but they knew that creating Flickr would cost less than getting Game Neverending up to scratch. But then, in mid-December, the team received an early, crucial Christmas present.

In 2002, Ludicorp had applied for funding from a Canadian new media agency called Telefilm, which offered small loans to promising film and digital start-ups. This initial application was rejected, but in 2003, Caterina and Stewart decided to try again, figuring they had nothing to lose. Just a few days before Christmas 2003, they received notice that their application had been successful, and a cheque for $450,000 (£279,000) was heading their way. Stewart recalls that had the loan come through in October (before he'd had the idea for Flickr in November) they'd have ploughed all the money from the loan into the game, and Flickr would have never existed.

The loan allowed the Ludicorp development team to begin a frenetic period of development, creating the structure that would underpin Flickr's rise to prominence.

Despite this small influx of money, the Flickr team relied on open source and – more important – free software tools. Not only did this help their still relatively small budget go further, but it also meant no licensing regulations to contend with. The development team worked hard to make sure the site would be really easy to use, and fast.

Meanwhile, the founders set about finding a name that was catchy and enticing. Finally, after endless brainstorming, one of their friends suggested Flicker, to describe the constant activity and interaction that would happen on the site. The reason they dropped the e? The guy who owned the web domain wouldn't give it up, so they made the spelling change and created the recognisable brand we know today.

Flicking on the switch

After two months of furious development, Flickr went live to the public on 10 February 2004. A trial version of the site was unveiled at the O'Reilly Emerging Tech conference, and a preview release followed shortly afterwards.

Essentially, this first form of Flickr was an instant messenger-style chat feature, where people could drop their photos into online conversations. Caterina remembers spending copious hours on the site, greeting every new member and asking how he or she was finding the site. She saw this was a crucial part in Flickr's growth – as, at the end of the day, it was meant to be social.

But the idea of thousands of people sharing pictures in real time soon fizzled out. In reality, even though users to the site grew quickly to over a thousand, the site only had a handful of people online at any one time. So the likelihood of you being online at the same time as a friend, in order to share photos, was very rare.

The photos would be the basis for a brand-new social network, an early incarnation of the phenomenon that would propel Facebook to global success.

Responding to this, the developers decided to shift the focus away from instant messaging, by putting photos on permanent web pages, with each image given its own distinct URL. This in itself wasn't particularly revolutionary; sites such as Fotonet, Fotolog and Snapfish had already been around for a while. But Flickr would be different – the photos would be the basis for a brand-new social network, an early incarnation of the phenomenon that would propel Facebook to global success. To help with development the founders sought outside investment from friends and contacts. Among those who bought into the idea was Reid Hoffman, who had founded LinkedIn in 2002.

The original social network

To create the social element of the site, the founders wanted to allow users to restrict access to their photos to friends, family or work colleagues. By keeping the photos within a user's network, the founders believed they could create new communities within Flickr, the sort of mini-societies that would later be crucial to the success of social networking.

So the development team set about creating a range of permission options. Using blogging platform LiveJournal for inspiration, the team decided on keeping it simple: LiveJournal only had two levels of privacy: public; and 'share it with my list of friends'.

From this basic start, the developers quickly came up with other ways to share images. In March 2004, Flickr allowed users to post photos to their blogs, and added an update feature, which notified users of their friends' recent activity. Templates were provided for blog posts and, in April, users were invited to try a feature that would create a unique URL for each of their photos.

Most significantly, the developers added a tagging function, enabling users to add labels to their images; and also letting their friends add text.

Users flock to Flickr

With the social network now firmly in place, Flickr's user base began to evolve. Caterina and Stewart had anticipated that people would use the site for weddings, school reunions and baby births, but it seemed they'd underestimated their users' imaginations. People began creating groups that they'd never even thought of, such as groups just for specific art projects.

Towards the end of its first year, Flickr's user base exploded. By February 2005, 12 months after its launch, Flickr was growing at a rate of up to 10% a week. The site's catalogue had expanded to encompass a then-staggering 3.5 million photos, with members uploading up to 60,000 new images every day. By December 2005, Flickr had 3.4 million users.

This growth is particularly impressive given that marketing spend was kept to a minimum. The founders were reluctant to risk money on expensive ads and promotional campaigns; although they did hire a PR company, its remit was to respond to incoming requests, rather than proactively seek coverage. Instead, the founders chose to focus on a viral strategy, confident that their product would market itself.

Flickr allows users to share their favourite pictures as part of a social network.

The strategy was hugely successful, owing much to Flickr's blogging tool. In the early days, nearly 80% of new users were lured to Flickr by the blogs of existing members. To boost their circulation by word of mouth, the company offered incentives such as extra storage to those prepared to recommend the site to their friends.

The founders chose to focus on a viral strategy, confident that their product would market itself.

Monetising the monster

In their quest to create the best user experience, Caterina and Stewart passionately believed that they couldn't over-commercialise their site. They were determined to keep the homepage free of pesky banner adverts, as they felt these would drive visitors away. But this left an obvious question unanswered – where would Flickr find an income stream?

They came up with a tiered subscription model: a vast base of free users would essentially be subsidised by a smaller band of paying subscribers.

Flickr was happy to give away many of its key services with the free model – such as photo sharing, online storage and tagging. However, these services were capped; for example, free users could only view their last 200 image uploads. Those prepared to pay a $25 (£16) annual subscription would get more storage space, and unlimited uploading. This was one of the earliest digital examples of what is now known as a 'freemium strategy', where a company attracts people to use a service for free, and hopes enough will upgrade to a paid-for service to make the whole business work.

Luckily, a substantial proportion of Flickr's user base was happy to pay – it's estimated that the site's free to paid conversion rate is between 5% and 10%. Right from the outset, the paid subscription proved particularly popular with independent professional photographers, who used Flickr to publicise their service and needed to upload hundreds of images every month.

The attractiveness of the business model played a key role in marking Flickr out from its competitors in the early days. At the outset, Flickr was hardly unique; several other sites were offering photo-sharing services. But by inviting people to try its core services for free, Flickr could show off its advantages and cutting-edge technology – and create an army of evangelists.

Yahoo!

On 20 March 2005, just 12 months after its launch, Flickr and its original parent company, Ludicorp, were bought by Yahoo! for around $35 million (£22 million). Gossip and speculation had been bouncing around the tech community for weeks; as Flickr's own blog proclaimed on the day of the announcement, 'somebody's very bad at keeping secrets'.

Despite Flickr's rapid growth in the preceding months, finances had remained an issue. The founders hadn't taken any external funding since that loan from Telefilm, and their reluctance to sell advertising on the site had cut off a potentially large source of revenue. The founders first met with Yahoo! back in the summer of 2004; but this didn't lead anywhere, until Yahoo! contacted them six months later wanting to talk again. The founders recall that some of the impetus for selling to Yahoo! relatively early in the company's life was the massive payback they could give their initial investors who had believed in them so early on.

In the aftermath of the announcement, Caterina told the Flickr community: 'We thought about lots of ways to keep Flickr going, growing, and getting better. We considered taking VC [venture capital] money, more angel investment, bootstrapping it and selling.

'When Yahoo first approached us, eons ago, we were pretty sceptical. But after meeting the people on the Yahoo! team and getting a picture of where they were going, we got religion. Maybe that's too strong. We realised we were all singing from the same hymn sheet.

'The things that were important to us were: being open, building innovative stuff and kicking ass. Were these people (Yahoo!) OUR people? Yes. See the stuff Yahoo!'s announced recently ... they're evolving in really interesting ways. And from our look inside, we know that there's a lot more coming.'

Selling to Yahoo! enabled Flickr to invest in key areas like storage space, and to build a brand-new data centre. Furthermore, Flickr was able to ramp up its engineering team with experienced Yahoo! staff, and tap into specialist people for all manner of nuts-and-bolts issues. Stewart later said that, following the Yahoo! deal, it was a relief to be able to call on an in-house lawyer, rather than having to hire one every time the company needed advice.

Meanwhile, with Caterina and Stewart at the helm, Flickr was allowed to maintain the independent spirit that had yielded such startling early growth. Although the company's entire operation was moved from Vancouver to Yahoo!'s headquarters in California, Flickr remained an autonomous entity, completely separate from Yahoo!'s existing image platform, Yahoo! Photos. To the outsider, it seemed that Flickr had the best of all worlds.

Constant evolution

The Yahoo! investment may have completed Flickr's transformation from plucky start-up to multinational über-brand, but the founders were desperate to keep improving. Caterina and Stewart may have received a substantial cheque and lavish new offices, but they were determined to show that Flickr hadn't lost its passion for improvement. So development continued at a strong pace. At one stage, the development team was updating the site 10 times a day.

Caterina and Stewart may have received a substantial cheque and lavish new offices, but they were determined to show that Flickr hadn't lost its passion for improvement.

This relentless pace of change brought a torrent of new features. The day after the announcement of the Yahoo! deal, Flickr unveiled an algorithm which ranked the site's most popular images; then, in October, Flickr announced that users could now order prints of their photographs. Each of these changes was intended to set the site apart even more from its competitors.

Where are they now?

Flickr's seemingly inexorable rise continued unchecked for several months. By November 2006, more than a million photos were being uploaded to the site every day. By May 2008, Flickr was attracting more than 44 million visitors every month; one industry expert speculated that the company was worth $4 billion (£2.48 billion).

In recent years, Flickr has faced lots of competition from Facebook and the burgeoning Google+, but it remains the number one site in the photos category worldwide, according to Comscore (January 2012). To keep up with the encroaching competition, the site continues to develop to make the experience for users fresher and more intuitive. In February 2012 the new-look contacts page, called the Justified layout, was announced, which claims to 'make it easier to see the stories your friends are telling with their photos'.

Meanwhile, Caterina and Stewart are long gone, having both resigned from Flickr in June 2008. In a subsequent interview, Stewart hinted that the Yahoo! deal may ultimately have constrained Flickr's development, saying: 'We just missed some opportunities that we could have tried, if we were independent and raised our own money.'

The founders are both now building new companies: Stewart has launched computer game company Tiny Speck, while Caterina is attempting to map every user on the internet with her new company, Pinwheel. But, no matter how well their new companies do, their original start-up has changed the world forever. With 750 photos now uploaded to Facebook every second, online image sharing is a phenomenon which shows no sign of burning out.

Wikipedia

A fount of knowledge

Founder: **Jimmy Wales**	
Age of founder: **34**	
Background: **Day trader**	
Founded in: **2001, USA**	
Headquarters: **California, USA**	
Business type: **Online encyclopaedia**	

Wikipedia, the online encyclopaedia, has opened up a whole world of information to us and has changed the way we access information for ever. Instead of turning to oversized, out-of-date books for answers, we can now search an online database of more than three million articles – and edit that information ourselves.

Founder Jimmy Wales was inspired by his love of encyclopaedias, and his thirst for knowledge. He envisioned a world where everyone could have access to information in their own language, and by using new technology in innovative ways, Jimmy was able to create a unique information source.

Not your typical business story, Wikipedia is run as a not-for-profit company, a result of the vision of its founder and loyalty of its users.

A thirst for knowledge

Jimmy's interest in encyclopaedias began at an early age. While attending a one-room elementary school in Alabama, he remembers supplementing much of his early education with sets of encyclopaedias, made famous by companies such as Britannica.

Jimmy had early entrepreneurial aspirations, harbouring a secret ambition to earn his first million by the time he was 40. After graduating with a master's degree in finance from the University of Alabama in 1994, he accepted a job as a day trader at Chicago Options Associates, where he rose to the position of Research Director. Jimmy did well at the firm, and after six years, he had earned a small fortune speculating on foreign currencies and internet valuations.

As he rose up the trader ranks, Jimmy became increasingly interested in the World Wide Web. So much so, that he decided to set up his first website in 1996, alongside his day job. The site he created, Bomis.com, was a basic search portal that focused on terms searched for mainly by male users. Jimmy funded the venture with money he'd made from trading, intending to generate money from advertising when the site was up and running. But for Jimmy, this venture was just the tip of the iceberg. What he really wanted to do was to merge his long-burning passion for encyclopaedias, and his new love of the web, creating some kind of online format.

The world of the print encyclopaedia was already well established, and during the 1990s CD-ROM technology drastically cut the cost of manufacturing and distributing such large volumes of information. Publishers such as Britannica and Microsoft's Encarta sold their encyclopaedias to millions of people, and the new CD-ROM format now brought sound and vision to what was traditionally one-dimensional, as well as making searches and cross-referencing easier and faster. Jimmy knew that he'd have to produce something innovative and different to stand out from the popular and well-entrenched market leaders, and putting an encyclopaedia onto the web seemed the obvious route.

Jimmy honed his idea while he watched the growing 'open software' movement in the mid- to late 1990s. Users were able to download software from the internet free of charge and improve it themselves. 'The open-source software movement was growing steadily and becoming more important – although at first people had tended to dismiss it', Jimmy recalls. 'Throughout the industry we were seeing programmers coming together in a volunteer capacity to create open software.' Collaborating was shown to be not only possible, but popular, and it could lead to some excellent results. There were many different types of software available, and Jimmy experimented with two popular open-source website development languages: Apache and Perl.

Freedom of information

After much tinkering, Jimmy decided to apply this open-source approach to create a free online encyclopaedia. He realised that by using this software he could create a site where *every* user – not just programmers – could write and edit web information, thereby making his encyclopaedia open to everyone. At the time, if people wanted to work together on a document with lots of other people, the only real option was to email it around, which was both impractical and time consuming. Open-source software provided a unique and viable way for people to collaborate online. If this worked in practice it would finally give him the means and method to get his vision for an online encyclopaedia off the ground.

'The idea seemed completely obvious to me and I went into a mad panic as I feared someone else would do it', Jimmy recalls. 'Encyclopaedias are low-hanging fruit when it comes to collaboration; it's pretty easy to do. For example, if you have an encyclopaedia article about the Golden Gate Bridge, everyone knows pretty much what the Golden Gate Bridge is and has a good idea of what an encyclopaedia entry should tell you. In a collaborative environment, it's really important to have a clear vision about what you are trying to accomplish.'

'The idea seemed completely obvious to me and I went into a mad panic as I feared someone else would do it.'

Unlike print encyclopaedias and CD-ROMs, Jimmy's online version would never go out of date; users would not need to buy upgrades or new editions to ensure they had the most current information. While CD-ROMs were seen as the height of new technology in the early 1990s, as technology rapidly developed, they were soon viewed as a slow and costly information source when compared to the free World Wide Web. And while traditional print encyclopaedias were still popular, a whole set of books could be very expensive, costing hundreds of pounds.

An early disaster

Going against the grain, Jimmy decided to not put together a business plan for his idea. He believed that the best businesses are not cooked up by those with MBAs and extensive business plans – rather, they are those businesses that meet the needs of potential customers in an innovative way. By 1999, he felt the time was right to set up his vision, which he called Nupedia. At the time, the market for internet businesses was booming and had reached peaks never seen before, let alone imagined. NASDAQ (the stock exchange favoured by high-tech growth companies) had risen by more than 85% in 1999.

Jimmy believed that the best businesses are not cooked up by those with MBAs and extensive business plans – rather, they are those businesses that meet the needs of potential customers in an innovative way.

Jimmy's encyclopaedia vision, based on open-source software, would be free to users, but the site would make money through advertising. He kick-started the business with several thousand dollars from his other business, Bomis.com. This supplied the internet access and a server, and paid for staff salaries. He then hired philosopher Larry Sangster (whom he knew through an online discussion forum and had met twice in person) as Editor-in-Chief and two programmers to build the site. The plan was that they would all work from home, and they'd recruit other people on a voluntary basis to update information and help develop the website.

But Nupedia wasn't the success Jimmy hoped for. Looking back, he admits his problems lay in the set-up of the business. He now believes that the site was far too academic in nature and too rigidly structured – it was also difficult to manage. The open-source software that Nupedia was using proved to be very clunky, and after a year of operating, there were only 24 articles on the site. Having spent all that time to have so few submissions was disheartening, to say the least.

Jimmy also found problems with how the contributors were being sourced. Originally, volunteers were recruited through online discussion forums and most of them had academic backgrounds. Anyone who wanted to contribute to the site had to submit credentials outlining why they would be suitable, most often by fax. These were then vetted online, and if they matched up, they were deemed suitable to contribute. It therefore took an incredibly long time to bring new volunteers on board, and even longer for them to edit and post articles. The process was far too lengthy, and Jimmy realised that the site was limiting its user base, thus missing out on all those people who wanted to contribute, regardless of their background or credentials, academic or otherwise.

Towards the end of 2000, 18 months after the launch of Nupedia, it became obvious that the site could not continue in its present state. Jimmy needed to find a way of improving how it was run. He and his volunteer contributors sent emails back and forth, debating ways that could make the site work better and assessing other types of software and tools. There were moments when he thought about shutting the site down, but Jimmy says that, ultimately, he was too passionate about the concept of creating a free encyclopaedia to close the site. 'That's when the idea really seized hold of me and I wanted to make it my life's work', he recalls. 'There was a bit of doubt about whether I could make it work, but there was never any serious question of quitting.'

Jimmy was too passionate about the concept of creating a free encyclopaedia to close Nupedia. 'That's when the idea really seized hold of me and I wanted to make it my life's work.'

But by this point, the market for internet businesses had turned sour, and in 2001 the economy began to lose speed. Many dot-com companies were running out of money, and it proved harder and harder for the remaining ones to prove their business models would work.

Turning point

Despite Jimmy's devotion, it was clear that getting Nupedia to succeed would take substantially more change than merely tweaking the site: it would need a complete software overhaul. It was one of his volunteers who first alerted him to the potential of using a new type of open-source software instead – a 'wiki' (Hawaiian for 'quick'). Howard Cunningham, an American computer programmer, had developed wiki in 1995. The volunteer had been using a wiki for some time and thought it would be a good way to encourage people to collaborate better on the web. It allowed people to link to different web pages, and users could easily create pages with new content. Its speed and abilities were significant improvements over the software Nupedia was using at the time.

So while Jimmy did not invent the wiki, he came up with a novel and inventive way of using it: to power his online encyclopaedia. It worked wonders: it was easy to use and implement and was relatively low-maintenance. The new online encyclopaedia, Wikipedia, was born in January 2001 and quickly took over from the Nupedia venture, as work gradually petered out in favour of focusing on this new technology. As a result of the dot-com crash, Jimmy (and the other Bomis.com investors) took the decision not to continue funding the role of Editor-in-Chief and Larry officially left Nupedia, and quit Wikipedia a month later too. Following Larry's departure, activity on Nupedia ground to a halt, and the site officially closed in September 2003.

Initial funds for Wikipedia were again provided by the Bomis.com venture. It paid for editorial staff, programmers and the required servers, and advertising would be sought when more funds were needed. Jimmy never considered asking users to pay to access the information: above all, he wanted to provide free content, where information sharing was the main focus of the business.

Early challenges

The same volunteers who worked on the editorial and technical side of Nupedia were invited to help develop Wikipedia. Excited by the groundbreaking use of new technology, many of them continued working with Jimmy, and the site was able to get off the ground quickly. When the first Wikipedia website was launched in January 2001 it used a type of programming software called Perl, which was very easy to implement – Jimmy recalls that he got it up and running in 10 minutes.

Perl was, however, quite basic and stored all articles as text files. As a result, the search facility looked for files in a pretty basic way and the site was slow to load pages. This made Jimmy realise that Wikipedia would need a proper database, and thankfully one of the voluntary programmers created a database of articles for the site free of charge.

There was no money to spend on marketing, but it turned out none was needed – due to the novelty of the idea it soon received attention from the media, and its loyal community of volunteers ensured they mentioned it online. Word of mouth spreads fast through academic and technological circles, and Wikipedia became a talked-about web phenomenon long before social media came to the fore. By the end of the first live month, there were around 600 articles on the site; two months later, this had grown to 1,300; by the end of May 2001, there were close to 4,000 articles.

At this stage, Jimmy took note of the effect that Google had on the site's profile. Each time the search engine browsed Wikipedia for information, more pages would be noticed by Google; and the greater the number of pages picked up by Google, the more people became members of the site. This in turn had a knock-on effect: the more contributors who got involved, the more pages there were for Google to pick up, fuelling the growth of the site. In January 2002, a year after launch, there were 20,000 articles on the encyclopaedia.

∩ot for profit

While Wikipedia had successfully launched at a time of economic uncertainty, the site was still greatly affected by the dot-com fallout of 2002. Bomis.com, the company that had funded the initial start-up of Nupedia and Wikipedia, was not faring well: it had more than halved its staff numbers from around 12 in 2000 to five in 2002.

Without Bomis.com to rely on, the intention had been to start selling ads on Wikipedia in 2002 to pay for staffing and operational costs. Even in the midst of the deepening dot-com fallout, the number of page views on the site appeared to support the argument for ads. But Jimmy knew this would be a controversial move – supporters of open-source software passionately disliked the use of online advertising and were likely to be up in arms at such a suggestion. The decision was made for Jimmy, however, when parent company Bomis.com failed to attract any advertising.

Jimmy had to consider other alternatives, including the potential of setting the business up as a not-for-profit organisation. Jimmy has always been adamant that his biggest motivation with his online encyclopaedia venture had always been to share information freely, and not to make money. He was also keen to keep onside his loyal network of contributors, some of whom had been working with him voluntarily since the beginning of Nupedia. So, in 2002 Jimmy decided to make Wikipedia a not-for-profit organisation and changed its web address from Wikipedia.com to .org to signify that it would not commercialise the site.

Raising funds

By the end of 2002, Wikipedia had grown so much that the site was being run off three servers. But at Christmas, two out of the three servers crashed, compromising the service and making Jimmy aware that another radical overhaul of the technology was due.

At the same time, there were other technology bottlenecks to manage. As the site became more populated with articles, the developers realised that the existing database server had about six weeks of disk space left. With no sign that the growth of the site was going to slow down, and without any money to buy new hardware, they were unsure about how to resolve the problem. So the developers asked Wikipedia's vast contributor community for advice, and through this they found a way of compressing the existing files to free up disk space.

Once again, Jimmy's loyal team had solved his problems, but the experience made him acutely aware that Wikipedia needed some new equipment to make its technology more robust. So, in the summer of 2003 he set up the Wikimedia Foundation, a not-for-profit charitable organisation, and donated all the business's assets (such as its domain names and computers) to the Foundation.

His first round of fundraising raised $20,000 (£12,400), which enabled them to buy and install the much-needed new servers. This money was raised through charitable donations directly from the site's users, as well as from major grants through grant-making foundations. Over the following years, income was also derived from business relationships and corporate donations from businesses that supported Wikipedia's purpose.

Information creation

As well as the technological problems the site encountered, Wikipedia also faced challenges with content. Many contributors started to confuse dictionary definitions with encyclopaedia entries, and Wikipedia had to make its users aware of this important difference.

A dictionary definition, for example, would simply explain what a word means, while an encyclopaedic entry gives background information and a history of the subject.

The Wikipedia team also realised they needed to ensure that users knew that it was not a place where original research could be published: all information on the site must be verifiable, and not still under development. To ensure the information was as accurate as possible, Wikipedia established some strict rules and guidelines. For example, unless the members of Wikipedia could verify the information on the site and cite sources to back it up, the site would not publish it. A community of contributors, built up during the Nupedia project, very quickly grew to include users from all over the world who were attracted to the open participation model – not just academics.

Jimmy also understood there would be constraints around certain articles, in particular biographies. 'If somebody is not very famous, or if they are only very famous for doing something bad, it is really hard to maintain the article; it is really hard to write a balanced one', Jimmy remarks. 'Those are the kinds of things where we realised that there were constraints in the social model on how detailed we could be and still maintain quality and accuracy.' Since being introduced, the guidelines have worked well, and new information is checked for provenance and any bias removed. There is also an interactive element to the editing process, where contributors can argue a point and agree on the right wording of a fact.

An invaluable source of information

The site continued to flourish; so much so that by the end of 2004 there were more than one million articles worldwide. In 2005 the business raised $100,000 (£62,000) to help upgrade the servers to cope with rising demand. Through the success of the site Jimmy had not only rivalled other encyclopaedic media, but had managed to virtually wipe out the existence of CD-ROM versions. Compared to Wikipedia's constantly updated entries, the CD-ROM just could not compete. Microsoft's Encarta eventually moved online, but in March 2009 the company announced the closure of both the online and disk versions.

Jimmy Wales, Achim Raschka and Daniel Arnold at technology conference 21C3 in 2004.

Where are they now?

In 2010, Wikipedia achieved its fundraising target of $16 million (£9.9 million), double the $8 million (£4.9 million) it raised the previous year. In 2011, the site raised a staggering $20 million (£12.4 million). Donations have continually risen year on year since the campaigns began in 2003, and every so often users are greeted with a plea from Jimmy as they enter the site.

Wikipedia is now the largest general reference work on the internet, and is the sixth most popular website in the world, hosting more than 20 million articles in 282 languages. In 2010 it set down some five-year targets, including increasing its global reach to one billion people and the number of articles in Wikipedia to 50 million.

The site also continues to remain socially responsive. In January 2012, Wikipedia participated in a 'blackout', taking its English-language site offline as part of the protests against anti-piracy laws in the USA. Jimmy's main ambition for the site has always been simple – to provide free information to as many people as possible – and his passion remains to this day.

Wikipedia has revolutionised how to look up information, and has become a verb in its own right while staying true to its open-source, not-for-profit roots.

mumsnet
By parents for parents

Mumsnet

A very maternal market

Founders:	**Justine Roberts and Carrie Longton**
Age of founders:	**33 and 35**
Background:	**City economist and later sports journalist, and television producer**
Flounded in:	**2000, UK**
Headquarters:	**London, UK**
Business type:	**Online community**

For many mums, Justine Roberts and Carrie Longton are the saviours of their sanity. When the pair launched Mumsnet in 2000, they saved many a mum from the isolation of motherhood, by creating a site that combined unique parenting information with a supportive social network and online community. From the outset, Mumsnet was unlike any other parenting site: it featured real-life parent to parent advice, instead of blanket advice written by 'experts'. Mumsnet launched just before the dot-com bubble burst, which caused thousands of fledgling sites to go under. Justine and Carrie, however, had bypassed the in vogue, ridiculous venture capital investments, and opted to grow organically. It was a wise move, and the site has gone from strength to strength, registering more than one million users a month and hosting thousands of forum postings every day.

Inspired by a 'holiday from hell'

Justine Roberts had worked in the City for 10 years as an economist and market strategist before switching to a career in sports journalism. During her first pregnancy in 1999, she met television producer Carrie Longton at ante-natal classes, and the two became friends. Throughout their pregnancies and with their newborns, they both agreed that the best source of parenting information was other mothers. The inspiration for Mumsnet came to Justine during a 'holiday from hell' in Florida with her one-year-old twins. They were supposedly staying at a 'family friendly' resort but she found the level of childcare at the resort appalling. Other mothers she talked to at the resort agreed that it would be a great if there was a website enabling parents to swap information on everything and anything – from recommendations on trusted family-friendly resorts to the best pushchairs to use.

They wanted a resource where parents could pool all their information together in one place that all parents could have access to. Home from holiday, the idea came together. Justine did some research to find out what else was out there. She found plenty of sites with parenting advice, but none that gave parents the opportunity to provide their own views, share ideas and give feedback. She wanted to create a site that offered both, and was sure this would be unique. 'Having done our research carefully, there wasn't really anything like our idea in the market at the time', says Justine. 'There was a site called Babyworld but it was more of an e-commerce offering rather than a resource for pooling information.'

'Having done our research carefully, there wasn't really anything like our idea in the market at the time.'

The idea for the business was an early version of the social networking sites that abound today, a place where user-generated content could be created and shared. Justine would recruit parents and mums- and dads-to-be to generate the content and would finance the site through advertising.

The idea was that the members of the site would fill in a brief questionnaire, and receive a range of benefits and incentives in return, such as regular emails highlighting the developmental milestones their children were approaching. They would also be encouraged to give advice and interact with each other. Once the site was up and running, the aim was also to negotiate special offers with relevant retailers for the site's members.

Spurred on by the novelty of the idea, Justine finalised her plans for the site in November 1999 and persuaded Carrie to get involved soon afterwards. Justine recalls another motivating factor for her: she really didn't want to go back to her job as a sports writer after maternity leave, as it involved too many weekends away from family life.

Booming possibilities

Justine and Carrie spent a month writing a business plan with the aim of having a test site ready by early 2000. At this time, the business climate couldn't have been better. In 1999, dozens upon dozens of internet businesses had emerged, buoyed by large sums of venture capital finance and a predicted growth in broadband technologies.

Many entrepreneurs boasted about securing money on the back of plans scrawled on business cards, so convinced were they that their idea was destined to be the next big thing. And it was clear that dot-coms were the next big thing, as even high street retailers made sure they also had an online presence and got in on the act. Buoyed by the economic climate, Justine and Carrie hoped to attract £500,000 worth of funding from private investors.

Late in 1999, work began on the site with the help of a friend of Justine's from university – a technical whizz who was willing to work on the site in his

Mumsnet provides parents with advice from fellow parents, and has lively discussion boards.

spare time. He managed all the technical aspects of building the site such as coding it and choosing a web host, while Justine and Carrie built the content pages, tested the site's navigation and came up with the design.

Both Justine and Carrie were working round the clock, juggling work and family life with evenings and weekends spent on the new business. Justine was reluctantly working most weekends as a sports journalist, and both had limited childcare available. Fortunately, they had the support of their husbands, whose jobs paid the mortgage and kept each family afloat. Writing all the original content themselves, Justine and Carrie spent many a day roving around London in search of reviews for the perfect pushchair. To get parents on board, they visited as many playgroups as possible.

Justine and Carrie spent a considerable amount of time discussing potential names for the business. The word 'Parentsnet', for example, did not seem snappy enough to them and while happy with the choice of Mumsnet, they were worried about alienating fathers and dads-to-be from the site. In the end, they decided to go with their gut instinct – the name was simple, clear and catchy and the strapline, 'by parents for parents' would include fathers.

By January 2000 the pair had already spent around £4,000 on content and technical expenses. They raised £25,000 from a friend, in return for a small percentage of the company, and began negotiations with other private investors to raise more.

From boom to bust

After months of work, the test site for Mumsnet was launched in March 2000. By this time, Justine and Carrie had recruited more than 500 parent reviewers through their contacts and research, and were actively seeking more.

Justine and Carrie were in the midst of negotiations to raise the funds they needed, when the economic environment changed considerably. Several high-profile dot-coms went bust, and people began predicting the end of the dot-com boom. One of the most infamous victims was e-retailer Boo.com, an online fashion retailer which collapsed in May 2000 through lack of funds, but not before it had burned through $120 million (£77.5 million) in venture capital. Once the darling of the dot-com world, Boo.com, which had launched in a fanfare of publicity at the beginning of 2000, had fallen victim to technology glitches and poor navigation, driving customers away in their droves. It was a wakeup call for Mumsnet. 'Boo failed in spectacular fashion and put everyone off the idea of dot-coms' recalls Justine. 'This meant our chances of funding disappeared too, almost overnight.'

'Boo failed in spectacular fashion and put everyone off the idea of dot-coms ... this meant our chances of funding disappeared too, almost overnight.'

That same month, IT consultancy Forrester published a report predicting that one in four UK internet companies would burn through their cash reserves in the next six months. The reasons for this were simple: many dot-coms had yet to make profits, most had low revenues and almost all of them had high burn rates (the speed at which they used up their venture capital funding). Consequently, venture capitalists pulled out of the dot-com market, leaving many companies without funds and on a downward spiral.

Failing to raise their initial funding target might have seemed a significant setback at the time, but Justine believes that ultimately, starting small helped to both save the business and shape its future. She feels the worsening economic climate made her and Carrie even more determined to succeed – they had already come so far that giving up was now not an option. As Justine explains, had the business secured additional funds from investors, the site would in all likelihood, like many a dot-com before it, have overspent on overheads and advertising, before running out of cash.

With precious little money in the business, and none on the horizon, both Justine and Carrie had to work out ways to cut costs down. This meant taking no salary apart from some money for expenses, and examining alternative ways of paying staff. By March 2000, as well as their technical expert, they had just taken on another friend from ante-natal class to work part-time. To overcome their lack of cash, they paid their technical expert by giving him some shares in the company.

Shrinking revenues

A lack of investment wasn't the founders' only worry. Soon after the site's launch in March 2000, it became clear that the revenue streams Mumsnet had originally planned for were not going to materialise. The site planned to make its money from the CPM (cost per thousand) model, where advertising costs are based on the number of page impressions it gets, that is the number of times an ad is viewed on the site. 'When we started, we had factored on getting £25 per 1,000 page impressions, a realistic figure at the time we had written the business plan', recalls Justine. 'But within a year or so, this had dropped to just £2.50 because of the dot-com crash and the subsequent economic climate. The original figures we worked out were just pie in the sky – the industry never recovered those levels again.'

Despite this setback, Justine and Carrie were actually able to use the tough economic environment to their advantage. With little financial reward available, there were no competitors entering the market. This gave Mumsnet

Gordon Brown took part in a live web chat at Mumsnet Towers.

the time to grow organically and build up its presence in the marketplace. With so many examples of other businesses that had needlessly burned through cash, Mumsnet was determined to learn from its mistakes. Thus far, it had managed on the initial investment of £25,000, and it was determined to succeed using only this.

Whatever the market conditions, and however hard it was to encourage advertisers to spend with them, there were some companies and products that Mumsnet would not accept advertising from. It believed the likes of Nestle, McDonalds, and products such as cosmetic surgery did not fit in with the site's philosophy.

On a shoestring

Mumsnet spent most of 2001 focusing on building up its user base and content, while keeping its outgoing costs as low as possible. According to Justine, the company spent hardly any money on marketing, bar printing leaflets to advertise the business in the first six months. Instead, Justine used her existing journalistic skills to raise their profile in the media.

This enabled them to place stories in relevant media, encouraging consumers to visit the site. As Justine explains, the site's users became the company's biggest marketers, creating original content and encouraging friends to join. Heated discussions in the forums often ended up being featured in newspapers, creating additional publicity. They learnt the power of word of mouth, and were able to grow their customer base with relative ease.

The site's users became the company's biggest marketers, creating original content and encouraging friends to join.

'An economic downturn can be a good time to start a business as long as you can afford to be austere about it', believes Justine. 'In a recession, it is best to adopt a lean approach. You have to be prepared to do everything yourself – we never had a secretary and I did our VAT returns on a Sunday morning at our kitchen table.'

Change in direction

By 2002, with online advertising sales continuing to slump, Justine and Carrie were forced to look at other ways of monetising the business. This prompted them to think about the value of their content and their member base, which amounted to around 10,000 registered users, and they made the decision to branch out into offline publishing. This had never been part of the original business plan, which had focused exclusively on the website, but was only made possible by the reputation the website had developed.

In March 2002, they launched the first Mumsnet book, *Mums on Babies*, a guide to the first year of parenting gathered from comments posted by users on the site. This was followed two years later in January 2004 by *Mums on Pregnancy*. Two handbag-sized magazine guides have also been produced; *Mumsnet Best* is a compilation of the product reviews on the website. In autumn 2004 Justine and Carrie presented a television series for Discovery Health called *Mum's the Word*, again drawing from the shared knowledge on the site and helping to troubleshoot parental questions. These activities helped to boost the number of registered users, and any profit made was ploughed back into the business.

'In a recession, it is best to adopt a lean approach. You have to be prepared to do everything yourself.'

Legal battle

In 2007, the site came under threat after it became embroiled in a legal dispute with renowned parenting author Gina Ford, after allegedly insulting comments about her appeared on the site's discussion boards, posted by users. Mumsnet clarified that it did not support the comments, removed the statements and issued an apology. Despite this, the site, and its hosting services DCS, were threatened with a libel action. Justine wanted to fight part of the action but it was unclear whether the law would be on her side or not, as no precedent had yet been set regarding how quickly content that is deemed defamatory should be taken down.

The situation raised an important new issue for websites with user content: who is liable for comments made by users of online communities? After consulting with lawyers, it became clear that Mumsnet would be a test case, which would cost time and money to fight, and there was no guaranteeing a positive outcome. The site also had no insurance at the time, which would have covered the cost of fighting or defending the case. As Justine explains, the truth of the matter was that it cost the business less to settle than it would have even if it had won in court, because the full costs of the legal battle would not have been recovered.

For Justine and Carrie, however, the legal experience was, on balance, a positive one. For one thing, it brought the site additional publicity. It also meant Mumsnet clarified its legal position, and adjusted some of the site's policies, making its terms and conditions clearer.

Where are they now?

Mumsnet has continued to explore offline publishing opportunities, signing a six-figure deal with a book publisher in 2008. They now publish a series of Mumsnet Guides and released The Mumsnet Rules *in 2011. In March 2009, the site partnered with the National Childbirth Trust (NCT) charity to provide access to its forum, Mumsnet Talk, direct from the NCT site and has been involved in various national campaigns.*

In February 2008, the site underwent its first major redesign since it was launched, to include new content across areas such as conception, pregnancy and babies, with the aim of making navigation easier. In the last couple of years, the site has expanded content even further to include work, education, style, beauty and relationships.

The business also opened its first offices in Kentish Town, North London, known as Mumsnet Towers (staff originally worked from home), and now employs over 50 members of staff. The Mumsnet empire has also expanded in terms of products and services. In 2011, the team launched a sister site, Gransnet, as well as the Mumsnet Bloggers Network and the Mumsnet Family Friendly Awards Programme.

Mumsnet recorded a profit for the first time in 2007, and the bulk of its online revenues come from advertising (as initially planned), and from market research, with Mumsnet's user base completing surveys and product tests. In the last few years the site has seen impressive commercial growth and in 2012 it receives 2.3 million monthly unique visitors and has a yearly turnover of $5 million (£3 million).

The company's early lesson in cost-minimisation has stood the business in good stead in the recent global financial crisis. Being sensible about costs, says Justine, has meant the business has weathered the latest economic downturn. They have not used any additional investment, other than the initial £25,000 they raised back in 2000. Mumsnet's organic business story proves how careful nurturing and care can help a business grow, through even the most dire circumstances.

Groupon

Turning coupons into cash

Founders: **Eric Lefkofsky, Andrew Mason and Brad Keywell (shown, left to right)**

Age of founders: **42, 30 and 42**

Background: **Serial entrepreneurs and law students (Brad and Eric) and entrepreneur and public policy student (Andrew)**

Founded in: **2008, USA**

Headquarters: **Chicago, USA**

Business type: **E-commerce**

143

Vouchers and coupons have been around since the late 1800s, when Coca-Cola began sending out free Coke offers. More than 100 years later, a new company would put an internet spin on coupons – and create one of the fastest-growing companies ever seen. Sales exploded from $5,000 (£2,700) in 2008 to top $1 billion (£647 million) in 2011.

Groupon offered a new marketing avenue for small merchants: the online daily deal. The wild popularity of Groupon's deals attracted over $1 billion (£647 million) in venture capital, spawned legions of competitors, and led to an IPO that valued the start-up at a staggering $12.7 billion. The most improbable thing about Groupon's success, though, is that the shopping-deals site was launched as an afterthought, by founders whose initial goal was to make the world a better place.

Start up early and often

Eric Lefkofsky started his first business while studying law at the University of Michigan. Apex Industries sold carpets to incoming students and grew to $100,000 (£66,000) in annual sales. Next came a t-shirt company, Mascot Sportswear, which he built and sold off.

Eric then teamed up with law school pal Brad Keywell to buy clothing firm Brandon Apparel Group. The two borrowed heavily to grow the company to $20 million (£13.2 million) in sales. But then fashion trends changed, sales crashed, and Brandon went out of business. In the aftermath, the pair faced multiple lawsuits.

On his blog, Eric called Brandon 'a huge failure. We over-leveraged the company and it eventually crumbled under the weight of that debt when the industry began to consolidate against us.'

While the Brandon legal mess dragged on, Brad and Eric started their first e-commerce venture in 1999. Starbelly.com sold corporate promotional items. At the height of the dot-com boom, Starbelly raised $9.5 million (£5.88 million) in venture capital, and quickly sold to retail chain Ha-Lo Industries for $240 million (£148 million). When Ha-Lo failed shortly afterwards, shareholders filed class-action and civil lawsuits against Eric and Brad. Discouraged, Brad took a job with famed US business magnate Sam Zell.

Eric pressed on, though. 'I never thought of stopping', he wrote in his blog. 'I just put my head down and kept moving forward, kept working toward success.'

Eric's next company, InnerWorkings, developed proprietary software to enable printing companies to bid for jobs online. A key funder for InnerWorkings was found when Eric went to a university reunion, where a friend introduced him to venture investor Peter Barris of New Enterprise Associates (NEA). Eric would later also meet NEA investor Harry Weller, and NEA invested in the company. InnerWorkings went public in 2006 and today is a $400 million (£259 million) business.

In 2005 Eric teamed with Brad again, spinning out the supply chain and logistics division of InnerWorkings to found Echo Global Logistics. The following year, they co-founded MediaBank, a technology-enabled media-buying software company. In 2012 MediaBank announced a merger with competitor Donovan Data Systems to create a $1 billion (£647 million) company, MediaOcean.

For its part, Echo grew rapidly, receiving over $17 million (£10.9 million) in funding from NEA, and went public in 2009. But perhaps Echo's most notable achievement was hiring a certain idealistic young web developer: Andrew Mason.

Raised in Pennsylvania, Andrew also had the entrepreneurial itch. At 15, he started a food delivery service, Bagel Express. After high school, he moved to Chicago to attend Northwestern University, where he studied music. He played in punk bands and had a wacky side – for a long time, one of his social media profiles featured a shot of him in his underwear. But his true passion was social justice, and Andrew planned to get a master's degree in public policy.

Getting to The Point

To earn extra money while studying, Andrew placed a Craigslist ad for web development work, and was hired by Echo. He caught Eric's eye by pulling a round-the-clock work stint.

'He took it on himself to rewrite a program in six or eight weeks', Eric remembers. 'He was pretty young and he was sleeping at the office. I just thought he was super-talented.'

Soon after, Andrew left to return to university. Several months later, though, Andrew reconnected with Eric. Andrew had an idea for a website that would help people come together to work on social action projects. He called it The Point.

On the site, individuals could start campaigns – to raise money for a new park, for instance, or to pressure a corporation to recycle. People would pledge to help by taking action or donating. When a critical mass of people signed on, a 'tipping point' was reached whereby the campaign moved forward.

Intrigued, Eric offered Andrew a $1 million (£500,000) investment if he would quit studying and begin work on The Point immediately. So in January 2007, Andrew left campus life behind and started building the site.

In the original business plan, three potential revenue models were identified for The Point: advertising; taking a percentage of the money raised in fundraising campaigns; or charging a fee for helping groups of people buy items in bulk at a discount. But the initial goal was simply to build the site, draw big traffic and focus on the social change mission. Monetisation would come later. In the meantime, Andrew kept his burn rate low by hiring just a few developers to work on The Point's launch.

'We had the ability to iterate and experiment without spending a lot of money', Andrew says.

He paid rent for a small area in Echo's vast offices inside a remodelled former warehouse in Chicago. In November 2007, The Point went live, and over the next year drew only a small following. This made it unlikely that either advertising or fundraising commissions would generate substantial revenue.

The initial goal was simply to build the site, draw big traffic and focus on the social change mission. Monetisation would come later.

To raise more money for The Point, Eric reconnected with his longtime investors at NEA, Harry Weller and Peter Barris, who invested $4.8 million (£2.69 million) in January 2008. Harry remembered Andrew from InnerWorkings and says he jumped at the chance, even though The Point's business model was as yet unformed.

'This was a bet on the team', Harry says. 'We knew the idea would transform over time. We really thought highly of Andrew – he was a sort of inspirational, visionary guy paired with two strong operator/entrepreneurs.'

Under increasing pressure to generate revenue, Andrew began investigating the idea of group buying through the internet. To start, Andrew studied companies that had tried group buying and failed.

'Coming up with the idea', Andrew says, 'was a process of eliminating the reasons that the previous attempts at the concept failed.'

One Seattle start-up Andrew looked at, Mercata, had raised nearly $90 million (£62.5 million) before going bust in early 2001. Mercata let consumers band together to bid down prices on goods and services they wanted. Mercata's 'auctions' took too long, though, and customers lost interest. Merchants didn't want to participate either, as they made less margin. Mercata had focused on selling items such as consumer electronics, for which bigger competitors such as Amazon could offer lower pricing.

Get your Groupon

One day during this time, Andrew was inspired after taking an architectural tour around Chicago. He realised that local discount deals would work well for group buying. Theatres had empty seats, restaurants empty tables, museums needed more members. The merchants could make a discount offer to fill some of that unused capacity, and the extra revenue would be found money.

Each deal would last only one day, so customers could buy quickly. He'd also sell only one deal a day, which would allow for a focused marketing effort. There would be a tipping point for each deal that the merchant could set. If enough customers didn't buy the deal, nobody got it.

It wasn't hard to come up with a name. The product was a 'group coupon', or Groupon for short. At first the name was 'Get Your Groupon'.

The local deal idea offered a revolutionary new way in which small merchants could affordably advertise online. Groupon also used the internet in a novel way that NEA's Harry Weller says grabbed his interest: instead of encouraging people to stay at home and online, it encouraged them to go out and experience new things in their area. It wasn't world peace, but it was a positive goal.

'We could make life better for small business owners and increase buying power significantly for consumers', Andrew says. 'Somebody who makes $30,000 (£16,200) a year can live like they make $60,000 (£32,400). That translates into freedom and experiencing more life – and that's something we could all get very excited about.'

To sign up his first merchant, Andrew simply went downstairs. The owners of Motel Bar, a restaurant and bar on the ground floor of Echo's Montgomery Ward building, readily agreed to do a deal offer. In October 2008, Andrew put together the first Groupon, a two-for-one on Motel Bar pizzas. Customers would pay The Point and receive a voucher through the site, which they would redeem later at the restaurant. The Point would send Motel Bar its share of the proceeds.

'We could make life better for small-business owners and increase buying power significantly for consumers. Somebody who makes $30,000 (£16,200) a year can live like they make $60,000 (£32,400).'

'We went from idea to launched product in just over a month', Andrew says. 'And it was a success – 25 people had to buy in, and it tipped.'

Encouraged, Andrew tried more deals. But in 2008, Groupons were still a sideline to The Point. Revenue for the year was just $5,000 (£2,700).

For Andrew, a couple of key deals that came shortly afterward demonstrated the potential of Groupons. One was for a stay in a sensory deprivation tank, an offbeat service Andrew was unsure would sell – but it did. Another notable offer was for a $180 (£97) tooth-whitening treatment, a much higher price than Andrew had yet tried. When hundreds of people signed up, the team knew Groupons could be a real revenue stream for The Point.

'We realised we'd tapped into this insane demand', says Eric. 'People wanted to go skydiving, try that massage parlour, become a member of the Art Institute, or go on an adventure trip – but they needed something to push them. Groupon was that thing.'

In January 2009, Chief Technology Officer Ken Pelletier threw a party at his small apartment for the entire The Point staff, their spouses and friends. It would be the last time the company would fit in such a small space.

'People wanted to go skydiving, try that massage parlour, become a member of the Art Institute, or go on an adventure trip – but they needed something to push them. Groupon was that thing.'

It was clear that Groupon wasn't a revenue model for The Point – Groupon *was* the point. The company was reorganised and renamed that month, with Brad serving as a director. One year later, Groupon would have 300 employees. The year after that, Groupon would have a staff of 5,000.

A bumpy ride on a hockey stick

Chicago clearly loved Groupon, snapping up $100,000 (£63,900) worth of deals in the first quarter of 2009. But it was time to test Groupon deals in another market to see if Groupon would work beyond the founders' home turf. The second Groupon market, Boston, opened in March.

Any doubts about the business model were quickly laid to rest. Boston took off just as Chicago had. Everyone realised that Groupon wasn't just a good local money-making idea – it was a huge, global idea.

As it happened, Groupon's timing was perfect – the economy had just gone under, and bargains were hot. Bloggers raved, the mainstream media took note, and a media honeymoon began that would boost the company's early expansion efforts.

Corporate missives were often playful, as in a blog post noting that the black background of the Groupon logo 'symbolises the constant darkness that would plague a world bereft of daily deals'.

After Boston's success, board members urged Groupon to expand as fast as possible, fundraising aggressively to pay for staff and online advertising. Groupon needed to build brand recognition and acquire scale to operate efficiently. Also, the barrier to entry for daily deals was fairly low. Competitors would be coming soon, NEA's Harry Weller forecast – and in fact one of Groupon's most successful competitors, Living Social, launched that year.

Groupon quickly added New York, San Francisco and Washington, DC and second-quarter revenue shot to $1.2 million (£76,000). Another dozen markets were opened in the third quarter, the subscriber base grew to 600,000 and sales leapt to $4 million (£2.55 million). The pace continued in the fourth quarter, with another 13 markets opening. Groupon would close out the year with a total of $14.5 million (£9.26 million) in revenue.

The company was a venture capitalist's dream: an almost endlessly replicable model that promised good profit margins once each market was established. At year-end, the company raised nearly $30 million (£19.2 million) from Accel Partners and NEA to fuel yet more growth.

As it grew, Groupon asserted a fun, wacky corporate personality. The company hired squadrons of copywriters to create amusing ad copy for the deals. Corporate missives were often playful, as in a blog post noting that the black background of the Groupon logo 'symbolises the constant darkness that would plague a world bereft of daily deals'.

Beneath the light-heartedness, the rapid growth taxed the limits of Groupon's executive team. Ostensibly an investor, Eric found himself sucked into the day-to-day operations, reporting on his blog that he served as de facto Chief Financial Officer for nearly a year until Jason Child was hired at the end of 2010.

One big problem was employee pay. The sales staff was on a commission programme initially premised on modest sales. Instead, some Groupon offers sold in the thousands, and salespeople could earn as much as $300,000 (£194,000) a year. This enraged some salaried support staff, many of whom were working long hours as well. After one staffer sued for equitable pay, some raises were given.

On the tech side, the company was constantly scrambling to bring on enough talent. Andrew says his biggest mistake was not opening a branch office in Silicon Valley until 2010. Chicago was not a tech hub, and it was hard to lure Californians to the Midwest.

Merchant backlash

By 2010, more than 2,500 merchants had participated in Groupon deals. As each market could only do 365 offers a year, most cities had long waiting lists. While the majority of merchants were happy and often signed up again, a distinct minority were displeased.

Reports surfaced of merchants who lost money after offering a Groupon. In a widely circulated blog post, Posies Café owner Jessie Burke in Oregon said she had to pay $8,000 (£5,180) in payroll out of savings after throngs of customers bought her half price Groupon deal, which was a money loser.

In a university study, 40% of Groupon merchants said they wouldn't do another offer. Groupon countered that the vast majority of merchants were happy, and the number of participating merchants continued to climb. It became clear that offers needed to be carefully structured, though, to avoid burning the merchant.

International explosion

In 2010, Groupon continued its stiff pace of entering new US markets, adding 13 more in the first quarter alone. The company began acquiring small competitors to add more markets quickly, along with tech companies to expand the platform. But the year's defining event was the acquisition of CityDeal, for a reported $100 million (£64.7 million).

Forbes magazine would proclaim Groupon 'the fastest-growing company ... ever'.

Overnight, Groupon was a global brand, adding major European markets including London and Berlin. Groupon was able to scale these markets at a breathtaking pace, taking the London market from $1.7 million (£1.1 million) to $27 million (£17.5 million) in revenue just over a year later, for example. Masterminding much of the overseas expansion were CityDeal's owners, brothers Marc, Oliver and Alexander Samwer, savvy Germans with a history of creating acquisition-worthy European clones of US companies.

A screenshot of Groupon's website today.

In all, Groupon entered 45 new countries in 16 months flat, a mind-boggling feat. Eighty markets were added in the second quarter alone, taking Groupon from zero to more than $100 million (£64.7 million) in overseas business in 2010. Investors liked what they saw. In April, Groupon raised $135 million (£87.4 million), from Accel, NEA, Battery Ventures and Russian tech mogul Yuri Milner's Digital Sky Technologies. In August, *Forbes* magazine would proclaim Groupon 'the fastest-growing company … ever'.

Besides its overseas expansion, Groupon broke new ground by offering its first national deal. An offer for $50 worth of clothes for $25 from apparel chain Gap sold 433,000 Groupons for $10.8 million (£6.99 million). The Gap deal generated tons of press and, better yet, 200,000 new subscribers.

With small imitators springing up in many cities, Groupon differentiated itself by introducing a 'Preferences' feature, enabling subscribers to receive offers in categories of interest only. The company also introduced a Groupon Rewards program, in which customers earn more discounts by shopping more frequently at a particular merchant.

No sale

By now, Groupon had grown successful enough to attract not just media attention, imitators and investors, but also buyout offers. But the team wasn't keen to sell, preferring to continue growing the company themselves.

In mid-2010, Yahoo! made an offer rumored to be between $3 billion (£1.9 billion) and $4 billion (£2.5 billion), only to be quickly rebuffed. The struggling search engine had its own problems, and the Groupon team wasn't interested in an alliance.

The next offer was harder to turn down. It was from Google, for a whopping $5.75 billion (£3.7 billion). But reports were that antitrust concerns shot the deal down. Instead, Groupon again turned to private equity investors raising $450 million (£291 million) at the end of the year, which dwarfed 2010's $313 million (£203 million) in revenue.

The funds kept flowing in, with Groupon raising another $492.5 million (£319 million) in early 2011. Interest from funders grew as the inevitable next step for the fast-growing phenomenon neared: a public offering.

IPO or 'disaster'?

As the company prepped its IPO (initial public offering on the stock market) in early 2011, the executive team seemed to crack under the strain. First,

President and Chief Operating Officer Robert Solomon quit in March after one year, followed by founding CTO Pelletier, who cited exhaustion. His replacement, former Google executive Margo Georgiadis, lasted only a few months. One communications head, Bradford Williams, lasted just two months. The high-staff turnover foreshadowed the rough waters ahead.

After Groupon filed its IPO papers in June 2011, the company was criticised for both the form and content of its filing. It used unconventional financial reporting methods, prompting restatement requests from the US Securities and Exchange Commission (SEC). Eric and Andrew made statements that leaked to the media and were viewed as potential violations of SEC 'quiet period' rules. An aura of suspicion enveloped the company.

Groupon's restated figures showed $1.1 billion (£712 million) in revenue for the first three quarters of 2011 and a $214.5 million (£139 million) loss – a surprise, as Andrew had said that Groupon was profitable the prior year. Also news: over $940 million (£608 million) of the $1.2 billion (£770 million) in venture capital Groupon raised had been paid out already to its founders and a few early backers, rather than being used as working capital at Groupon. As a result, the company had more payables due than cash in hand. The filing also revealed that the number of US merchants placing Groupon deals had begun to decline in the second quarter, although the international merchant base continued to grow.

Critics charged that Groupon's daily deal model was too easily replicated and would be outdone by competitors such as Google Offers, which launched in April 2011. Others opined that group coupons were a fading fad.

'Groupon is a disaster', proclaimed financial analyst Sucharita Mulpuru in one widely circulated article. Meanwhile, the US stock markets tanked in summer 2011 after Standard & Poor's downgraded the nation's credit rating, putting the IPO on hold.

In the end, investors turned a deaf ear to the media din, as did Groupon subscribers, who continued to buy. Groupon's IPO effort survived all the travails, and the company went public in November 2011. The IPO priced at $20 (£12.90) a share, above its planned $16–$18 range, raising $700 million (£453 million) in the highest-valuation IPO since Google in 2004.

Where are they now?

At the time of its IPO, Groupon offered more than 33 million deals in a single quarter, to nearly 143 million subscribers in 175 cities across 45 countries. Sixty per cent of Groupon's business is now international.

In early 2010, Eric and Brad co-founded the venture fund LightBank, which focuses on disruptive technology start-ups. Eric also serves on the boards of several non-profits. Brad serves on several company and non-profit boards, and he and Eric teach at the University of Chicago's Booth School of Business. Andrew continues as CEO of Groupon.

In May 2011, the company introduced Groupon NOW, which enables merchants to implement short-term flash sales. In early 2012, the company reported that it was nearing its breakeven point.

Etsy

Etsy

A handcrafted success

Founders: **Rob Kalin (shown), Chris Maguire, Haim Schoppik and Jared Tarbell**

Age of founders: **All early-to mid-20s**

Background: **New York University (Rob, Chris and Haim), New Mexico State University (Jared)**

Founded in: **2005, USA**

Headquarters: **New York, USA**

Business type: **Online marketplace for independent creative businesses**

I n 2005, Rob Kalin was a 25-year-old student, carpenter, photographer and painter looking for a good way to sell his wares. He would join with two other friends at New York University to create exactly that: an online marketplace for handcrafted goods. He gave it a short, nonsensical name: Etsy.

From a website cobbled together in just a few months in Rob's Brooklyn apartment, Etsy would grow in five years to move more than $300 million (£192 million) in merchandise, be valued at more than $300 million by investors, and employ more than 250 people.

The ironic secret of Etsy's success? Rob put more energy into helping the crafter community and promoting the lifestyle of buying handmade goods than he did into making Etsy a viable business. That philosophy would cause much conflict and turmoil at the company, but would also draw an enthusiastic user base and enable Etsy to succeed.

'Profit isn't a focus', he said flatly in a 2010 video interview with the influential technology blog TechCrunch. 'To me, the most important part of commerce is the social aspect. This is a huge opportunity to reinvent what e-commerce means. That's our goal.'

A little client project leads to a big idea

In 2005, Rob and his friend Chris Maguire were hungry New York University (NYU) students doing freelance web development work to try to cover their tuition fees. Chris was just 21. The pair formed a design company, iospace, but quickly tired of client work and wanted to create their own online business. The question was what it would do.

Rob's time at NYU overlapped only briefly with Haim Schoppik's, but the two had something in common besides NYU: both were high school dropouts. Boyish, redheaded Rob had basically dropped out of high school and then bounced through six different colleges before landing at NYU. He only made it into the school through subterfuge, faking a student ID at Massachusetts Institute of Technology (MIT) and then using a recommendation letter from an MIT professor he'd met to gain admission.

For his part, Haim dropped out of high school at 16 to pursue his first love, computer programming. After a couple of years in the workforce, including stints as a site administrator for Goldman Sachs and Reuters, Haim went back to school. All three studied at NYU's Gallatin School of Individualized Study, where students create their own majors.

Entrepreneurial ideas seemed to grow in Rob's head like weeds, Haim recalls, though many were of dubious value, such as opening a photo-scanning store. One early idea of Rob's was to create an online community productivity software application. He even wangled $10,000 (£6,120) in financing to develop the idea from a local property mogul, Spencer Ain, for whom Rob had built a home bar.

'Rob's hidden ability is talking rich people out of their money', Chris says. 'That's what he's best at.'

Unfortunately, the concept flopped shortly after Rob got the money. The pair needed another website idea that could justify the investment money they were quickly spending.

'To me, the most important part of commerce is the social aspect. This is a huge opportunity to reinvent what e-commerce means.'

The turning point proved to be the duo's pro bono revamp of a crafters' chat forum site, GetCrafty.com, which was owned by an NYU professor's wife, Jean Railla. The project gave Chris and Rob the chance to work on community forum software. More important, they had a chance to chat with many of the site's members online.

'People kept saying they wished they had a better place online to sell their stuff', Chris says. 'eBay was too big, too expensive, and too ugly for what they wanted. And we were like, "There's an idea. We could build that."'

Three months with three men and three cats

The idea of a crafters' e-commerce website caught Haim's interest. At 25, Haim was the most seasoned worker of the group, bringing needed site administration and design experience to the project. The trio soon converged on Rob's Brooklyn apartment, which became the designated launchpad for the site.

'eBay was too big, too expensive, and too ugly for what they wanted. And we were like, "There's an idea. We could build that."'

The apartment had several bedrooms, but Rob's flatmates had moved out, leaving just Rob and his three pet cats. Chris and Haim would rarely make it back to their own homes over the next few months as they worked frantically to build the as yet unnamed website.

'We literally lived there', recalls Haim. 'There are unflattering pictures of me asleep with my mouth open, drooling. We'd wake up and go to work and work until we crashed.'

As the team built frantically and ran through its capital, the question quickly became how much site to build before launch. Rob was taking counsel from his grandfather, who had worked at both IBM and GE. He advised the trio to wait until they had a fully featured website and a solid business plan.

Haim working away in their first 'office', Rob's apartment.

But Rob was also talking to a friend from his Brooklyn neighbourhood, restaurateur Sean Meenan, who had created several successful eateries including popular Café Habana. The two had cemented their relationship when Rob built Sean a cool computer made of orange plexiglass for an internet café. He liked Rob's hustle: before the site's launch, he noticed Rob out distributing flyers about the site at a Brooklyn craft fair.

Sean had the opposite opinion from Rob's grandfather: launch as soon as you possibly can, and add more features later. This latter theory won out, and a fairly bare bones version of the site would launch after nearly three months of work, in June 2005.

During this frenetic period, Rob was also out raising more money. He returned to Spencer Ain for more funding, who also brought in his brother, Judson Ain. Sean was the third investor in the start-up's $315,000 (£193,000) first funding round.

Why would Sean write a 25-year-old, first-time entrepreneur a six-figure cheque for an as yet unlaunched e-commerce website?

'I was a big believer in Rob', he says. 'He has a unique perspective and he's really smart. And there was something really sincere, innocent and hopeful about this project.'

Origin of a made-up name

As the site neared launch, Rob hunted for a name for the new business. He knew he wanted it to be something short – short website addresses are easier to remember – and he wanted a made-up word around which he could build a brand.

Watching the Italian director Federico Fellini's classic film *8½*, Rob kept hearing the actors say 'etsi', Italian for 'oh yes'. He also noted that in Latin it meant 'and if'. Americanised with a 'y' ending, the company was christened Etsy.

The free launch

In June 2005, Etsy launched as a free e-commerce site for crafters. Why? The billing system wasn't built yet. Etsy had no way to assess, track or collect payments.

Sean had the opposite opinion from Rob's grandfather: launch as soon as you possibly can, and add more features later.

It would be several more months before Etsy would be able to institute its initial fees: $0.10 (£0.06) per listing and a 3.5% fee on items sold. For now, crafters could get onto the site, put up listings and pictures of their wares, and sell them. Search tools for customers were rudimentary. Still, Etsy was up and going, and crafters took notice immediately.

'The biggest landmark is after we launched, we actually saw someone list something', Haim recalls. 'Holy shit, somebody actually used us! And later on, somebody actually bought something. That was a real moment for me. From there, it just grew and grew.'

As crafters signed on and began to use the site, the team continued to work madly on fixing problems and adding features. For instance, sellers of vintage items wanted more categories for their wares.

The breakthrough addition was chat forums. The team had seen the power of forums on the GetCrafty site, but never imagined how crafters longed to share their problems and ideas. By the year's end the team would be moderating 100 forum posts a day. (By 2008, it would be 15,000 posts.) Of course, managing all this took work, work and more work for the small team.

'Our work arguably never stopped', says Haim. 'There were always improvements to make and bugs to fix. We were literally always building it.'

Quickly, it became clear that more robust search tools would be needed to sift through the growing piles of merchandise – jewellery and sock puppets, paintings and hand-sewn pillows. Rob knew a visual artist in New Mexico, Jared Tarbell, who was adept at working in the graphics program Adobe Flash. Jared had been hesitant to join before the launch, but once the site was up, he began working remotely from New Mexico on new search features.

His first search tool allowed users to search for items by colour, a useful feature for decorators. Etsy ended up patenting the technology, which is used by many retailers today. Other features added later were more whimsical, such as one that would select Etsy sellers who were celebrating their birthday. A geolocator was also added so that shoppers could view goods from a particular country or city.

Rob, Chris, Haim and Jared in California, circa 2006.

'Our work arguably never stopped', says Haim. 'There were always improvements to make and bugs to fix. We were literally always building it.'

While the tech team had their heads down, Rob had his eye on the big picture. He considered Etsy's marketplace nothing short of revolutionary. He wanted it to be a tool to enable consumers to abandon mass-produced, cheap goods in favour of getting to know small merchants and purchasing their wares. On the seller side, more people would be empowered to make an independent living.

'Etsy is about offering viable alternatives to mass-produced objects in the world marketplace', he told the *Financial Times*.

While it wasn't done intentionally, launching as a free site had its advantages in attracting crafters. Once the pay model was introduced several months later, many users would accept the fees and continue to be Etsy sellers.

By the end of 2005, several thousand crafters had sold $170,000 (£104,000) of goods on Etsy. Of course, there was little profit in it for the team, since the site was free for about half of its six months of operation.

It wasn't clear in those early days if Etsy would grow large enough to become profitable. Most of the products were low-priced, so Etsy's commissions were small. But crafters loved the site, and shoppers were buying.

Rob, Chris and Haim's California adventure

Now that the site was up and enjoying modest success, the budding company grappled with growing pains. As more users came on, the site developed problems and sometimes crashed. When it was down or a feature didn't work, users would see a cartoon of a flaming Haim known as 'Haim on Fire' with the caption, 'Don't worry – Haim's working on it!' After one major 2007 outage, Etsy crafters expressed gratitude for Haim's round-the-clock efforts to restore the site by making crafts incorporating the Haim on Fire image.

The cartoon Etsy put up when their website crashed.

Etsy needed more powerful computer servers, more staff – and more money. Fortunately, word had spread rapidly about the little start-up. The tech press loved Jared's innovative Flash features, while crafting magazines printed glowing tales of crafters who'd seen success on Etsy and had been able to turn crafting into a full-time business.

To connect with Silicon Valley venture capitalists, Rob laid plans to visit California. Rob's Brooklyn pal and investor Sean Meenan came along as his wingman.

Rob had contacted Flickr co-founder Stewart Butterfield via email, expressing his admiration for Flickr and asking him to take a look at Etsy. He did, and he liked what he saw. Flickr had recently sold to Yahoo! for a reported $30 million (£18 million), putting Stewart and his co-founder/spouse Caterina Fake in the investing business. Both were enthusiastic about Etsy and would take the lead in helping to secure Etsy's first round of venture funding.

Through Fake and the social bookmarking site Delicious.com founder Joshua Schachter, whom Rob had met at a New York party, Rob met a couple of heavy-hitting venture capitalists at Union Square Ventures: Fred Wilson and Albert Wenger (who had briefly been president of Delicious.com).

Together, these investors committed $1 million (£592,000) in November 2006 to Etsy in its 'Series A' venture funding round. Union Square would invest over $3 million (£178,000) more the following year. The negotiation was a triumph for Rob, who was nervous pitching Union Square as he'd heard the firm wanted at least a 20% stake to invest in a start-up. Rob didn't want to give up that much ownership.

He boldly offered Union just 1% of the company, take it or leave it. Wilson immediately agreed, and Union Square was in. Albert says investing in Etsy was a no-brainer.

'They didn't have to pitch', he says. 'I could go on the site and see people were genuinely excited to have a marketplace just for them. The existing venues – craft fairs and consignment shops – were incredibly inefficient. I thought, "This is what the internet is for – connecting people and enabling this kind of commerce that has a personal component to it." Plus, they had youthful enthusiasm aplenty.'

The money was raised to fund 'Etsy 2.0', a major upgrade of the site. To stay close to their new funders, the Etsy trio rented a house in San Francisco and set to work coding the new version.

One bright spot in the frantic money-raising and site-rebuilding of 2006 was that Etsy doubled its listing rate to $0.20 (£0.12). Haim says there was some griping from sellers, but as the fees on Etsy were still substantially lower than eBay's – and far simpler to understand – most accepted it.

During this time, Etsy picked up a marketing manager, former rock band member Matt Stinchcomb. To this point, Etsy had put almost no money into marketing. Matt created 'street teams', bringing together Etsy sellers by market area or interest group. The groups offered support for crafters and put on local craft fairs and how-to events. This promotional method got the word out about Etsy and built crafters' loyalty to the brand.

Etsy closed out the year having handled $3.8 million (£2.25 million) in sales for its merchants. But the New Yorkers didn't take to California, and returned home after just a month. Soon Chris and Haim would be coding at Haim's house, with Chris crashing on the uncomfortable couch they dubbed 'the spine-crusher'.

The team continued in this way until Etsy got its first Brooklyn office in 2007. It was a heady time: the company had just seen its millionth sale, and two million items would be sold before the end of the year. With its first real office, Rob started Etsy Labs, installing silk-screening machines and other craft supplies and holding events where crafters could create goods on site.

The company also added a new revenue stream to its business model, offering sellers the chance to pay a $7 (£4) fee to have their product featured prominently in Etsy's 'Showcase'.

In Rob's view, Etsy sellers were like the tiny fish that band together to repel scary big fish in the children's story *Swimmy* by Leo Lionni. Bringing crafters together on the site, he hoped, would enable them to better compete with big chains and shopping centres.

Some crafters found a dark side to being an Etsy seller, though. Crafters reported toiling 14-hour days at what amounted to less than minimum wage to create their wares. On the flip side, success could get you banned from Etsy. The site's rule was that all goods must be handmade. If sellers became popular and wanted to make more goods than they could personally handcraft, they had to leave the site.

Doubting Thomas

Sales volume skyrocketed in the next few years, hitting $26 million (£15 million) in 2007 and $87.5 million (£51.3 million) in 2008. With growth, though, came chaos. The company staff expanded to 60 without a planned structure for how they would interact. Cracks developed. Teams lost focus. The site struggled to keep up with crafters' demands for more features.

At the same time, the site's explosive growth drew more interest from investors. Etsy was able to raise much more investment in 2007: $27 million (£15.6 million) from Accel Partners, Acton Capital Partners, Hubert Burda Media and Union Square.

With investors looking on and increasingly anxious for the site to turn a profit, Etsy needed someone more seasoned to create a stronger corporate structure. Former Amazon and NPR Digital Media manager Maria Thomas was hired as Chief Operating Officer. Maria was quickly elevated to CEO, with Rob stepping away from day-to-day responsibilities to focus on creating a charity that would help empower crafters.

The leadership change was a breaking point for Chris and Haim, who were burnt out from the years of long hours. In particular, Haim had been working in the company's rented New Jersey data centre under hellish conditions, locked alone inside a security cage in a noisy, cold, poorly lit, windowless cavern he dubbed 'a raver's prison'. The two identified pressing problems and told Maria about their proposals to solve them, and were rebuffed. They asked to do research and development work for new Etsy projects. Again, the answer was no.

'She said, "I have no interest in any of this – I'm bringing in all my own people"', Haim recalls. 'It was time for us to go, because this was never going to work. If you don't have board seats, you don't have power – that's the most valuable lesson we learned.'

In 2009, Etsy moved to larger, art-filled offices on the fifth floor

The Etsy site today.

of a former printing company in Brooklyn's arty DUMBO neighborhood (the acronym stands for 'down under the Manhattan Bridge overpass'). The new space would allow Etsy to add employees and offered more room for Etsy Labs activities.

The return of Rob

Maria accomplished some critical milestones during her time at Etsy. Most important, the company turned profitable in 2009 and saw over $180 million (£115 million) in sales transacted by its merchants. Revenue increased sevenfold during her tenure. The company laid plans to open its first foreign office, in Berlin, and made its first acquisition, buying online advertising start-up Adtuitive for an undisclosed sum.

But there was a feeling among both staff and crafters that the company had lost its way on the creative side. A community council was formed to try to involve crafters and respond to concerns, but the discontent persisted.

Ultimately, Rob was drawn back to the helm. In December 2009, Rob returned as CEO of Etsy, and Maria left the company.

Where are they now?

In 2010, Etsy had seven million registered members and 400,000 sellers. Ten million items were listed for sale, and the site received 940 million page views. The company saw revenue of $40 million (£6 million) on over $300 million (£194 million) in merchandise transactions. By September 2011, Etsy had already exceeded the previous year's sales, with nearly $358 million (£229 million) in revenue.

In August 2010, Etsy raised an additional $20 million (£12.8 million) from Accel, Hubert Burda, Acton and Index Ventures. In all, the company has raised more than $51 million (£32.6 million). Etsy is the subject of regular rumours of a public offering, but as of autumn 2011, no plans had been announced.

Post-Etsy, Chris and Haim work together at the start-up Postling, which makes social media management tools.

In July 2011, just eight months after his return, Rob announced he would depart Etsy again. Chief Technology Officer Chad Dickerson, who had joined Etsy at the same time as Maria, assumed the CEO mantle. Union Square's Fred Wilson said this second departure felt like goodbye.

'Rob is so very much that founder who cares intensely', Wilson wrote on his blog, A VC. 'He has given so much to the company over the years, and he just completed a product road map that provides a guidepost for what Etsy will become in the coming years. Etsy is his creation and will always be.'

eBay

Buying power

Founder: **Pierre Omidyar**	
Age of founder: **28**	
Background: **Software engineer**	
Founded in: **1995, USA**	
Headquarters: **California, USA**	
Business type: **Online auction site**	

Fifteen dollars might seem an insignificant amount, but it was the sum of money that sparked the business known today as eBay, the global auction site with $11.7 billion (£7.6 billion) in revenue.

Founder Pierre Omidyar, a software engineer, was experimenting with online auctions as a hobby and advertised a broken laser pointer for sale. He was amazed that someone would consider paying just under $15 ($14.83 to be precise) for an item that didn't work, and it convinced him that there was potential in a business that catered to people's passion for collecting.

The laser pointer was duly sold and dispatched and has gone down in history as eBay's first transaction. Today eBay is the world's largest online marketplace and one of the most successful companies of the dot-com era – and is still making headlines around the world.

Technology guru

Born in Paris, Pierre moved with his family to Washington, DC in 1973 when he was six years old, and he was fascinated by computers and technology from an early age. While other kids were out playing sports, he was more likely to be found indoors tinkering with hardware and learning how to program computers. He taught himself to program in BASIC and used his technology skills to get his first job, computerising his school library's card catalogue for $6 an hour.

Unsurprisingly, Pierre later decided to major in computer science at Tufts University near Boston, where he nurtured a passion for Apple software. It was an early sign of his entrepreneurial flair and desire to do something different. At the time, Apple was seen as a trendy, non-traditional technology company, a minnow challenging established giants such as IBM. With a beard, sunglasses and his long hair tied back in a ponytail, Pierre sported a look that was well suited to his love of Apple.

In the late 1980s and early 1990s, he worked as a Macintosh programmer, securing a number of jobs at software companies in Silicon Valley before deciding to venture out on his own. Together with friends he founded Ink Development Corporation, which aimed to produce software for pen-based computers, forerunners of the Palm Pilot. This part of the business, however, did not take off as rapidly as he had hoped, and a year later Pierre decided to focus on another offshoot of the business – online commerce. The company was subsequently renamed eShop, and it operated as an electronic retailing company. While the concept of the internet was gathering momentum around the world, the pace of technology was still too slow for Pierre's liking, and he quit eShop in 1994 in order to pursue a business that would propel him one step closer to the internet. Pierre retained a stake in eShop, however, and in hindsight this proved to be a wise move. Barely two years later, eShop caught the attention of software giant Microsoft, which acquired the company and made Pierre a millionaire before his 30th birthday.

All things internet

By this point, Pierre had caught the internet bug. Luckily, he was in the right place at the right time, as a host of other online businesses were now starting to emerge. Pierre cultivated his interest in the internet by joining mobile communications start-up General Magic. It was during his time here that the idea for AuctionWeb, which would eventually become eBay, took shape. Like many great business ideas, Pierre's creation stemmed from a bad personal experience. A few years earlier, he had placed an order online for shares in a company that looked promising, but he soon discovered that the stock had soared by 50% before his order had been fulfilled.

He thought it unfair that some buyers were favoured with one price, while others had to settle for another. Pierre believed an online auction was a better way of arriving at a fairer price for all concerned, and with the development of the internet such a concept could become a reality. 'I've got a passion for solving a problem that I think I can solve in a new way', he said at the time. Pierre wanted to test the web's ability to connect people around the world and offer a platform where buyers and sellers could share information about prices and products.

'Instead of posting a classified ad saying I have this object for sale, give me $100 (£63), you post it and say, "Here's a minimum price"', he once said, recalling his early strategy in an interview. 'If there's more than one person interested, let them fight it out.'

The bigger picture

It was going to take time and patience to develop his business idea, but Pierre relished such a challenge and worked around the clock, holding down his day job during the week and working on AuctionWeb in his spare time in the evenings and at weekends. In fact, he wrote the initial code for eBay in one weekend. It was a labour of love and an all-consuming hobby. With his concept for an online auction, Pierre wanted, above all, to promote the idea of a community on the internet, one that was built on fairness and trust.

Once the code was complete, Pierre launched the site; however, he had no idea what types of things people might want to buy and sell. As an experiment, he advertised his broken laser pointer for sale, and to his surprise, he found a buyer who was interested in broken ones. Pierre created a handful of categories – including computer hardware and software, antiques, and books and comics – in which users were soon listing, viewing and bidding on items.

Because he intended to offer the service for free, it was imperative that he keep overheads as low as possible. To this end, Pierre ran the site from home, paying $30 (£19.60) a month to his internet service provider (ISP). He also decided to register the business and picked the name Echo Bay Technology, which he thought 'sounded cool'. But when he tried to register it, he found that it was already registered to a Canadian mining company, so instead he chose the closest alternative, by shortening the name to eBay.

To boost traffic, Pierre avoided advertising and PR and deals with other sites in favour of generating awareness by word of mouth. He posted announcements about the site in online newsgroups to attract attention, and this had the desired effect: computer geeks and bargain hunters emailed one another with details of the site. Despite the lack of paid advertising, eBay soon gathered momentum, and healthy numbers of visitors began listing and buying all manner of goods. Toward the end of 1995, Pierre's ISP began to charge him $250 (£158) a month, suspecting that the growing volume of traffic was putting a strain on its system. This marked a turning point for Pierre and signaled the moment when he decided to turn what was until now just a hobby into a fully fledged business.

Pierre wanted, above all, to promote the idea of a community on the internet, one that was built on fairness and trust.

'That's when I said, "You know, this is kind of a fun hobby, but $250 a month is a lot of money"', he has since recalled. Pierre had designed the

eBay's headquarters in California.

site to be able to collect a small fee based on each sale. Implementing this charge now would provide him with the necessary money to fund overheads and expand the business. He decided to charge 5% of the sale price for items under $25 (£16) and 2.5% for items above this threshold. Later he would add a charge for listing items.

Going for growth

With the new fee structure, the fees collected began to surpass his salary at the time, which made it an easy decision to quit his job and devote his full attention and time to eBay. In June 1996, with the site recording more than $10,000 (£6,400) in revenues for that month and 41,000 registered users, Pierre hired his first employee, Jeff Skoll, who had previously been involved in two high-tech start-ups. Pierre also set up feedback capabilities on the site to enhance the buying and selling process and reinforce his original mission of creating a trusted community. A year later, eBay was attracting more consumers than any other online site.

'By building a simple system, with just a few guiding principles, eBay was open to organic growth – it could achieve a certain degree of self-organisation', Pierre said in one interview.

In 1997, with the business growing at a phenomenal rate, Pierre invested substantially in advertising for the first time and helped design what has now become the business's iconic logo. The year marked another milestone as the one millionth item was sold on eBay: a toy version of *Sesame Street*'s Big Bird. By 1998, the site was making a name for itself as the best place to trade for Beanie Babies, tiny stuffed animals that were fast becoming a collectors' item.

Fortune continued to favour Pierre's sense of timing. Towards the end of 1997 and throughout 1998, business communities around the world were experiencing the dot-com boom, and seemingly everything online at the time became attractive to investors and consumers alike. Pierre recognised that the business was becoming too big for him to handle alone and that the time was right to seek outside help and expertise. He had already filled several roles, among them Chief Financial Officer, President and CEO, as well as chairman of the board.

Pierre decided to seek outside funding and sold a 22% stake in the business to venture capital firm Benchmark Capital in return for an injection of $6.7 million (£4.7 million), which some reports have suggested was the most lucrative investment ever made in Silicon Valley. Benchmark began the search for an experienced management team, and the new recruits included Margaret (Meg) Whitman, a Harvard Business School graduate who had previously worked for Disney. She took the role of President and CEO, while Pierre remained as chairman. Meg poached senior executives from the likes of PepsiCo and Disney who helped to take the company public in 1998 and presided over a big investment in advertising.

The IPO, too, was a phenomenal success and provided funds for further expansion. Pierre and Meg watched the share price jump from $18 (£11) to $50 (£31) in a matter of minutes, and within two months of listing, the price had reached $100 (£63). By early 1999, Benchmark's stake was worth $2.5 billion (£1.55 billion), equating to a staggering return of 50,000%. After a secondary offering, eBay's valuation peaked at $26 billion (£16 billion).

Teething troubles

Rapid growth came at a price, however. In June 1999, following a site redesign, eBay suffered a number of breaks in service, with one lasting 22 hours. This had a severe impact on consumer interaction with the site and knocked more than $8 (£5) off the price of its shares. Further outages occurred, and company revenues took a severe hit. According to reports at the time, the service interruptions cost eBay $3.9 million (£2.4 million) of its second-quarter revenues after it refunded listing fees and granted extensions on auctions.

At the time, the 22-hour outage was one of the worst internet crashes in history, and a backlash quickly ensued as users wasted no time registering their complaints on an internet newsgroup dedicated to the site. Others raised questions about the robustness of the technology.

Keeping the customer foremost in mind had always been Pierre's aim, and he set about reassuring customers about the quality of eBay's service. Staff worked around the clock to address technical problems, and eBay made some 10,000 phone calls to the site's top users, alerting them to the problems, apologising for the inconvenience and assuring them that everything possible was being done to get the site back up and running.

A few users however, began turning to other sites that were giving eBay a run for its money with their own versions of online auctions, most notably search engine Yahoo! and online retailer Amazon. The latter had launched online auctions in March 1999 with a model similar to eBay's, including a commission on sales and a rating and feedback system. New competition, however, appeared to be a good thing, as eBay beefed up its services in response. It expanded the range of products on offer, streamlined the buying and selling processes – and set its sights on global growth.

Worldwide expansion

In 1999, eBay launched sites in the UK, Australia, Germany and Canada, and Pierre and Meg also implemented a strategy that involved selling more expensive goods on the site. This entailed launching a series of regional sites, which they believed would facilitate the sale of larger items that would be cumbersome and expensive to shift, such as vehicles. eBay also began to focus on making targeted acquisitions, and a year later the company bought online retailer Half.com, which allowed users to buy goods directly without going through an auction process.

eBay's well-known bright signage.

By 2001, eBay had added Ireland, Italy, Korea, New Zealand, Singapore, Japan and Switzerland to its portfolio of international sites, and its user numbers had swelled to 42 million. Such rapid expansion was an impressive feat in itself, more impressive for having been achieved against a backdrop of doom and gloom in the dot-com community. Many internet businesses had sought a public listing and seen their shares and valuations soar in the same vein as eBay's. But by 2001 the landscape had changed, and one online business after another went bust.

Such rapid expansion was an impressive feat in itself, more impressive for having been achieved against a backdrop of doom and gloom in the dot-com community.

As for eBay, it wasn't all smooth sailing either. The Asian market, for instance, proved very difficult to crack. By 2002, just two years after its launch, the company had pulled the plug on its operations in Japan, admitting that it was struggling to make inroads in a market where competitors such as Yahoo! already had a well-established auction model. According to reports, eBay was able to offer only 25,000 items on its Japanese site, while Yahoo! Japan offered close to 3.5 million. But as one door closed, another one opened. eBay's entrepreneurial spirit and appetite for global challenges persisted, and the management team set its sights instead on China, buying a third of Eachnet.com, the country's leading online auction site.

eBay also looked at ways of improving its services, and in 2002 it bought electronic payment system PayPal in a deal valued at $1.5 billion (£99 million). PayPal was the leading player in the online payment market, and eBay's own payment system, Billpoint, had failed to dent PayPal's market share. It seemed to make sense to team up with PayPal's winning formula, and Meg hoped the acquisition would help speed up eBay's existing payment processes.

In 2004, eBay introduced the 'Buy it now' function, enabling sellers to bypass the auction process and sell immediately to consumers. A year later, it launched a business and industrial category, offering items from the industrial surplus market. Its most surprising move came a year later, however, with the acquisition of internet telephony provider Skype in October 2005, at a cost of around $2.6 billion (£1.5 billion). At the time, eBay said it planned to integrate Skype with its auction website to smooth the sales process in those categories that called for better channels of communication, such as used cars and high-end collectibles. The deal also enabled eBay to extend its global reach by accessing an audience in Europe and Asia, areas in which it had so far failed to gain a strong foothold.

Survival of the fittest

While some analysts questioned the logic behind the eBay–Skype deal, and others said eBay paid too much, one thing was clear: by the time it celebrated its 10th anniversary in 2005, eBay had proved itself many times over as an internet business that was here to stay. It had peaked during the dot-com boom and survived while other high-profile, venture capital-backed brands such as Boo.com, eToys and Webvan had disappeared altogether.

Although eBay's foray into online auctions in China ultimately proved unsuccessful (it closed the website at the end of 2006 and instead

The inside of eBay's headquarters.

entered into a joint venture with a Chinese company), eBay had more success with Skype. In 2007 Meg Whitman said that Skype had more customers in China than in the USA, and the growth rate in China was higher than anywhere else.

Fittingly for an internet business, eBay has not been slow to capitalise on other technology opportunities, as it now offers a site enabled for mobile devices, an iPhone app, text-message alerts and blogs. It has also further diversified its services to offer 'Best of eBay', a site dedicated to finding the most unusual items advertised, and 'eBay Pulse', which provides information on popular search terms and most-watched items.

More recently the company has branched out into other international markets and expanded its auctions business into event ticketing and comparison shopping, while navigating its fair share of challenges. The company has seen the overall growth of its core auction business slow down, and it has had to deal with numerous incidents of fraud carried out on the site. What's more, eBay has faced intense competition from search engine giant Google, which in 2006 launched Checkout, its own online payment system. Amazon, too, has begun to attract independent sellers, the core of eBay's business.

The company's success has been credited in part to its ability to innovate as well as to adapt, a vision that has been with the company since the very beginning, and that continues to hold true today.

Where are they now?

As of 2011, eBay had around 100 million active users globally. Its three biggest markets are the USA, the UK and Germany. In Forbes's 2010 list of the world's billionaires, Pierre Omidyar was listed at number 148 with personal wealth of around $5.2 billion (£3.37 billion). He remains Chairman of eBay but has kept himself busy with other ventures, such as Omidyar Network, a philanthropic investment firm.

In April 2008, Meg Whitman stepped down as CEO (and in 2010 ran unsuccessfully for Governor of California). She was succeeded by John Donahoe, President of eBay's Marketplaces division, who remains CEO today.

In 2009, eBay sold 70% of its share of Skype for $2 billion (£1.25 million), having paid $2.6 billion for the online communications company in 2006. But in 2011 Microsoft acquired Skype for a massive $8.5 billion (£5.33 billion), valuing eBay's 30% share at $2.8 billion (£1.76 billion).

The full-year 2011 revenues showed an increase of 27% on 2010 levels to $11.7 billion (£7.6 billion). The company generated net income of $3.2 billion (£2 billion). PayPal also saw significant rise in revenue, with a 28% year-on-year revenue increase to $4.4 billion (£2.85 billion), with the payments provider adding a million new accounts every month in 2011.

The company's success has been credited in part to its ability to innovate as well as to adapt, a vision that has been with the company since the very beginning, and that continues to hold true today. The site introduced new measures to make its auctions and fixed-price listings easier to use, revamped its feedback mechanisms and strengthened its anti-fraud provisions in a bid to make eBay a safer place in which to trade. As Pierre explained in an interview in 2000: 'What eBay did was create a new market, one that wasn't really there before. We've had to evolve our strategies and policies from what I built in the beginning, which was a self-policing community of people, to one where we take a more active role in trying to help identify the bad actors.'

MADE.COM

Growth by design

Founders: **Julien Callede, Ning Li and Chloe Macintosh**

Age of founders: **29, 30 and 37**

Backgrounds: **Julien: private equity, financial analysis and development management; Ning: co-founder and CEO of Paris-based furniture company Myfab; Chloe: architect and headed the design department at e-tail venture MyDeco.**

Founded in: **2010, UK**

Headquarters: **London, UK**

Business type: **Design-led furniture e-tailer**

179

I n the space of just a couple of years, Made.com has charted a course from unknown start-up to a genuine player in the UK's home furniture and fittings market.

The company began with grand ambitions, but a simple idea: to create designer products at affordable prices. Expanding on a direct to consumer model already tried and tested in France, Made.com's three entrepreneurs planned to revolutionise the furniture market. With no storage costs to contend with and designers lining up to take part from the get go, Made.com's profile has been on a steady incline and the online retailer is now synonymous with trendy, non-extortionate furniture. After ironing out a few niggles with delivery times and customer service, surely the site can only go from strength to strength.

A wealth of experience

Made.com's founders all bring something different to the table. Business-minded Ning Li worked for investment bank Rothschild before co-founding MyFab, a Paris-based furniture retailer with a very similar business model to Made.com – sourcing products directly from factories. Julien Callede had a wealth of experience in operations and management, as well as a solid business background from experience in venture capital and start-up management. And Chloe Macintosh brought a creative element, having spent 10 years working as an Associate Partner at top architectural practice of Norman Foster. Chloe's move into retail e-commerce stemmed from a friendship with digital entrepreneur Brent Hoberman – best known as founder of Lastminute.com – who asked her to head up the design operation at his online furniture retailer MyDeco.com.

As it turned out, Brent was instrumental in getting Made.com off the ground. 'He was very interested in the "direct from the factory" business and reached out a few times to me when I was still CEO of Myfab', says Ning. 'I had the idea of a direct to consumer business model, but was living in Paris and most of my contacts were in France. I wouldn't have come to London to start Made.com without the backing of someone like Brent.' Ning finally responded to Brent's friend who had introduced them – at this point Ning had cashed out from Myfab and embarked on a one-year round-the-world trip. Brent persuaded Ning to come to London.

Here, Brent introduced Ning to Chloe and, as the business model for Made.com began to take shape, Ning brought in his friend from business school,

Julien Callede, who brought some much-needed design and operational experience to the business.

A concept emerged

At its heart was the direct from the factory model, but, as Chloe is keen to stress, Made.com's business plan was not simply about the processes associated with keeping costs down and offering cheaper prices to the public – it was also about design. 'We wanted to offer a platform for designers and offer them a route to market', she says. 'We wanted to be really aspirational and compete with both the likes of Ikea and Conranshop.'

The business model was deceptively simple. Made.com would commission designs – tables, chairs, beds, lighting, etc – which would be marketed through its website. The items would be manufactured only when a customer placed an order, and the goods would then be shipped from the factory, via a UK depot and on to customers' homes. With minimal storage required, and with no expensive high street shops, costs could be kept to a minimum and the savings passed on to customers. Thus, design-led quality pieces could be offered at a greater discount than from competitors.

Ideas into reality

To achieve their objectives, Made.com's founders had to place a number of ducks neatly in a row. Before they could even think about coming to the market, they needed finance, suppliers and the all-important co-operation and participation of talented designers.

With Brent as chairman, the project had financial backing and business experience from the start.

Finding the funding was challenging. However, the founders – Ning in particular – had a track record, and the business model had been tested in the French marketplace. Equally important was the fact that, with Brent as chairman, the project had financial backing and business experience from the start. Together they raised an initial funding round of £2.5 million for the UK launch of Made.com.

Arguably the market conditions were favourable. In 2009 and 2010, the UK economy was beginning a fitful and often faltering recovery. Consumers had an appetite for well-designed furniture, but conventional suppliers were struggling with the realities of costly warehousing and retail floor space. At the same time, a large segment of the buying public were paying off debt and seeking out the best available prices. Witness the collapse of Habitat. Made.com's low-cost model was ideal for this marketplace.

Chloe herself invested in the project, but the bulk of the funding – about £2.5 million – was raised from third parties in a first round investment led by venture capital firm Profounders Capital, and also including Jaina Capital, Brent's MyDeco and John Hunt, founder of the Seattle Coffee Company.

The second challenge was to find suppliers – which was far from straightforward. Following Made.com's unconventional business model, a minimum order quantity must be reached before products are actually manufactured, meaning that orders for the suppliers are not guaranteed. Unsurprisingly, suppliers did not find this prospect particularly appealing, as they would traditionally agree to a number of minimum orders before they sign a contract. 'In a market where price and economies of scale were driving everything, we had to get manufacturers to trust us and invest in new product development as well as quality and service levels', Julien explains.

As a new company it was something of a gamble. With no track record on sales, the founders knew that some producers might understandably shy away from gearing up to deliver on contracts that might only generate a trickle of orders. Larger manufacturers were unlikely to be receptive to the Made.com pitch; and, although smaller companies might be happy to take on the work, from the founders' perspective there was a risk that they would lack the resources to provide a stable run of production.

Made.com therefore focused on the middle range, says Chloe. 'Manufacturers who weren't too big or too small. And what we set out to do was work with them as collaborators – as partners.'

Made.com selected factories in Asia, including China and Vietnam, depending on the skills and expertise on offer. However, they also started with a UK supplier (who now manufactures about 30% of the products). 'In the case of big upholstered items there are issues surrounding fire retardant standards and transport costs, and it makes sense to source from British suppliers', Chloe explains.

Initially, Chloe's expectation was that the company would be working with relatively young and inexperienced designers. This was, after all, a new

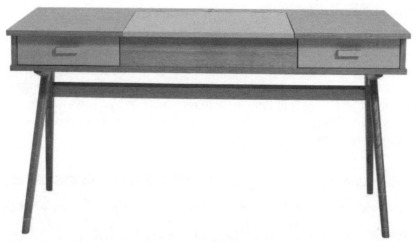

Steuart Padwick's designer desk is now one of Made.com's staple products.

and untried concept and therefore potentially a risk for established names. Young designers, fresh out of college, would see the opportunity rather than the risk. But one established designer saw the potential from the outset. Steuart Padwick was the first designer to come on board with a desk that Made.com sells for £300 – the bespoke version on Steuart's website costs £2,000. This product was the result of the first designer collaboration, a hit with the press (appearing in more than 50 publications to date) and remains one of Made.com's bestsellers today. The company's creative roster now includes a mix of designers from James Harrison and Dare Studio to Allegra Hicks and Jimmie Martin.

In Chloe's view, this was partly attributable to the speed at which Made. com can bring its products to the market. 'With a conventional retailer, it will take at least 18 months for a product to travel from the drawing board to the shopfront', she says. 'We can bring a product to market in about four months. That is very attractive to designers. It means they can get their ideas into the marketplace very quickly.'

The ability to work with designers via collaborations is crucial to the process. The designers always work closely with the Made.com team during the development of their products.

The web address

For an internet-only business, the web address is effectively the brand name. As such the moniker Made.com played a vital role in helping the young company establish a recognised online presence. Selecting the right name wasn't easy. The founders knew they needed to find a memorable, four-letter word – easy to type, easy to remember and with associations to the product. Almost two decades on from the dawn of the internet, such names were in short supply and the best ones came at a cost.

The founders knew they needed to find a memorable, four-letter word – easy to type, easy to remember and with associations to the product.

Arguably, it's not perfect. Unlike a URL such as furniture.com or chairs.com, it doesn't provide a 'does what it says on the tin' summation of what the company is about – and that's a disadvantage when it comes to search engine rankings. However, it hasn't proved too much of a problem: the team worked hard to develop the name into a brand which exudes a certain 'cool' that is in keeping with the product, and favourable extensive press coverage has fuelled organic search.

Appealing to customers

Once the site had its front page and a couple of products to sell, the next stage was to plan marketing efforts, followed by getting orders to suppliers. The site launched in March 2010. The founders then had to convince customers that the unique approach would work.

As a start-up, Made.com knew it would be competing with the big and established names of the industry. Yes, Made.com may have been doing something interesting and fresh in terms of both its business model and its products, but somehow it had to make its voice heard above blue-chip competitors such as John Lewis, Next and Laura Ashley.

Chloe explains that the key was the product range, and its value pieces. A glance at Made.com's website reveals prices that are genuinely well below those of designer furniture companies. And while the products are design-led, price is the main incentive. 'Price is key in the current market', says Chloe. 'Customers are looking for bargains and the prices they are prepared to pay can be extremely challenging for conventional retailers. So people are coming to us because of the prices we charge.'

The business was also attracting attention from other retailers. 'We could see many of the high street brands on our distribution list', Chloe continues. 'And some were ordering products from us. I recall an afternoon just after the weekly launch of a new collection, when we received a call from the supplier asking us to remove the new product from sale. A very renowned high street retailer who was selling a similar product from the same supplier was putting pressure on them. We had sold 50 pieces that day, almost twice the amount that the retailer sells in a month. We, however, agreed to stop selling the product to avoid creating issues for the supplier.'

Against the low prices, customers have to bear the wait for the goods to arrive. A consumer who keys in a credit card number today may not see the product for several months. It's not an experience for those who are seeking instant gratification – but then again, buy a sofa from John Lewis or Heal's and you'll often get the same wait. With Made.com, it just also counts for lamps and cushions.

Relying on PR

From the start, Made.com planned to use PR to drive customers to their site. The lifestyle press is always on the lookout for companies offering good deals on well-designed products and Made.com fitted the bill. The founders began by contacting editors and putting forward both its products and its business model, and found the press very receptive to their offering. 'We knew that endorsement was important', Chloe recalls, 'especially for an unknown online company that does not have a physical showroom or shop.' The company started to secure write-ups in publications ranging from the *Daily Telegraph* and *Evening Standard* through to glossy magazines such as *GQ*, *Elle Decoration*, and *House & Garden*. 'Initially most of the sales came as a result of PR', Chloe attests, 'and today the majority of our traffic is still organically driven.'

But the founders were also aware that raising your profile through press coverage can be a hazardous business. While favourable coverage can work wonders when it comes to driving sales, negative coverage can inflict serious damage. Thus it's not only important to secure press coverage but also to manage it carefully.

Chloe recalls an order from an influential newspaper editor for a Steuart Padwick desk about six months after they launched. Immediately, she knew what she had to do. 'I was petrified in case something went wrong', she recalls, 'so I decided to make the delivery myself.'

It was probably a wise decision. At that point, Made.com had benefited from a series of positive write-ups in newspapers and magazines – coverage that had been instrumental in raising the profile of the business and driving sales. In the first few months, the business had been seeing around 100 orders a week. Winning an order from a senior journalist was clearly a coup, but there were also risks. Put simply, if the customer was dissatisfied there was a real danger that Made.com could find itself generating column inches for all the wrong reasons at a very early stage in its development.

So Chloe went to the customer's house, assembled the table and took time to listen to the thoughts of the recipient. 'I came back with a lot of feedback which we were able to learn from', she says.

Not all of that feedback was positive. Aside from a later than expected delivery date, the customer was less than impressed by the bulk of the packaging. However, by turning up in person Chloe not only brought that personal touch, but also witnessed first-hand the practical problems associated with delivering and assembling bulky items of furniture. 'Since then I've always insisted that we assemble every product line in the office before we begin shipping to customers.'

Selling on the web

Unusually for a digital start-up, the company decided not to pump money into online advertising, instead relying on PR and natural (free) search engine traffic.

In order for this tactic to work, Made.com needed to achieve a high search ranking, and ensure that they appeared near the top on the first page of results. Made.com populated their site with keywords that people would search for, and articles in online magazines and newspapers (with links to Made.com) helped give the company a strong presence on the search engines. Type in, say, 'designer furniture cheap prices' and the chances are Made.com will come up close to the top in the unpaid rankings.

Founders Julien, Ning and Chloe all bring different specialties to Made.com.

The strategy worked, with about 80% of Made.com's business coming from organic searches. By the end of the first year, Made.com was getting around 500 orders per week.

Clever advertising

Towards the end of their first year the company started advertising online to accelerate growth. New developments in online advertising began to play a major part in attracting customers. Normally, online ads are sold to appear in a particular place or on a specific website, but now media agencies can use technology to track the internet user – noting what they are searching for, or browsing – and then place display banners that are thought to be relevant to the consumer, with that assumption based on previous online activity. Made.com decided this new approach was perfect for them.

One-time visitors to the site often find that ads for a particular Made.com product pursue them around the internet. Wherever they go, they see the Made.com name. 'It's a very clever way of advertising', says Chloe. 'It makes it look like you're advertising everywhere and that you are much bigger than you are.' And, of course, it keeps the Made.com name and product portfolio at the forefront of the customer's mind.

Customer service: the biggest challenge

Given the apparent ease with which Made.com's founders raised cash, struck deals with suppliers and were embraced by the media, it would be tempting to conclude that the business has had a relatively easy ride. But there has been one major challenge, which remains an ongoing source of concern: delivery and customer service.

Online companies thrive or dive according to the quality of their service. Placing an order on a website is something of an act of faith. What the customer is looking for is rapid fulfilment – preferably a delivery the next day or within a clear time frame – and a means of tracking the order. Additionally, once the credit card details have been placed, nothing shatters the faith of the customer more effectively than a poor fulfilment service.

Made.com faced some very specific challenges in this regard. Unlike, say, Amazon, which can store its bestselling books and CDs in a central warehouse, Made.com ships directly from overseas factories to the UK, where individual orders are redirected to the customer.

While customers knew they had to wait for their orders to be manufactured and shipped, the company found they weren't necessarily aware of – or sympathetic to – the logistical challenges involved in getting a bulky package from China to Bradford, London or Aberdeen. Thus, at points, the positive publicity enjoyed by the company was tempered and arguably undermined by some very negative customer feedback on websites and in the press. In particular, Made.com was criticised for failing to deliver in accordance with a customer-friendly timeframe, for instance failing to provide a morning or afternoon delivery slot and therefore requiring the customer to wait around for the whole day.

The danger for Made.com was that the limitations of third party hauliers would reflect directly (and negatively) on the brand. Put simply, the man with the delivery lorry is the public face of Made.com. If the drop goes wrong, it is the retailer rather than the haulier who suffers a reputational hit.

The founders soon acknowledged this problem, and recognised that its ability to alter the practices of the haulage industry was limited, to say the least. 'Managing your growth is one of the most important and complicated things to deal with', Julien says. 'When you grow by 20% every month, and sometimes 100% month on month, you quickly outgrow both your team's and your fulfilment partners' capacities. It became our biggest challenge when we realised that even the largest home delivery companies out there were not always able to deal with our peaks in deliveries.' Nevertheless, the company took what steps it could to limit any damage by stepping up its customer service operation. 'We've grown our service team to look after our customers. The key is to ensure that we can keep customers informed. If there is a problem we will tell them what it is and find a way to make up for it.' Chloe explains that once they pinpointed this issue, the bulk of their initial investment went into creating back office functions for the website – in particular systems that allow the customers to track the progress of orders through from manufacturing progress to shipping and delivery.

Put simply, the man with the delivery lorry is the public face of Made.com. If the drop goes wrong, it is the retailer rather than the haulier who suffers a reputational hit.

The company also realised the need to manage demand. Now, if the sales of a particular product are in danger of outstripping manufacturer capacity, the company can take it off the site.

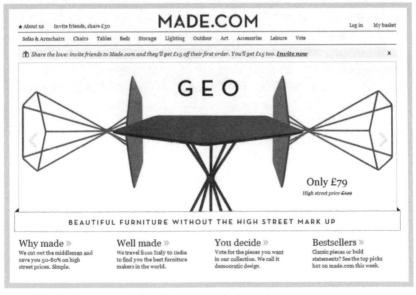

The Made.com website showcases their newest designer pieces.

Where are they now?

Two years on from its launch, Made.com is making good progress and – as the company puts it – it now connects more than 100,000 customers with leading designers. A second round of funding has been completed, raising £6 million from venture capitalist Level Equity and the original investors, and the stage is set for more domestic and international growth.

However, the founders are cautious about pursuing growth at the expense of profits. 'The investors want us to spend more to drive growth', says Chloe. 'But we also want to become profitable. We have ambitious growth targets, but the growth curve is not the only thing that we – the managers – are looking at.'

Made.com's founders successfully started and grew a company at a time when the UK economy as a whole was looking shaky. In many respects it was a business perfectly attuned to the times, offering low-cost products that nonetheless spoke to the aspirations of the design-conscious consumer. But success was not a given. On paper, the founders had everything going for them: knowledgeable and influential backers; a tried and tested business model; and founders with collective experience running from design through to logistics and operations.

But making an internet business work requires more than a sound business idea and an understanding of e-commerce. It requires the ability to stand out from the crowd, build a brand in a crowded marketplace and the ability to not only sell products, but to keep customers satisfied. From the evidence of its first few years, it looks like Made.com is set for continued growth and success.

discover fashion online

ASOS

Dressing the digital generation

Founders: **Quentin Griffiths and Nick Robertson OBE**	
Age of founders: **32 and 33**	
Background: **Advertising/media planning and co-founder of Entertainment Marketing**	
Founded in: **2000, UK**	
Headquarters: **London, UK**	
Business type: **Fashion e-commerce**	

With nearly four million customers worldwide and growth of 50% in 2011–12, if you don't already know about ASOS, you soon will. The online-only apparel business, best known for its young, fashion-forward collections, is the largest online fashion retailer in the UK. Furthermore, the website's collection of womenswear, menswear, footwear, accessories, jewellery and beauty products is attracting an increasingly global customer base, with international sales soaring 150% in 2010–11.

However, despite the current popularity of the fashion site, ASOS started in 2000 as a portal for celebrity-linked furniture and products under the name As Seen On Screen. The following decade has seen the business evolve into much more than just a fashion e-commerce site; it has become one of the defining brands of a generation.

So, how did a man who left school with his tail between his legs create one of the most respected digital businesses in the world?

Cutting the cloth

With Austin Reed, founder of the eponymous British menswear retailer, as his great grandfather, you might think it obvious that Nick Robertson would enter the fashion industry; but in his early years it didn't look as though Nick would follow in his footsteps.

The son of a high-flying advertising executive, Nick enjoyed a comfortable upbringing in suburban Surrey and attended a £28,000-a-year private boarding school in Dorset. By his own admission, he didn't make the most of his privileged education, describing his school results as 'diabolical'. He achieved a mere two Ds and an F at A level.

After leaving school at 18, he spent the first years of his adult life as a 'ski bum' in Meribel, France. However, upon his return to the UK, aged 20, he decided to follow his father into advertising and picked up a job as a media buyer for advertising agency Young & Rubicam in 1987. It was here that Nick cut his teeth, developing a real understanding of consumer behaviour, which would underpin the rest of his career.

After nearly four years with Young & Rubicam, he crossed over to work for rival agency Carat – the UK's largest media planning and buying business. But Nick was restless and growing frustrated at working for other people. He had seen his brother Nigel set up business directory firm Scoot in 1991 and a few years later decided to take the plunge into entrepreneurship himself.

The first template

Having seen an opportunity to cash in on the popularity of cult television programmes such as *Friends*, Nick founded Entertainment Marketing with Quentin Griffiths in 1996. The marketing services business was among the first to work with advertisers to, for example, get Weetabix featured in *Eastenders*, by offering the product to the television programme's producers as a free prop.

The business model, which relied on the power of celebrity to sell products, proved to be a success and Entertainment Marketing was soon attracting big-name clients including Carlsberg, Coca-Cola, Ford, Mars, Pepsi, Tetley and Samsung. While Nick worked closely with the television and film industry over the next four years, the idea for a sideline business – As Seen On Screen – emerged. He came to his new venture from an unconventional angle, he recalls: 'Entertainment Marketing was a product placement business, where we were being paid by big brands to associate them with celebrities. The idea spun out of that.'

The idea that emerged from their product placement business was to create a website where viewers could source, for example, Meg Ryan's coat in *You've Got Mail* or Jamie Oliver's pestle and mortar in an episode of *The Naked Chef* – or else a very good knock-off. Nick explains the inspiration for this idea further: 'We read a stat back in 1999 that when the programme *Friends* aired, NBC got 4,000 calls about some standard lamp in one of their apartments asking where it could be purchased. So that was the real idea behind the business', Nick says. 'Anything that gets exposure in a film or TV programme creates desire among the public, so we based the shop around that.'

But far from having visions of what ASOS has now become, in its earliest incarnation, the founders weren't especially focused on clothing at all.

'We read a stat in 1999 that when *Friends* aired, NBC got 4,000 calls about a standard lamp in one of their apartments asking where it could be purchased. So that was the real idea behind the business.'

Finance and fashion

Leaving Entertainment Marketing behind, Nick and Quentin launched As Seen On Screen online in June 2000, just after the dot-com bubble had burst. With the good fortune of having entrepreneurial families who were willing to back the venture, the pair raised a total of £2.4 million in start-up capital and purchased a variety of celebrity-linked products to launch the business. Nick's brother, who had sold Scoot two years earlier for £30 million, invested £1.1 million in the venture.

Although the full extent of the comedown from the dot-com boom was yet to become apparent, launching an online business in the mid-2000s was still a risky business. Yet the co-founders were undeterred. 'It was always going to be an online business, because of the amount of products that came up after being on TV. It needed to serve that function', Nick says, highlighting the wide reach and fast turnover of e-commerce. 'Also, our expertise wasn't in the "normal" high street, so this was more comfortable for us.'

While the founders had a wealth of business knowledge, Nick acknowledges that they had little background in consumer spending – something that would be crucial in making their business an online success. So one of Nick and Quentin's first hires was buyer Lorri Penn, whom they scouted from Arcadia – Sir Philip Green's umbrella retail group, which includes Topshop and Dorothy Perkins. She believed deeply in the potential of focusing the business on fashion (rather than furniture and other goods) – and they trusted her judgement.

'It wasn't until our first buyer came in, who was a fashion buyer, that we were pushed in that direction', Nick says, recalling the As Seen On Screen's first few months. 'Fashion is where we got the most returns for the business. Rather than saying "here's a standard top", we could say "here's a top that Jennifer Aniston wore in *Friends*".'

The founders acknowledged customer demand, and shifted As Seen On Screen from a website for odd celebrity-linked products to a focused haven of fast fashion. Targeted initially at 18–24-year-olds wishing to 'steal' an icon's style, the company homed in on the popularity of starlets such as Kate Moss and Sienna Miller, selling replicas of their most-touted ensembles using smaller designers, who were easy to get on board, to supply the products. It was the right formula, and, with some strategic PR and affiliates, sales started to grow. In 2001, As Seen On Screen reached sales of £250,000.

Frayed edges

The first year may have looked promising, but behind the scenes times were tight.

Nick now admits that for several months of 2001 he struggled to pay salaries. However, unwilling to abandon the investment his friends and family had made in his big idea, he kept his head down and pushed ahead.

In October 2001, after little more than a year in operation, Nick decided to go public and floated As Seen On Screen Holdings plc on the Alternative Investment Market (AIM). In the wake of 9/11 and the collapse of the dot-com boom, shares were falling towards one of the worst market collapses for a generation.

Nick persevered, focusing on proving the value of the business to investors by delivering his visions of growth. For Nick – who openly admits that he's no expert on youth fashion – this vision centred on two things: developing his business's talent pool; and increasing the website's reputation to encourage big brands to the site. 'We were constantly changing and developing', he recalls, 'but we accelerated that by getting in new buyers and new areas of expertise. We originally relied on one or two buyers buying across the board.'

At the time, As Seen On Screen had yet to attract larger fashion labels to supply the site. Later on, the business would launch its own-brand collections, but to begin with, they relied on existing smaller labels that were easy to secure. However, to grow customers and sales, they needed bigger names on board. Nick realised that building the website's reputation was crucial in attracting these larger fashion labels to the site. 'On day one, we weren't dealing with the big brands and developers because they didn't want to deal with us. Our reputation and those relationships have got bigger to the point where the big brands do want to deal with us', Nick says. 'You can't just open a shop door and expect them to come through; it's not going to happen like that. You need to build a reputation. You need to be financially sound because brands are precious about where they sit and what they sit next to.'

Nick's patience and perseverance paid off and by 2004, ASOS was selling stock from a number of prestigious brands – which in turn attracted more customers to the site.

As its customer base did grow, it became apparent that the brand awareness the business had developed with its fans was not As Seen On

195

The ASOS site today.

Screen, but ASOS. Just as the founders had responded to their customers' demands for fast fashion, they acknowledged that consumers no longer favoured As Seen On Screen for its celebrity links, but for its wide and affordable range of apparel. In 2003 the nimble start-up adapted to its market again, renaming the company with the acronym its customers had adopted for it.

> '*You need to be financially sound because brands are precious about where they sit and what they sit next to.*'

Drawing a new pattern

As ASOS reached profitability in 2004, two notable events occurred that would forever become landmarks in the company's history.

First, in September 2004, Quentin walked away from the company in search of a new challenge. For Nick, the thrill of business was to follow a start-up through. 'I'm as passionate now as the day I started', he said in 2006. 'And for the first time in 10 years I feel I'm loving it and making a positive contribution.' For Quentin, on the other hand, ASOS was just the first in a long line of entrepreneurial ventures, most notably, his latest venture ACHICA – the UK's first members-only luxury lifestyle store.

In the same year that Quentin departed the business, Nick married his wife Jan. On the morning of their first wedding anniversary, 12 December 2005, they were woken in their hotel room by the news that the Buncefield oil depot in Hertfordshire had exploded, and ASOS's sole warehouse had been destroyed in the blast.

'I got a call at 8.30 in the morning', Nick recalls. 'It was very patchy but the security guard on the site had seen it all from a distance and, thank God, we knew nobody was hurt.'

It was a devastating blow for the business nonetheless, and the worst possible timing for such a disaster to affect a product-based retailer: the day before its busiest week of the year. With 19,000 orders to fulfil and no access allowed to the site for at least two days, Nick made the brave decision to halt operations for six weeks during the Christmas period, temporarily suspending shares in ASOS from trading. 'It was a painful decision, but the right one', he says. 'I was still working blind and had no idea how bad it was or when we'd be selling again so there was no alternative but to suspend the shares.'

Nick prepared a statement for the press and a board meeting was scheduled for 8.30 the next morning, to put together an action plan. 'There was a small disaster recovery (DR) plan in place but we're a growing company; we hadn't got the substantial DR plans other companies probably have', he recalls. 'That said, when you're forced to focus on sorting out a problem it's surprising how quickly things come together. Within an hour of the meeting we started refunding the 19,000 orders, emailing customers and had changed the temporary message on the homepage.'

Three more anxious days went by before Nick was allowed to inspect the warehouse premises. When he was eventually permitted on site he found the roof lifted, doors blown off, and, worst of all, a burst sprinkler pipe, which had damaged £3.8 million worth of stock. Of the business's total assets, 45% of the stock was irrecoverable. 'Ironically, if we'd known the warehouse had been totally destroyed we could have started sourcing a new one straight away', says Nick, 'but we just had to wait.'

With 19,000 orders to fulfil Nick made the brave decision to halt operations for six weeks during the Christmas period, temporarily suspending shares in ASOS from trading.

Darning the damage

While ASOS rolled out its DR plan, its insurance brokers Seymour Pierce requested an assessment of the damage. Arcadia's Sir Philip Green – who had clearly forgiven Robertson for poaching Lori four years earlier, and was with the same broker – felt for the plight of a fellow fashion entrepreneur and sent his personal insurance assessor to Nick's aid. 'He turned up in a chauffeur-driven Bentley, which immediately put my mind at rest', says Nick. 'Green and his company were absolutely brilliant.'

By the following day, ASOS had received its first interim payment from the insurer to cover cashflow; a process that was scheduled to continue for 12 months, until the business was back on track.

Reflecting on the catastrophe a month later, Nick said: 'Personally, and from a business perspective, we've been through worst. We can pay salaries and nobody was hurt. We were absolutely insured to the hilt so with cover for loss of gross profit and assets, we shouldn't be any worse off at all. If you take the positives out of it, we've had more coverage from this than anything else we could have done.'

Indeed, ASOS's loyal customers were undeterred and when operations recommenced on 16 January, the business received a record 10,300 orders in 24 hours – double its previous best.

Speaking the following day, on 17 January 2006, Nick said: 'On yesterday's orders we have come back stronger than ever before and I'm confident of full recovery and a much stronger year. Our insurers are paying for an ad campaign we wouldn't normally have had and our share price today is up 2p on the day the disaster happened.' Robertson's predictions were right and year-end results for the business in March 2007 showed a dramatic recovery, with growth of 116% in 12 months – and revenues of £42.6 million.

Where are they now?

Those figures now seem modest compared to the annual turnover of £1 billion expected by 2015. Nick used ASOS's strong comeback from the Buncefield disaster to draw out a long line of innovations, including the debut of the free ASOS magazine in 2007. With a distribution of 456,000, this is now the second biggest women's fashion monthly in the UK and currently makes the business around £3 million in advertising alone.

ASOS has bucked the trend of the recession with consistently impressive growth. However, with the UK providing just 3% of global internet traffic, Robertson's growth strategy now is to focus on the 97% outside the home market and in 2010 he launched three country-specific sites – ASOS France, ASOS Germany and ASOS USA. These were followed in 2011 by ASOS Spain, ASOS Italy and ASOS Australia and will no doubt be followed by several more. Already, the brand's 1,000 staff cater to customers in 160 countries around the world. To aid growth, Robertson has invested £20 million in finding larger facilities, choosing a warehouse that can accommodate an initial capacity of £600 million in stock – almost double 2011's sales of £324 million.

For his success with ASOS, Nick has been hailed as one of the greatest entrepreneurs of the twenty-first century. On 15 November 2011 he was made an Officer of the Order of the British Empire (OBE) at Buckingham Palace, in the Queen's birthday honours list. Having defied the critics, led his business through several storms and become the definitive retailer of a generation, there is speculation that Nick will soon exit his online empire. But in the short term, he is enjoying the business too much to bow out – and no doubt he will want to see his fledgling celebrity product brand reach the £1 billion mark in 2015.

NET-A-PORTER.COM

The NET-A-PORTER GROUP Limited

Luxury online

Founder: **Natalie Massenet**	
Age of founder: **46**	
Background: **Fashion journalist**	
Founded in: **2000, UK**	
Headquarters: **London, UK, New York, USA and Shanghai and Hong Kong, China**	
Business type: **e-commerce fashion**	

With the launch of NET-A-PORTER.COM in June 2000, founder Natalie Massenet changed for ever the way women – particularly wealthy, successful women – shop. In the process, she created a business worth over £350 million in just 10 years.

In 2000 luxury goods manufacturers were reluctant to embrace the internet. They claimed that it didn't allow you to see the quality or to get an impression of the skills that went into the products, and that ordering online meant having to wait days for your order to arrive. Fast forward to today: on NET-A-PORTER you can buy anything from a pair of tights costing £15 to a dress costing over £7,000 and have it delivered in luxurious packaging, by a courteous and well-dressed courier, on the same day.

The eureka moment

Natalie spent her early life in Paris and Los Angeles following her journalist father and fashion model mother around the world. Following in their career footsteps, by the late 1990s she was working as a fashion journalist in London writing and styling fashion shoots for *WWD* and *Tatler*.

However Natalie wasn't afraid to try her hand at starting a business. First, she wanted to open a coffee shop, although after listening to business experts who told her there was no money in it, she scrapped the idea. She then looked into expensive candles: 'I took samples to several designer stores in LA, but they all said that nobody would pay more than a dollar for a candle.' So she scrapped that idea too.

The inspiration for NET-A-PORTER came in 1999, while Natalie was shopping online. She was looking to buy a pair of Chloé designer jeans she had seen in a fashion magazine, but couldn't find anywhere that stocked them. She remembers her confusion: 'I blindly assumed [the retailer] existed because of how brilliantly companies like Amazon were revolutionising service.' But she was wrong: there was no way to buy the designer label's products online and get them delivered; you had to set foot in a shop. And that's when it hit her: 'I thought, for a luxury brand, what better way to give the best service to clients than actually linking the browsing of a fashion magazine to the ability to shop at the click of a mouse and delivering to their door. That was the eureka moment.' Natalie's idea was simple: merge the magazine and the shop to enable women to purchase luxury goods and designer products online with ease, and – crucially – deliver them quickly and reliably.

'I thought, for a luxury brand, what better way to give the best service to clients than actually delivering to their door. That was the eureka moment.'

The scarf that started a business

While the purchase of some Chloé jeans created the eureka moment, the impetus to actually start the business herself came from yet another garment – a pashmina scarf. Back in 1999, the craze for the pashmina was taking off. 'When the pashmina was the big world-wide craze, suddenly overnight every woman from London to Hong Kong needed to have a pashmina, and they had to have them in every colour. A friend of mine was importing them and selling them to John Lewis and Harrods, and I said to her, "Why sell it as a wholesale proposition when you can go direct to the consumer?" I asked if she had seen the internet, and told her you could just create a website and sell pashminas to every woman around the world and take the entire margin. And she said, "No, no, no, I don't even know how to turn on a computer." I tried to convince her, and I then tried to convince other people to do it.'

But instead of leaving it there, Natalie decided that perhaps she should do it herself instead. 'As a journalist, you see some amazing ideas come along, and you write about them. I thought, "maybe this [selling online] is one that I can throw myself into. I'll do it." And with absolutely no idea of how to start a business, but with an end goal in sight, I started it.'

Getting the funding

Natalie began work on her site in 1999, and used her existing contacts in the fashion world including designer Anya Hindmarch and Jimmy Choo founder Tamara Mellon as a starting point. An initial backing of £830,000 came from friends, family and angel investor Carmen Busquets. Carmen was early to recognise the digital opportunity for luxury goods and, in 1998, began building a private portfolio of online companies. 'I was very lucky that I had amazing people around me from the very first day, who were able to advise me, and to contribute towards the business. It started really from a desire that it *should* exist.' Fundraising in the middle of the bursting dot-com bubble was not easy. Add to this the spectacular crash of fashion retailer boo.com in May 2000 – they had burnt through over £125 million of venture capital from luxury goods manufacturers (including one of the largest luxury brands LVMH) – and you would have said Natalie was, at best, foolhardy to start her online business at this time. 'They had an idea and a business plan', said Carmen Busquets. 'I invested £250,000 and afterwards I invested another £250,000. I knew the project would take at least £12 million to £16 million but I kept reinvesting because I really believed.'

'I remember reading Natalie's business plan for NET-A-PORTER in the Caribbean on Christmas day in 1999. Natalie was having a hard time. I phoned her up and said: "Don't worry. I'll put the rest in. I am willing to go all the way." I knew people would buy from a picture. Now nobody can tell me that online doesn't work.'

Although she was successful in getting her initial backers on board, she remembers many people being unimpressed with her idea. 'There were a lot of unimaginative private-equity people who said that women would never shop online. I think about those people a lot. I'm sure their wives are having NET-A-PORTER bags delivered to their homes every day.'

But her idea was to prove harder to put into practice than expected: historically, luxury goods websites have been very slow to populate the internet. In 2004 Gucci's then director of e-commerce said: '[Gucci is] still unsure whether Ready to Wear will be available as an ecommerce offering. But we live and learn and will test it eventually.' Back in 2000, when the majority of online customers surfed using slow dial-up connections, the number of luxury companies willing to take the digital plunge was even fewer. So it was a brave decision for a journalist with no entrepreneurial background to attempt to launch a website selling luxury clothing – especially as nobody was even sure whether the target demographic were internet users.

Nobody was even sure whether the target demographic were internet users.

The designers get on board

Natalie's fashion contacts were also helpful in establishing the initial list of designers that were to be available on the site – Anya Hindmarch and Tamara Mellon were again among the first to agree to be involved.

However it was backer Carmen who was to be one of the biggest helps in getting initial suppliers on board. Carmen ran a boutique in Caracas called Cabus. Part of what made Cabus special was the way Carmen would attend the catwalk shows in Europe, take photographs of the fashions and send the images to her best clients, who could then pre-order items through her shop. It also meant that when Carmen personally vouched for NET-A-PORTER's creditworthiness to designers with whom she had long-standing relationships, they listened and agreed to be involved.

But it would take years to convince other designers that this could work. Natalie was very emotional when they finally managed to sign some big names. 'One season we met with Marc Jacobs, Michael Kors and Chloé, and they all said yes. I remember bursting into tears when the team from Marc Jacobs said they'd sell through us', Natalie says. Marc Jacobs went live on the site in 2002.

Building luxury online

The next fundamental problem Natalie faced with selling luxury clothing on the internet was making it feel, well, luxurious. She was very aware that when buying online, there's no ambience, no feeling of being special that is associated with designer labels. The prospective NET-A-PORTER audience were used to walking into exclusive stores, where the staff were attentive and helpful, and everything would give the air of luxury, including the glossy packaging your goods come in.

Natalie understood this, and it was one of the first issues she had to deal with. The site had to be easy to use, it had to look good, and that luxuriousness had to continue right to the customers' door. So from the start, Natalie made receiving a package from NET-A-PORTER a memorable moment: products would arrive exquisitely wrapped in a black Balacron-covered box with a bow.

The site had to be easy to use, it had to look good, and that luxuriousness had to continue right to the customers' door.

Natalie also realised that one of the key elements of the site would be the images of the clothes. So she ensured that all goods were accompanied by high-quality graphics. When the site launched, it included ultra high-quality photography that allowed users to zoom in to see the individual threads on the fabrics.

The next piece of the luxury jigsaw that needed to be recreated online was service and fulfilment. Natalie realised that her time-poor, cash-rich audience weren't prepared to wait days for their goods. So she made sure that the goods arrived in her customers' hands as quickly as possible, wherever they were in the world. 'It's important to control the entire customer experience, and we certainly never forget that we are also a service and fulfilment company. From day one we were shipping to every country in the world.'

While many businesses would have stopped there, Natalie believed that this still wasn't going to be good enough for her customers, many of whom – particularly the VIPs – were used to being able to ring up and have things

The NET-A-PORTER site as it appears today.

delivered immediately. 'We worked with companies such as DHL so we could send things worldwide, and we created a taxes and duties system so that products could be expedited through customs, overnight delivery throughout Europe, two-day delivery to the Far East and Asia. And then we sped things up because people want same-day delivery in London, same-day delivery in Manhattan, which are two of the most important markets for us.'

The final piece of the puzzle was to create a community, which in NET-A-PORTER's case was the online magazine which launched on day one and has remained at the core of the business. The digital magazine proved very successful for NET-A-PORTER – not only does it bring in potential new customers through online searches, but it also indirectly created another revenue stream. The readers of the magazine are a very covetable audience for any advertiser and NET-A-PORTER are reaping the benefits with ad slots in the magazine.

Going live

Even in the face of the sceptics, Natalie knew she had enough support from colleagues and designers to proceed. She chose the name, NET-A-PORTER – a pun on prêt-à-porter, the French for 'ready to wear'. After flicking through a fashion dictionary for inspiration, she initially wanted to call it 'what's new pussycat?' but was dissuaded by friends who said it might attract the wrong sort of traffic.

Work began on the development of the site, eventually going live on 10 June 2000 – six months after Natalie had originally planned. During this time, she worked on getting her proposition as sleek and perfect as possible: her clientele would expect the best, so the site needed to perform.

However, the launch was not as smooth as Natalie would have liked. 'We had all this inventory just hanging there in our studio, becoming less and less valuable. We'd been sitting there compiling a list of what still needed to be done, and this poor IT guy who had been working without sleep for a month just put the website live without talking to us and went to bed', she remembers.

The business was based in a small artist's studio in Chelsea, London, with three members of staff. The rooms were stacked with stock and black packaging boxes, they had the capacity to deliver 1,000 orders a year.

But any preliminary teething problems soon dissipated. Initial publicity for the site came through Natalie's contacts and through her investors' networks, which created some strategic PR in the retail, business and fashion press including *American Vogue* who declared the website the 'chicest new boutique in the world'. They had reached their audience, and the first few sales came in. 'What was exciting was when an order came in and nobody around the room could say, "Oh yeah, that's my aunt." It was, like, "Oh my God, it's someone we don't know."'

The £350 million retail business

While it was tempting to grow fast and get a large capital investment soon after launch, Natalie instead decided on a more cautious approach to business growth. Expansion came only when cash was rolling in, and even then the shadow of failure loomed large.

'We'd watch companies fold that were funded with hundreds of millions of pounds. We'd buy equipment from websites that had gone under. We'd get calls from friends saying, "We've just gone down; do you want to buy our furniture?" I remember thinking that I never wanted to have to make that call.'

Natalie and her team still struggled to convince sceptics that her site was truly a revolution in buying designer goods online. 'In the first four years there was a lot of desperate hand-wringing, tears and pleading with brands ...', she recalls. 'You'd go through a pitch and say: "and then you can click and buy it from pictures and it's delivered anywhere in the world." And they'd listen and they'd nod and then afterwards they'd say: "Just tell me one more thing: where is your store?"'

'We'd get calls from friends saying, "We've just gone down; do you want to buy our furniture?" I remember thinking that I never wanted to have to make that call.'

Despite the early warnings NET-A-PORTER became very successful very quickly. The business became profitable in 2004, and by 2010 around three million visitors were logging on to the NET-A-PORTER site every month, with an average of 14,000 new customers arriving every month, and an average order value of £500. And while £500 is the average order value, there are a select few customers who spend considerably more: these VIP clients represent just 1% of NET-A-PORTER's customer base, but due to their immense spending power they account for 20% of sales.

With this fast growth and healthy profitability, it was only a matter of time before NET-A-PORTER attracted offers to sell the business. In 2010 she accepted an offer from Swiss luxury brands group Richemont, owner of the Cartier, Mont Blanc and Dunhill brands and an investor in NET-A-PORTER since 2002 – with a 28% stake in the business. The offer valued the business at over £350 million, and made Natalie a personal fortune overnight – although she immediately reinvested £15 million after cashing in her shares.

VIP clients represent just 1% of NET-A-PORTER's customer base, but due to their immense spending power they account for 20% of sales.

NET-A-PORTER's glamourous London headquarters.

Where are they now?

NET-A-PORTER's total number of monthly visitors now reaches over four million. Mark Sebba joined the NET-A-PORTER GROUP Limited in 2003 as Chief Executive, and has led the company's rapid expansion. Today the business has an exceptional management team and the original employees have been joined by more than 2,000 other employees across offices in New York, London, Shanghai and Hong Kong. Deliveries are still made on the same day in London and Manhattan, with 170 countries able to receive express shipping from a catalogue of over 350 of the world's leading designers.

Life is now very different from the early days, when it was hard to convince designers to be involved: now brands are clamouring to be considered: Stella McCartney, Yves Saint Laurent, Alexander Wang and RM by Roland Mouret are among the designers who have created capsule collections for the site. NET-A-PORTER has also diversified: THE OUTNET, the most fashionable fashion outlet, was launched in April 2009 and in February 2011, the company launched MR PORTER, a NET-A-PORTER for men, selling everything from a £5,000 leather coat to £20 Calvin Klein underwear.

Where next for Natalie Massenet? 'If we come up with an idea and someone says it's never been done before', Natalie answers, 'that's when we get going. We haven't even begun to see just how many transactions are going to take place online. I attend internet conferences all the time and they literally make the hairs on the back of my neck stand up.'

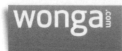

Wonga

Getting cash to consumers

Company: **Wonga**	
Founders: **Errol Damelin and Jonty Hurwitz**	
Age of founders: **36 and 36**	
Background: **Serial entrepreneurs in Israel and London**	
Founded in: **2006, UK**	
Headquarters: **London, UK**	
Business type: **Short-term consumer finance**	

Wonga is a young company, innovating within a very mature market. Its nimble response to the lumbering giants of the financial world has seen it crack the hard shell of the banks' stronghold over loans and consumer credit, to create a highly attractive financial solution for the digital generation.

In a climate where consumers' purse strings are the tightest they've been for decades, Wonga found its niche, and quickly found its simple approach to credit was a hit with consumers. Following in the footsteps of online innovators such as Google and Paypal, Wonga provides fully automated, efficient access to finance – delivering cash into customers' bank accounts within 15 minutes of them leaving the website.

As CEO of Wonga, Errol Damelin has described his role as not a job but a mission. There's no doubt that his mission – to bring transparency and ease of access to very short-term consumer credit – has been controversial. But, having won a mass of loyal customers and an impressive succession of awards, and quadrupled turnover between 2009 and 2010, Wonga has defied its critics to become one of the fastest growing companies in history.

Entrepreneurial entrée

The story of Wonga begins in South Africa, where Errol was born. During a degree in business science at the University of Cape Town in the late 1980s, Errol first showed his tendency to go against the established norm, sitting on the student representative council in the dying days of apartheid and speaking out against the separatist regime.

After a move to Israel and a master's degree in management science through Boston University's School of Management, Errol launched a successful career as an investment banker and remained in Israel for eight years. He became inspired by the dynamic, entrepreneurial spirit of the country – which he has compared to Singapore, Hong Kong and Silicon Valley – while working at YLR Investment Management, where he worked closely with entrepreneurs, helping them transform their dreams into reality. Soon, he too was bitten by the entrepreneurial bug; he decided to leave his job as an investor to become an innovator.

Errol's first venture, started in 1997, was Barzelan Ltd, an advanced steel wire production company, which he co-founded with a small team of associates.

The business is still trading today, but Errol, by his own admission, 'can't sit still for long', and by 2000 he had itchy feet again. He wanted to do something bigger still, and was drawn to London for two reasons: first, its position on the global business stage, and second, the Blair government's focus on entrepreneurship.

Errol moved to Europe, the third continent that he'd lived and worked on, in May 2000. Here, he founded Supply Chain Connect Ltd, which provided innovative software for blue-chip companies to manage their logistics. The venture was quite a leap from his previous start-up, but revealed the beginnings of a theme in Errol's entrepreneurial career: he is motivated by disrupting business sectors and taking on challenges others deem too difficult, rather than limiting himself to any particular field.

'I've always believed life's what you make it, and business success can be yours if you have the right ideas, attitude and a bit of luck', he muses.

Errol evidently has all of the above, as Supply Chain Connect quickly grew into a global business and opened offices in the USA. In 2005 – just five short years after it was founded – the firm was acquired by ChemConnect Inc., and Errol started scouting for his next business challenge.

The path to disruption

Errol left Supply Chain Connect in November 2005 but did not found his next company until 2006. In those 13 months, the ambitious entrepreneur worked tirelessly to explore markets and expand his network, looking for a groundbreaking opportunity with which he could make his foray into consumer markets. He recalls looking for an opportunity that would be scalable, responsible and user friendly. 'I was looking quite objectively at how the internet was disrupting large consumer markets and looking specifically at consumer credit', he recalls. 'Consumer internet was evolving, mobile was evolving and there were some very disruptive businesses in a bunch of consumer sectors – but retail financial services just hadn't been touched. It hadn't been innovated in.'

Errol had found his niche; seeing an obvious, immediate need to provide much faster, simpler, more flexible access to short-term credit than the raw deal he perceived customers to receive from existing solutions. 'People had been providing short-term credit for thousands of years, so it wasn't new in the sense that people need cash, but no-one had worked out how to innovate within the sector', he says.

Errol had found his niche; seeing an obvious, immediate need to provide much faster, simpler, more flexible access to short-term credit than the raw deal he perceived customers to receive from existing solutions.

The way to breathe new life into short-term credit in the noughties, Errol decided, was to design an online solution that catered to an internet-savvy generation's expectations of speed, choice and flexibility – which they'd become accustomed to from consumer giants such as Amazon, Facebook and Google. This was an opportunity the high street banks could easily take advantage of, if only, Errol says, they weren't 'weighed down in legacy systems', which prevent them from innovating. But none of them was even trying it.

That may be because the challenges were enormous. How could Errol convert the laborious process of credit assessment into a system that would work smoothly on the internet? How would he get the attention of a scrupulous online audience (and build their trust)? Could he, a lone entrepreneur with little over a decade's business experience, really break the banks' dominance?

'The problem with being digital was, would customers even know that an online digital solution existed for this kind of problem? And how to communicate that', Errol says.

Could he, a lone entrepreneur with little over a decade's business experience, really break the banks' dominance?

He acknowledged that he could not act alone, and scoured his network for a candidate with the expertise to co-found his risky venture. Errol chose fellow South African Jonty Hurwirtz, with whom he had become friends while sharing office space at Supply Chain Connect. A serial innovator himself, Jonty had started financial reporting platform Delve Reporting in a

Covent Garden back room in 1996 and grew it through the dot-com wave before selling to Statpro plc in 2005.

Power in numbers

Bringing nearly 15 years' experience in the financial sector to the partnership, Jonty joined forces with Errol in early 2007. They had £3 million worth of start-up capital behind them, raised by Errol from venture capital fund Balderton Capital and early-stage investor TAG the year before. TAG co-founder and experienced entrepreneur Robin Klein – an early investor in lastminute.com, whose own mail order company Innovations was the first UK business to allow payment transactions on the internet – also joined the company's board, as Chairman.

Errol says raising the money was 'pretty straightforward'. By which, he explains, he met Klein on numerous occasions in a Hampstead café in 2006 and they both talked over the challenges and honed the idea, realising it was a big opportunity to shake up a neglected market and meet the expectations of customers who had long demanded speed and flexibility for short-term financial solutions.

'We very deliberately chose who we wanted to be involved in the business and made it work with those guys', Errol recalls. 'It wasn't that it was hard

Errol joined forces with experienced Jonty and they took the business forward together.

to raise the money; it was much more about who we want to be partners with over the long term.'

The new team's plan was to make the process of borrowing money over the short term (up to a month) completely automatic and free from human intervention. The aim was to rid the loan process of its cumbersome, subjective and bureaucratic nature, making it instantly appealing and accessible to consumers. They would start with the UK consumer credit market.

The aim was to rid the loan process of its cumbersome, subjective and bureaucratic nature, making it instantly appealing and accessible to consumers.

As Chief Technology Officer, Jonty spent the best part of 2007 developing the first automatic, real-time processing system, which used sophisticated algorithms that could assess a customer's creditworthiness in less than a second. It was painstaking work and required the gradual addition to the team of first one, then two, outsourced developers.

'A major technology challenge was to automate the process of taking a loan and make an old-style process completely digital. It was massively complicated and we consumed thousands of pieces of data', Errol recalls. 'We joined up dozens of data sources and encountered tonnes of challenges to make it digital.'

The first loan

In October 2007, from an office in London's St John's Wood, Errol's team of 10 launched a beta site under the name samedaycash.co.uk. They had undertaken no pre-launch marketing, except for investing £50 in Google AdWords; turning on the pay-per-click account for the first time at the same moment as the web page and bidding on phrases such as 'small loan' to drive traffic. Within 10 minutes, a customer applied to borrow £100 and inadvertently became the first person on the internet to receive a fully automated loan, with no human approving the transaction.

With such an untested, high-risk business concept (and with samedaycash.co.uk putting its own money into customers' bank accounts) this pilot was crucial to test the technology in a controlled manner. The speed with which the first application came through was a relief for Errol, proving that people were actively looking online for a solution to their credit issues. A few days later, the site had its first customer to default on a loan – apparently a respectable man working for a well-known bank – further proving Errol's hunch that personal appearances can't be trusted; and highlighting the importance of fully automated credit assessment.

On the surface, the business strategy looked like commercial suicide. Defaults were happening all too often, and with loans coming out of samedaycash.co.uk's own pocket, it was not shaping up to be a business plan to lure further investors. But this was all part of the master plan. By adopting this approach with samedaycash.co.uk, the founders could gather vital intelligence on customer behaviour, enabling the company to profile its users and learn what type of people repaid loans – and crucially, who didn't.

This data all fed into Wonga's signature technology: an algorithm that completely automated the credit-checking process, assessing a customer's creditworthiness by analysing a whole range of data about them, then returning a decision. Once completed, this technology was groundbreaking; analysing data from numerous sophisticated sources, including the electoral roll and Facebook, to make fast, more reliable credit decisions. This reduced the default ratio significantly, laying a foundation for sustainable growth.

'We've never seen anyone else build a fully automated process in all the years since we launched', Errol reveals. 'So it's not a trivial, technical challenge in terms of what we've achieved. We haven't seen anyone else do it in any country of the world.'

'We've never seen anyone else build a fully automated process in all the years since we launched.'

Show me the Wonga

With the technology ready for commercial launch, the founding team began working with branding agencies to generate a company name that would be compelling and memorable, eventually settling on 'Wonga' – English slang for money.

'Jonty and I tossed around a whole bunch of ideas and in the end we just liked the word', Errol recalls. 'Most of the agencies were strongly against using the name Wonga but we felt we could build a true brand around it.

'There were other words that were more descriptive and could have been optimised differently to acquire customers more easily early on, on AdWords. But the intention from day one was to build a consumer brand.'

Wonga had its full commercial launch in July 2008 and featured two horizontal sliding bars on the homepage. The first let customers choose exactly how much they'd like to borrow – climbing in increments of £1 to £400 for new borrowers and £750 for returning customers – and the second controlled the period of the loan in days, before the total repayment amount was calculated. This function was key to the founders' vision, putting ease of access and flexibility at the business's core by allowing customers to control the size, length and cost of their loan for the first time.

The website enjoyed instant popularity and within a year Wonga had issued 100,000 loans, worth more than £20 million. The business reached profitability within its first 12 months, and generated around £15 million from loan interest. The start-up couldn't have launched at a better time: the UK was on the brink of a recession, household budgets were squeezed and banks were more cautious than ever about lending. By promising to place the loan in customers' bank accounts initially within an hour of their application (and later within 15 minutes), Wonga's offering was hard to compete with.

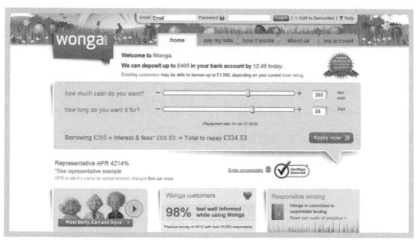

Wonga's current homepage still features the easy-to-use sliding bars.

However, the start-up's early success was met with a backlash of protests about the website's 4,214% representative annual percentage rate (APR – which legally has to be listed in all promotion, although it is misleading for a business with a maximum loan term of a month).

This is a theme which has continued to haunt Errol since Wonga's launch, and when the business employed the promotional strategy of sponsoring free public transport in London on New Year's Eve 2010 – using the poster slogan 'Sometimes you need some extra cash …' – a documentary on BBC Radio 4 blamed the business for luring customers into a destructive cycle of expensive loans.

'I think it's a controversial business because people have pre-conceived notions of short-term credit', Errol ponders. 'We've built the best-known brand in the area, so I think opposition comes with being disruptive and innovative. Facebook have lots of issues on data and Google have too, with some of the geography they chose to market to. When you go against the grain you knock into stuff around the edges.

'I don't think our customers think the cost of our product is 4,000%. It's just stuck with us because it was an equation required by law, but created for an old set of products in an old world. We happen to be in a new place, but customers really want to know the actual cost of repayment and that's often hard to find with traditional credit products.'

Cutting its losses

Demand for Wonga's loans rose so rapidly that by February 2009 the start-up required a second round of funding – securing £14 million from Accel Partners, Greylock Partners and Balderton Capital four months later.

'It's a complex business in that the more successful you are and the faster you grow, the more money you need to raise.'

'Wonga as a business is quite capital-intensive, because we lend our own money and we had to build our balance sheet to be able to do that', Errol explains. 'So it wasn't that we had spent the money, it's just that we were lending it. It's a complex business in that the more successful you are and the faster you grow, the more money you need to raise.'

Errol also took to the press to defend the reputation of his business, taking part in interviews to bust some myths and fight back against critics. He argued that the default rate on their loans has consistently fallen and is now in single-figure percentages, compared to the typical banking industry expectation of around 10% of credit card debt being uncollectable. Besides, far from being a predator on the vulnerable, Errol argued, Wonga rejects two out of every three applications it receives – only lending to those with an outstanding credit rating.

Where are they now?

Errol has remained unshaken in the face of criticism, focusing instead on ensuring Wonga delivers the highest customer service experience it can. The investment appears to have paid off, as the business won an army of loyal customers – it had approved over three million credit applications by the end of 2011. Furthermore, according to a 2012 survey by Populus, 92% of Wonga's customers would recommend the Wonga experience.

Wonga has now approved more than 3.5 million loans in four years. The founders have continued to focus on innovation – the website technology, although seemingly unchanged, is in its 30th incarnation. Returning customers can now borrow up to £1,000, and customers can also apply for credit on the go, through Wonga's iPhone and Android apps.

The key to Wonga's exponential growth is found in its business model. In contrast to the long period it takes organisations providing mortgage finance to profit from their investment, Wonga's fast turnover of customers has allowed it to maintain a regular income and a healthy balance sheet – providing the capital to continuously invest in growth. To support this, the founders secured a third round of investment in February 2011, worth £73 million, from Oak Investment Partners, Meritech Partners and the Wellcome Trust.

Next on Errol's growth strategy is to launch the website into new territories, as well as making further innovations in the broader space of consumer banking. If Errol's success to date is anything to go by, we should expect Wonga to grow substantially further.

moneysupermarket.com
the price comparison site

MoneySupermarket.com

A wealth of experience

Founder:	**Simon Nixon**
Age of founder:	**32**
Background:	**Mortgage broker**
Founded in:	**1999, UK**
Headquarters:	**Chester, UK**
Business type:	**Price comparison website**

n 1999, the UK's first personal finance price comparison site for consumers was launched by mortgage broker Simon Nixon. MoneySupermarket.com provided a wealth of information and aimed from the outset to be a 'consumer champion'. It is now visited by more than 3.5 million unique visitors a month in the UK, floated on the London Stock Exchange for £843 million, and, although the web has been flooded with replicas, it retains its position as the leading comparison site. Simon began with a solid background in providing accessible mortgage information, which he was able to adapt to his new venture. He was also able to use an existing business model to make MoneySupermarket.com's creation relatively painless.

An entrepreneurial mind

This extraordinary story starts in 1989 when Simon dropped out of a much-hated finance and accountancy degree at Nottingham University in his first year; he had no idea which career path to pursue, much to the distress of his parents. They presented him with the job section in their local newspaper, the *Chester Chronicle*, and 'basically forced' him to apply for the first post he was vaguely suited to, which turned out to be a position as a financial consultant.

Simon warmed to the idea of 'making some money', but, at only 20, he didn't like the idea of selling life insurance and pensions. Following this logic, he decided to specialise in the more relevant area of mortgages. He quickly found that 'the harder you work and the more innovative you are, the more money you make' as he was effectively self-employed, working on a commission-only basis.

Simon realised that if he teamed up with a local sales office, he might be able to get sales representatives to contact him directly to set up mortgages for their clients. He approached the nearby Chester Persimmon Homes office and asked if his services would aid their sales, quickly discovering that one in two people who wanted to buy homes from them could not as they had been refused mortgages.

Simon made himself first port of call for this sales office and started getting five or six mortgage enquiries a day. Soon, having only been working a few months, he was the top sales person in his office. The Managing Director of Persimmon Homes then asked him to provide information for three or four of their other offices. Simon describes how 'all of a sudden, I had someone helping me arrange mortgages'.

Simon made himself first port of call for this sales office and started getting five or six mortgage enquiries a day. Soon, having only been working a few months, he was the top sales person in his office.

This experience gave Simon a taste for the success of ingenuity. He also spotted an opportunity: there was no resource in the market for financial advisers like himself to find the best mortgage for their customer. Realising this, Simon bought an Apple Mac computer and in his spare time put together a fortnightly trade magazine, *Brokers Update*, listing the best deals and every product for reference. He initially sent out 500 free copies and charged £11 per month on standing order, with the first month free. Simon recalls that for every 100 copies he sent out, he received 10 standing orders. It was so successful that within three or four months he was making more money from magazine subscriptions than from arranging mortgages.

Simon recognised that he had to focus on either the magazine or mortgage brokering and decided to pursue the magazine – he thought it had more potential and found it more interesting. He recruited two people to work with him, bought a printing press with his savings and leaped into the world of publishing.

The magazine performed well but within two years, subscriptions started to plateau as mortgage brokers began relying more on computer technology. Information could be accessed immediately, so the magazine was already a couple of days out of date by the time it landed on their desk; something had to change. Simon, innovative as always, used funds saved from his magazine and took the format to begin writing a software package that was updated daily over the internet, allowing brokers to enter criteria and find the most competitive mortgage. He was joined by software programmer and then-business partner Duncan Cameron. Mortgage 2000 launched in 1994 and Simon estimates that this software is currently used by about 40% of all mortgage brokers in Britain. He acknowledges that had he just kept the magazine going, it probably would have died a few years later and he emphasises the need to keep 'spotting opportunities' and 'move with the times'.

To house his business initiative, Simon initially rented a room in the Chester Enterprise Centre, where they helped new businesses get on their feet. Eventually he was able to buy a terraced house in the Hoole district of Chester, where the company stayed until 1998. It then purchased its first purpose-built office on the then new Chester Business Park, from where they still operate today.

Breakthrough

Simon's 'real break' came in 1999 when Freeserve introduced free access to the internet. He wanted to create a site that used the information from Mortgage 2000, but changed the interface so that consumers themselves could use it. Simon also decided to broaden the information they could access to include other areas of personal finance, including loans and credit cards, to create a price comparison site.

Extending research to other areas was easy: with a solid background in mortgages and having produced financial information for several years, the transition was 'bread and butter to us'. Simon took on more researchers who specialised in personal finance, recruited internet developers and purchased some servers. He feels that it is important to have an in-depth knowledge of the business you are dealing in. While some entrepreneurs will jump into a market they think will be lucrative, Simon warns that without sound prior knowledge, there is a greater chance that business will not be successful.

'In business, if you work really hard, you take two steps forward and one step back.'

It was while setting up Mortgage 2000 that Simon went through the hard process of establishing a business from scratch, and not in his second venture – he warns that 'in business, if you work really hard, you take two steps forward and one step back.' Therefore, MoneySupermarket.com was able to lean on Mortgage 2000 and benefit from its legal and administrative infrastructure and personnel, of whom there were 40 or 50 by this point.

In total, Simon estimates that MoneySupermarket.com cost around £100,000 to set up, most of which was spent on PR, and because of Mortgage 2000's success, the new venture already had cash reserves in place. Unlike a lot of internet start-ups, which have to find an investor and 'blow it all on TV advertising', Simon already had a successful business under his belt and had already learned the principles of being in business. He advises entrepreneurs to follow a 'no frills' policy in setting up.

'People like to shop around and brag to their friend in the pub that they got a bargain.'

When MoneySupermarket.com was launched at the end of 1999, Simon felt that he had created a truly useful site – the challenge now was to direct internet traffic to visit and use it. Despite having more money in the bank than most start-ups, there was no million-pound fund to facilitate a vigorous TV advertising campaign, so Simon and his team had to be more imaginative with their marketing strategy. He notes that he was sure people would use the site, as he believes the average UK consumer is 'very price driven'. He explains, 'they like to shop around and brag to their friend in the pub that they got a bargain.'

Growing interest

MoneySupermarket.com makes its money every time a consumer clicks on a link to a financial provider such as Barclays or Capital One. So before MoneySupermarket.com could make a profit from their site, they needed to set up deals with financial providers and convince them they could provide high-quality internet leads. Simon remembers this process as being extremely difficult – companies were of course very sceptical, as this method of partnership had never been attempted before.

MoneySupermarket.com also anticipated that their information might be used by others, sourced through their website. The strategy was to pitch to the big web 'portals', such as BT, Yahoo! and Freeserve (who already had lots of readers but relatively 'poor content', according to Simon), and offer them MoneySupermarket.com's price comparison tools, splitting any e-commerce revenue 50:50. Simon approached the main players and pitched his novel

MoneySupermarket.com's homepage as it is today.

idea, but was categorically turned down. The companies were not interested in a revenue share and were asking for a fee from him of millions up front, which MoneySupermarket.com could not offer. Simon's last appointment in the first week of pitching was to the *Daily Mail'*s financial website, thisismoney.co.uk. They liked the content that MoneySupermarket.com were offering so much that they took a gamble and agreed to a revenue share in early 2000.

'Once you have enough inertia behind you, they fall like a pack of cards.'

Simon remembers how after this break, other portals 'sat up' and thought, 'Hang on a minute, they've got better information than us and they are our competitor.' Once they saw the information in practice, MoneySupermarket. com secured the internet portals that had at first declined.

It also became much easier to set up deals with the financial providers that would provide the income, and Simon describes how the deals slowly 'dripped' in: 'once you have enough inertia behind you, they fall like a pack of cards.' A slow yet rewarding process, within six months (which seems like an age in the internet world) MoneySupermarket.com had secured deals with five or six providers and therefore could start producing revenue.

Although MoneySupermarket.com did no advertising, Simon did recognise the importance of good press coverage, as this was essential in driving traffic to their site. He recalls that they spent nearly £100,000 on PR, using both PR company Lansons, of London, and PR staff employed in-house. Simon ensured that his researchers talked to all the national financial press every month – from the *Sunday Times* to the *Daily Star*: financial journalists would obtain figures and statistics from MoneySupermarket.com and quote their source in articles. He 'knew straight away that this was one of the most effective ways to drive traffic and raise your profile.' Simon describes this endeavour as a 'little bit cleverer than just spending money on advertising.'

'You have to put your foot down on the accelerator or people will catch you up very quickly.'

Although they faced a challenging start, Simon believes this was inevitable as he was pitching a unique idea, essential, he feels, in succeeding. If your idea is not unique, it must at least be a variation of what exists in that market at the time. He believes that if you follow what everyone else is doing, 'how do you stand out?' MoneySupermarket.com was the first price comparison tool for consumers in early 2000, and by the end of the same year had been joined by others cashing in on their success. Simon believes that because they were first in the market they had the advantage, but it was crucial to capitalise on this: 'you have to put your foot down on the accelerator or people will catch you up very quickly.' He's proven this to date, as MoneySupermeatket.com remains ahead of its competitors in their field.

Moving with the times

In the first year, MoneySupermarket.com made a respectable £500,000 and received around 50,000–60,000 hits a month. In a way, Simon comments,

MoneySupermarket.com were 'victims of our own success': their servers crashed several times to begin with, as they had underestimated the server capacity they would need to cope with the amount of hits they would get. Simon had to quickly adapt their servers to allow for the demand they had generated and he describes the 'steep learning curve' the company went through to rectify the problem.

MoneySupermarket.com had one very close call: in 2001, the year of the dot-com boom, London bankers followed lastminute.com's example and advised Simon to float the business, estimating he would get £100 million for it. Obviously intrigued by this estimate (turning over half a million a year), Simon went ahead with the long process of floating the company. However, not long after lastminute.com was floated, their shares crashed and the dot-com boom rapidly turned into a bust. MoneySupermarket. com had to pull their floatation four weeks from completion and Simon remembers this as a very painful process that made him a more cautious businessman. He waited another six years before attempting to float the business again.

In 2002, Simon and his team developed some clever technology, which Simon admits was groundbreaking then but is probably commonplace now. It worked like a 'spider robot': after the consumer keys in their details, the robot searches hundreds of sites and brings back the results on one page, making the site faster, more efficient and fully inclusive in its searches.

Alongside this, the business branched into the insurance market with InsureSupermarket.com in February 2003. Later the same year, the company launched TravelSupermarket.com and burst into the highly competitive travel market. This move may have been a risky one as this was a step out of the financial market they had dominated, yet Simon made sure that TravelSupermarket.com had something new to offer consumers – their technology ensured they searched every travel provider including, for example, charter flights and aggregators, while existing sites only searched deals from the traditional airlines or agencies. Again, Simon ensured that MoneySupermarket.com differentiated itself from any competitors as it explored new markets.

Where are they now?

In 2007, the company floated on the London Stock Exchange – but not before Simon had to convince initial business partner Duncan Cameron, who had not been involved in the company for six years, to sell his 50% in the business back to the company. Only then could the company float, and Duncan took some persuading. He finally agreed to sell the majority of his shares only a month before the flotation, with MoneySupermarket.com paying £162 million for 90% of his stake. The company eventually floated in July 2007 for an impressive £843 million. Simon remembers that this was actually a disappointment, as the valuation had been tipped to be over £1 billion – but bad timing meant the flotation occurred just as the recession hit hard.

Simon pocketed £103 million from the IPO, and stepped back from his role as CEO at the beginning of 2009 to start a new venture, Simonseeks, a travel- and property-focused business. He remains on the board as deputy chairman and continues to influence the development of the core product. Peter Plumb now sits on the board as CEO.

The site's growth has continued unabated and in 2011 the company announced revenues of £181 million, up 22% on the previous year. In a move away from Simon's initial no-advertising rule, MoneySupermarket.com ran its first ever TV advertisement in 2006. In 2011 the company spent £77.5 million on marketing and this is set to rise in the years to follow.

The reason for this? These campaigns are crucial in helping the site retain its number one spot – price comparison brands are the biggest advertisers on TV. Going up against the likes of talking meercats and Italian opera singers, the launch of the 'You're so MoneySupermarket' advertising campaign as well as sponsorship of ITV show Britain's Got Talent has firmly established the MoneySupermarket.com brand in the eyes of consumers; and all competitors are still snapping at their heels.

Cheapflights Media™

Cheapflights.co.uk

Taking to the skies

Founder: **John Hatt**	
Age of founder: **48**	
Background: **Travel journalist**	
Founded in: **1996, UK**	
Headquarters: **London, UK**	
Business type: **Flight price comparison site**	

t is so easy now to book a flight or holiday through one of the many online travel sites that you're unlikely to remember the days when making travel arrangements was a much harder process. Not long ago you'd have to slog through page upon page of potentially outdated classified ads or head to a high street travel agent in the hope that they might be able to offer you a good deal.

It is, of course, a different story today: armed with a credit card and a laptop – or even your smartphone – an affordable return flight to a remote African city can be yours in minutes. It was the travel journalist John Hatt who played a key part in this revolution, when he set up flight price comparison website Cheapflights.co.uk in 1996.

The website paved the way for the competitive online travel market we see today, but it was far from a straightforward process, with many in the industry reluctant to share their prices openly, and dubious of the site's popularity with consumers.

Proving doubters wrong at every step, and billing itself as a consumer champion supported by an advertising model that enabled it to remain independent, Cheapflights.co.uk became one of the top 10 travel sites in the UK whilst still operating from the small attic of founder John Hatt.

By 2000, the price comparison site had lured more than 200 advertisers on board and monthly page visits passed two million. Investment came from David Soskin and Hugo Burge, whose management buy-in grew the company from a South London attic operation to an international global brand.

Revolutions in the skies

As a veteran traveller, John, who had previously edited the travel pages of *Harpers & Queen* and written travel books, was well aware of the difficulties in obtaining good deals on flight prices, particularly for those travellers who wanted to visit cities that were off the beaten track. In early 1996, after being introduced to the internet through an American magazine for which he worked as a freelancer, John had the foresight to realise that the new online technology could provide an excellent way of giving potential customers access to great real-time deals on flights.

John was helped by the shift in the travel industry itself. With the deregulation of the airlines, and the familiar 'no-frills' flights being introduced, travel was becoming more accessible, if consumers could only access this information. Flights from the UK to South Africa at the end of the 1980s, for example, cost as much as £1,000, whereas today's travellers can get to Johannesburg for less than half that.

Search, not sales

John's light bulb idea was his decision to publish flight price data, rather than trying to create an online version of the travel agency model. This might sound simple, but in the travel industry, it was groundbreaking.

In the mid-1990s, digital entrepreneurs were focusing on the potential of online technology for portals and e-commerce, but John foresaw that, within the travel industry, an online search facility, rather than a sales function, could be equally profitable and carried with it less risk – overheads could be kept low because he wouldn't have to fund sales agents, issue tickets, take payments or provide an after-sales service to users. Armed with this vision, John set about creating the first online price comparison site in the UK travel industry.

To get started, the website would initially simply provide fares reproduced from other advertisements, primarily the classified ads. John would publish the fares online for free as a way of building up a user base that would then allow him to approach potential advertisers and ask them to pay to publish their deals on the site.

But setting up as an online publisher of flight prices at the dawn of the digital age wasn't necessarily straightforward, as David Soskin, who came

David Soskin took over as Cheapflights. co.uk CEO and now serves as Non-Executive Director.

on board Cheapflights.co.uk in 2000 following a management buy-in, explains: 'John's model turned the traditional publishing model on its head. Traditionally, you pay people for content. In his case, he was being paid by the people providing the content.' So, from his advertisers, he would gain not only advertising revenue but also the actual content for his site.

For this to work, John first needed to convince potential advertisers that the internet was where customers would be looking for flight deals from now on. He needed to persuade them that if they put their flight price data on his site, Cheapflights.co.uk would bring them genuine leads. No mean feat in 1996, when many had yet to be convinced about the possibilities arising from the internet.

John's light bulb idea was his decision to publish flight price data, rather than trying to create an online version of the travel agency model.

Despite John's confidence in the potential power of the web to generate valuable leads for his advertisers, inevitably many of the airlines and travel agents that he approached were sceptical. To try and assure prospective advertisers that online bookings represented the future of the travel industry, John offered them an enticing deal. He first explained the shift that he saw happening in consumer behaviour: more and more people were going to move away from traditional media and search for flight prices online instead. In the online world the customer has the potential to access flight price data from a range of agencies in real time, giving them multiple opportunities for a great deal. He then used what David terms the 'magic' line: 'Try us for a month – I don't want a long complicated legal contract with you – and if you're not delighted with the response we'll tear up the invoice and go our separate ways.'

It was a risky tactic, but it paid off. In 1997, the first paying advertisers signed up – initially, a handful of small travel agents, with Air Tickets Direct and Austravel coming on board later in the year. Bigger players soon followed as they began to realise the potential offered by the internet for the travel industry. Easyjet, KLM and Journey Latin America signed up in 1998 and Dial A Flight in 1999. And John's risky strategy worked: not one advertiser ever tore up their invoice.

But this start-up phase wasn't easy – although he outsourced all the technical work, he alone was responsible for persuading advertisers to come on board. 'British business was on the whole quite astoundingly slow to take it up, even though there was no risk for them. Trying to get people on board was a struggle – I worked very hard and the hours were enormous', he recalls.

John chose the domain name Cheapflights.co.uk because he wanted a name that reflected this ethos. And, of course, the name does exactly what it says on the tin.

Such a straightforward and memorable name clearly helped with marketing the site. In the early days of Cheapflights.co.uk, overheads were kept very low and spend on marketing was minimal. Although John used his professional experience and contacts in journalism to help create media coverage, he spent very little on advertising, relying instead on word of mouth to promote the site and drive up user numbers.

Keeping Aunt Agatha happy

John placed a real emphasis on providing a quality product, believing that if you had a positive online experience you would tell other people about it. It was a strategy that worked – six months after its launch, the website was receiving 290,000 monthly page impressions, and this had increased to more than 500,000 by the end of the first year. In 1998, Cheapflights. co.uk exceeded one million monthly page visits – with minimal outlay on advertising or marketing.

John believed that the key to a good website lies in the detail. It isn't just the layout of the page that is important but the font that is used, the navigation, the copy and the functionality. But that didn't mean he developed an all-singing, all-dancing website – simplicity was always key at Cheapflights.co.uk. From the outset, John introduced what he termed the Aunt Agatha test – if the mythical Aunt Agatha, an inexperienced computer user, couldn't master the technology on the website, it was no good. Cheapflights.co.uk was aiming to be a mass market product and the technology underpinning it had to tally with that.

John placed a real emphasis on providing a quality product, believing that if you had a positive online experience you would tell other people about it.

John's professional background as a travel journalist gave him credibility in the industry but he had no technical experience to speak of. Rather than growing the company with new recruits, John decided to outsource the technology and web development functions. This left him free to focus on sales, design and PR and also helped keep his overheads low, enabling him to develop the business from his small attic. Until 2000, the only recruit hired to work alongside John was a part-time personal assistant.

By keeping overheads down, the start-up costs of Cheapflights.co.uk were minimal. John didn't raise any finance because he wanted to own 100% of the company's equity. He initially relied on his own savings, managing the business out of cashflow once it started generating an income, but finances were always very tight. It was a frugal approach that contrasted sharply with many of the nascent dot-coms of that era, but it paid dividends. It had only taken a year to turn a small profit and by 2000 turnover had reached £400,000, unheard of for a digital company at that time.

Adopting a 'long tail' approach

John realised early on that a key aspect of Cheapflight's appeal lay in the potential for a range of smaller niche players in the travel industry to reach out to customers. By offering these companies access to highly targeted leads that they simply wouldn't have been able to reach before, it gave them the chance to compete on the same stage as the main players. This 'long tail' (going after lots of smaller deals, rather than a few big ones) approach was critical to the early success of the company, according to David. 'Cheapflights.co.uk was a very original long tail company. It was long tail in two respects – not just because its list of destinations was very comprehensive, but also because it dealt with a very long tail of small companies as well as all the very grand travel companies. This was crucial, absolutely crucial.'

This democratic approach applied not just to paying advertisers, but to visitors to the website as well. By offering users access to a broad range of both major airlines and the smaller travel agencies, it differentiated Cheapflights.co.uk from the classified print ads. Niche travel firms could ill afford to advertise on the pages of national broadsheets. This meant the classifieds were filled with ads for the same old places. Great if you wanted to go to New York, Paris or Rome but not very useful if you wanted to get a good deal on flights to Caracas.

John wanted the site to appeal to all tourists and travellers. He knew that nobody wants to pay over the odds for a flight – whether you're a multimillionaire or an impoverished student. And so, by offering such a broad range of flights and agencies, this long tail approach benefited both the customers and John's bottom line.

By offering users access to a broad range of both major airlines and the smaller travel agencies, it differentiated Cheapflights.co.uk from the classified print ads.

Hatt sells up

It was this strong consumer offering – together with the site's solid revenue stream and lean approach – that attracted David Soskin to the company. By 2000, John felt that he had worked long and hard enough and it was time to leave the company in somebody else's hands. The timing worked well for John – by selling up before the overinflated dot-com bubble burst he made himself a tidy profit from the sale of the company (although the figure has never been disclosed publicly).

Current CEO Hugo Burge remains as committed to Cheapflights.co.uk as ever.

David, who was lured from a corporate role as Head of Global Media at banking firm ABN AMRO, said he saw the potential that Cheapflights.co.uk offered straight away. 'I thought it was the most brilliant opportunity. I think it played to my own skills and I recognised that there was scope to expand way beyond the UK. Also, I was passionate about the product – I'm a keen traveller myself, I love flying.'

Together with Hugo Burge, David co-led a management buy-in in March 2000. Hugo is the current CEO of Cheapflights.co.uk Media and has a property and entrepreneurial background. He says that Cheapflights.co.uk represented a beacon of business sanity when he first looked at the company. 'It was growing, profitable and delivering a real consumer transformation in flight deals. Compare this to the multitude of business plans I saw which were nothing but a piece of paper, some hot air, five years of losses and a lot of talk about initial public offerings.'

Occurring only days before the dot-com bubble burst, the timing of the management buy-in may have appeared inauspicious to outsiders, but David remains adamant that the digital crash did little to dent his confidence in the prospects of the business. Underpinned by a sound business model and plenty of traffic, he was convinced Cheapflights.co.uk was only going to grow. Although revenue from banner advertising dropped as a result of the crash, the impact of this was balanced by falls in technology and hosting charges.

As well as leasing a serviced office around the corner from John's home (finally moving out of his attic), one of the first steps taken by the new management was to recruit a sales manager – Ceri Davies, who remains with the company to this day. By the end of 2000, staff numbered 10. This enabled the company to ramp up its sales efforts, attracting more than 200 paying advertisers by the end of the first year under David and Hugo's leadership.

In the same year, David and Hugo transformed the company's business model by introducing pay-per-click, and were the first travel price comparison site to do so in the UK. This was a shrewd and crucial move for the company: previously advertisers paid to publish their price data on the site in fixed monthly fees, but with this model, Cheapflights.co.uk was finding it difficult to financially capitalise on the growth in traffic to the site. Pay-per-click provided a solution by asking advertisers to pay a fee each time a Cheapflights.co.uk user clicked through to their site. It also took the sting out of renegotiating monthly fixed prices. Burge explains that using pay-per-click 'was warmly embraced by the travel industry and became the engine of growth for us'.

Expansion beckons

By 2002, the number of paying advertisers on the site had grown to more than 300 and in the same year, traffic exceeded one million *unique* users for the first time. Having established clear market leadership in the UK, David felt the time was right to start growing the company overseas. The US market was a clear choice and although the travel habits of Americans are very different from those of the British, a foothold in the world's biggest market would give the company a critical base from which to expand into a truly global business. At that time, there was only one competitor in the USA – Sidestep – publishing flight prices, but this was a desktop application and as such didn't represent serious competition.

In 1999, John had acquired the Cheapflights.com domain name – not because he had visions of expanding into the US market, but because .com is the default name for so many websites. It was a fortuitous decision because without this domain name, it would have been very difficult to break into the US market in 2003. To this day, a framed copy of the invoice hangs in the company's boardroom.

In 2002 Hugo relocated to Boston to found the website and build up a team of people. It launched in May 2003 and now business in the USA

The purchase of the .com domain name proved to be extremely fortunate.

generates more revenue than the original UK website. According to David, getting established in the USA only took a matter of months, but he admits that luck was on their side. As in the UK, the growth of the company in America was helped by wider developments in the travel market. Post-9/11, the US travel industry was desperate to get passengers on to planes because people weren't keen to fly. At the same time, there was an explosion in low-cost airlines in the USA, making the market more competitive.

Expansion for Cheapflights.co.uk didn't just take the form of breaking international markets. In 2001, the company launched Cheapnights.com, a sister site providing a portal to global accommodation. It was re-launched in 2002 as a price-led site displaying accommodation deals for over 500 destinations. In 2003 the site was rebranded Cheapaccommodation. com, mainly due to the fact that, in the USA especially, Cheapnights was sometimes mistaken for offering much more intimate (overnight) services. An additional sister site targeting the package holiday market was launched in 2004 displaying 200,000 holiday deals.

In 2006, both sites were sold to IBG Group, after the decision was taken by David and Hugo that it made better business sense to focus on international expansion rather than diversifying into new areas of the travel market. Burge explains that the other sites 'were growing businesses and doing pretty well but we had a dilemma – at the time the US was growing so well that we decided that it was better to focus on launching the Cheapflights.co.uk product into new markets. We believed that the Cheapflights.co.uk product was nicely differentiated and the international opportunity was huge.'

The distraction of hotels and package holidays did little to dent the rise of Cheapflights.co.uk, both at home and in overseas markets. In 2004, data from the internet monitoring agency Hitwise indicated that Cheapflights. co.uk's website was the third biggest referrer of leads to airlines and the fourth biggest to travel agencies.

Where are they now?

In 2005, Cheapflights.co.uk was awarded Innovative Business of the Year at the 2005 London Business Awards for its work as an independent online travel price comparison site.

In 2010 the company rebranded itself Cheapflights Media – to emphasise the nature of the company as a provider of published information rather than an online travel agent. Monthly global traffic now regularly exceeds 11 million visits and the company was awarded a place in the Sunday Times Microsoft Tech Track 100 fastest growing UK technology firms for seven consecutive years up to 2010.

International expansion remains an area for ongoing focus at Cheapflights Media. In 2010 the company launched in Australia and Spain and in March 2011 the business acquired the Danish travel website Momondo and its parent company Skygate, which enabled Cheapflights Media to strengthen its presence in the Scandinavian and Russian markets. As a meta-search site, Momondo complements Cheapflights.co.uk's business model and continues to operate as an independent brand. However, plans are under way to leverage technology, data and advertising partnerships across both networks in the future.

Hugo remains at the helm of the company, as Chief Executive Officer, and David is a Non-Executive Director. Both David and Hugo also teamed up together on another digital venture, launching HOWZAT Media, an internet investment fund, in 2006.

As for John, after the management buy-in, he also sold his travel publishing business, Eland, and took early retirement, although he has been involved in charitable work both at home and overseas.

Gocompare.com

Experience pays

Founder: **Hayley Parsons**	
Age of founder: **31**	
Background: **Worked at Admiral and Confused.com**	
Founded in: **November 2006, UK**	
Headquarters: **Newport, Wales**	
Business type: **Aggregator**	

If the words 'go compare' make you think of a large, singing Italian **man** with a curly moustache, then Hayley Parsons has done her job well. After leaving school at 16 and building up an impressive CV within the insurance industry, the internet entrepreneur decided to go it alone in 2006 and launch her own price comparison website, Gocompare.com.

In many ways, Gocompare.com was a classic kitchen table start-up, poised to succeed from the get go due to its founder's insight and perseverance, even in the face of competition from consumer giant Tesco and snubs from some of the largest insurance companies in the UK.

But Gocompare.com was not an overnight success: it took Hayley 15 years before she was ready to break out on her own, with the help of some pragmatic advisers and an innovative plan for her site. And although Gocompare.com cannot claim to be the first – or the number one – price comparison website, it has established itself as a successful, significant player in its market.

Discovering a people focus

Born in Cwmbran, Wales, Hayley Parsons left school and took her first steps in the business world at the age of 16. As a young woman Hayley was never a big fan of academia; all she ever wanted to do was work, make her own money and stand on her own two feet. Her father advised her to 'always work for yourself'. He wanted to set Hayley up with her own business, and he suggested that she become a hairdresser. But Hayley rebuffed his kind offer, preferring instead to go it alone.

So she left home to get herself a job, any job. She applied for everything she saw, including a job with a local insurance broker. The interview for the broker was the first interview she ever had. Luckily for the insurance world it was successful.

Hayley was hired by a small husband and wife-owned local insurance broker, and her job was to make tea and coffee, write cover notes and do the filing and the general admin. However, she was a keen learner and she was prepared to have a go at anything. One day, when the owners were out at lunch, a customer came in asking for an insurance quote. Instead of asking them to wait for the owners to come back, Hayley instead helped them with their quote. It was at this point that Hayley realised that she was 'customer-focused'. She also appreciated just how much money a broker could save people, a lesson that was to help her make her fortune later.

After her show of initiative, the owners began trusting Hayley with more and more responsibility and she began to find a real passion for business and helping customers.

Her next move was at just 18, when she moved to be a branch manager at broker Safeguard, where she worked for two years learning the ropes. It was while she was at Safeguard that she learnt about new start-up insurance company, Admiral. The new business appealed to Hayley and she decided to jump ship. It was a big risk and she had to take a step back to work for them, giving up her branch manager job for a sales role. After a year in her sales role she put herself forward for a position within the company to launch Gladiator, an online insurance business that, if successful, would be used as a model for bigger businesses further down the line.

Launched in 1998, Gladiator was a success, and Hayley was asked to move on to another big start-up project at Admiral; something that would shape her future career more than anything else in the years to come. The project was to develop a business that, instead of selling insurance, would actually allow users to enter their insurance needs and see a basket of different prices from a range of insurers.

Launching Confused.com

It took two years of hard work to launch what became Confused.com, and during that period it went through a number of different models. Hayley describes the launch of Confused.com in 2002 as an 'educational process' – for customers and for insurers. Until Confused.com came along the insurance market consisted of just two channels; the traditional broker channel, and the direct channel.

Thirty years ago, most consumers bought their insurance through brokers; quite possibly the same brokers their parents and grandparents had used. Then 20 years ago, insurance companies such as Direct Line encouraged consumers to cut out the middleman and go directly to them. Confused.com brought back the broker, but this time the broker was digital, and could compare tens of quotes at a time and show the customer the cheapest deal in just seconds.

'We had to completely change the business, I had to go out and explain to insurers that the way they sold insurance needed to change.'

This shift to an online broker model wasn't well received by the insurance companies or easily understood by consumers, but this is where Hayley came in. Hayley's part in Confused.com was to go out to the insurers and convince them to provide prices and quotes to the customers through the Confused.com website. It didn't always go smoothly. Direct Line was, unsurprisingly, not impressed (the fact that there is no middleman is their USP) and instead of a meeting to 'agree to disagree' Hayley was instead physically ejected from the building. It wasn't an easy job by any means. 'We had to completely change the business, I had to go out and explain to insurers that the way they sold insurance needed to change.'

Hayley's work, however, paid off, and Confused.com grew quickly. By 2004 it was showing a profit of £2.3 million; in 2005 profits had increased to £8.7 million and by 2006 profits hit £23.1 million. Customers were flocking to the site: by the first half of 2006 it was supplying more than 3.8 million quotes, an increase of 124% over the 1.7 million in the first half of 2005. However, despite this meteoric success, Hayley still felt the urge to go it alone, and work for herself.

Making a giant leap into the unknown

In 2006 she decided that it was time to make a break. 'I had worked on three start-ups and I had always been a number two or a number three in those start-ups. It was my time to become number one.'

Hayley had also realised that there was nowhere for her to go within Admiral. 'It's important to be realistic and to realise when you have reached your limits with your employer. I've had a number of situations where I've thought to myself, "I've got as far as I'm going to get in this company and now it's time to move on."'

While she was at Confused.com, Hayley had been watching the comparison market grow and watched as new competitors such as MoneySupermarket. com emerged, but she realised there was something missing. 'Confused. com and MoneySupermarket.com were both very successful, but they didn't have the incentive to move the industry on.'

In Hayley's eyes, what was needed was more information. Users had become accustomed to aggregators producing long lists of insurance companies and prices, but this only told the customer's side of the story. What was missing was more detailed information about the companies and the add-ons and features available –such as courtesy cars, protected no-claims bonuses and free windscreen repairs. This extra information would then enable the customer to finally compare like with like. Hayley wanted to 'produce a solution that gave the customer all the information they needed. I realised that the only way to do that was to get off my backside and do it myself', she recalls.

Users had become accustomed to aggregators producing long lists of insurance companies and prices, but this only told the customer's side of the story.

The impetus to start on her own partly came from seeing an old colleague make a move to price comparison site U Switch. 'I thought this is one of those points in your life where you need to change, and I looked at my colleague and I thought, "If he can do it, then I can do it too."' Once Hayley made her decision, she didn't hang around. 'I am not one of those people who can work on a business in the background while I work on my current job. If I make my mind up to do something then I just need to do it. So I literally woke up on the Monday morning and decided that I was going to leave', and by Friday she was out.

The first steps of the start-up

Gocompare.com was started with a small team of people who had loyally followed Hayley from Confused.com. One of those people was Lee Griffin – now COO of Gocompare.com– 'Lee started working with me when he was 17. On the day I was leaving Confused.com I asked Lee where his loyalties lay and he answered, "I'm coming with you, of course", and we both left that day.'

While Hayley had plenty of experience at starting up new businesses, this new venture was significantly different from all of her earlier start-ups. In her previous start-ups she had always had the backing of a large parent business. All of the office basics, desks, phones, IT, etc were all provided. Gocompare.com was a lot different. 'The business started with us all working on my dining table or working from home. It was a big change for all of us, we were completely on our own.'

An early version of the now infamous price comparison site.

But, unlike many start-ups, Gocompare.com was well financed from the start. 'I secured finance the day before I resigned. I had a meeting on Wednesday morning in Oxford with an old friend, Tom Duggan, and within 20 minutes I had confirmation that hewould give me a loan of £500,000 and he was willing to invest up to £1.5 million in the idea.' As a serial entrepreneur specialising in the insurance market, Tom was the perfect initial investor.Hayley was up and running.

Now all she needed was a name. 'We spent weeks agonising over the name of the company. It had to tell people exactly what we do and, more importantly, we needed to be able to find both .com and .co.uk domains. Me and Lee Griffin, who's now Gocompare.com's chief operating officer, trawled through lots of different sites and domains in our search for "the one". Then, one day, I got a text from Lee at two o'clock in the morning saying "Gocompare?" I replied immediately with "Yes!"

'We love the name because it communicates what we do but still gives us the flexibility to develop the comparison services that our customers need. The Gocompare.com domain was owned by a company in America who we approached to see if we could buy it. After some negotiating we managed to secure the domain and the rest, as they say, is history.'

With a strong brand name in place, creating the new business and website was a straightforward process for Hayley. The technology was built by a team with whom she had worked before, and the relationships with the insurance companies were once again built by Hayley. And, like all of the other aggregators, Gocompare.com was built on the familiar broker revenue model, with insurance companies paying a sum to the site for each insurance policy sold through leads from Gocompare.com.

The work on Gocompare.com started in April 2006, and by November the website was launched with a team of just seven people and with household names such as Swiftcover, More Than, Norwich Union and Endsleigh signed up from the start.

Building a monster not a me-too

Another turning point for Hayley came quite early on in the life of Gocompare.com. 'On the very first day our plan was to create a decent business, with the customer at the heart of everything we do. I didn't think we would be building the monster that we have today. But when we launched I realised that what we had produced on the dining room table was head and shoulders above everything else on the market, and that was when my plans changed.' Additionally during the pre-launch process Hayley got wind that Tesco were about to launch a price comparison site of their own, Tesco Compare, and that worried her. 'I realised that we had two choices, we could just launch the site, or we could really go for it.'

Hayley Parsons, founder and CEO of Gocompare.com.

Many would have looked at their business plans at this point and thought, 'Should we bother?', but to Hayley it was all the incentive she needed. Instead of being happy to be a respectable third or fourth place player in the market, while providing her unique like-for-like offering, she decided that she instead wanted to be the biggest in the market, and launch before Tesco could grab the advantage and drown out the Gocompare.com launch.

However, to fight a business with deep pockets like Tesco and to launch quickly, Hayley was going to need more working capital. One of the key problems for most businesses is getting funding. However, Hayley doesn't seem to have ever suffered this problem.

The war chest needed to beat Tesco

For her additional funding Hayley turned to another friend, Peter Wood. Peter (and his business esure) was a fortunate contact – he had valuable experience and knowledge in the field, having founded Direct Line in 1985, and later, digital start-up esure in 2000 (home of women's insurance company Sheilas' Wheels). The investment on paper was a risk, but Hayley had proved herself on her previous launches and she had always delivered, and that was enough for Peter to agree to make a post-launch investment of up to a staggering £30 million for growth and to build an extensive TV advertising campaign that would get the brand noticed.

Hayley had looked at other options for funding, but the choice of a single investor was an easy decision. She was looking for an investor that would support her business and understood her business, and esure and its founder was just that.

As well as providing funding, Peter was also a good mentor to Hayley. She credits his influence for helping her focus and set the correct priorities in the early days of Gocompare.com. His best advice to Hayley was to 'ignore the red line, ignore the losses you incur and ignore the pain you are going to go through.' And Hayley did just that. 'When we made a £10 million loss in our first year, and then an £8.8 million loss in the next year we were overjoyed and not downhearted.'

'Ignore the red line, ignore the losses you incur and ignore the pain you are going to go through.'

Gocompare.com's current headquarters in Wales.

While Hayley's enthusiasm helped her persevere, there were some insurance companies that still just didn't get the concept behind Gocompare.com, and developing relationships with them proved difficult. Direct Line continued to refuse to play ball and actually launched an advertising campaign that claimed price comparison sites were not accurate, independent or comprehensive. However, this didn't deter Hayley. There are now over 100 insurance companies who feed into Gocompare.com and those companies include both Churchill and Privilege, sister companies of Royal Bank of Scotland's Direct Line (who still don't appear on any insurance and price comparison aggregators).

Love it or hate it ...

An important lesson that she learned while she was at Confused.com was that changing the public's and insurers' attitudes to the way they sold and bought insurance was 'an expensive process'. Luckily much of the groundwork had already been done by Confused.com, but the market still needed some educating, and that education has come from Gocompare.com's extensive (and extremely memorable) TV advertising. Gocompare.com spent more than £2.3 million on TV advertising in the first 12 months of trading, and increased its spend to almost £10 million in the second year.

As Hayley points out, even from the very first days their advertising was successful; their early advertising was all about 'pushing the brand and the brands that it compares'. However, once they felt this message had got through, it was time to 'have some fun'. Hayley believes that laughter should be a big part of the business for both staff and customers, and that has been helped by some very clever advertising, and the 'popularity' of the love-it-or-hate-it opera-singing GioCompario advert, an advert that seems to win as many awards for popularity as it does for irritating the public – it was voted the most irritating ad in *Marketing*'s annual poll in both 2009 and 2010.

GioCompario, also known as 'the Gocompare man' was the brainchild of Sian and Chris Wilkins, a talented husband and wife advertising team who also created the infamous Sheilas for Sheilas' Wheels and the cult Cadbury's Smash Martians campaign.

Hayley said: 'Our previous adverts had done their job, educating the consumer about the merits of price comparison sites. But with our new campaign we wanted to make sure that when people received their car insurance renewal letter, their first thought would be "Gocompare!".

'I told Chris and Sian that I wanted adverts that people couldn't forget – and that's exactly what we got!'

Hayley admits that a few people weren't 100% sure at concept stage. 'We knew that it would be a "Marmite" campaign because of the sheer amount of times it would be broadcast. We also knew that the jingle had that catchy effect and could potentially annoy people.'

But this risky strategy obviously paid off: since the launch of the GioCompario advertising campaign, Gocompare.com's brand recognition increased by 450%, customer numbers have increased by 60% and YouTube has recorded over 1.8 million views of the official adverts, as well as inspiring hundreds of users to produce their own spoof adverts.

GioCompario's latest Cinderella-inspired advert.

Where are they now?

In May 2008, Gocompare.com became the first price comparison site to be invited to join the British Insurance Brokers' Association (BIBA). In its press release at the time, BIBA praised Gocompare.com for 'its philosophy of comparing insurance products on their suitability to individuals' requirements as well as price', which it deemed was in line with their policy of providing consumers with fair information. This had been one of Hayley's aims all along, to give customers more detailed information, and it still gives Gocompare.com an edge over their competitors to this day. Gocompare.com remains the only comparison site with BIBA accreditation. Gocompare.com was named as the 'One to Watch' in Growing Business's 2008 Fast Growth Business Awards, and in March 2009 Gocompare.com became the first price comparison site in the UK to compare over 100 different car insurance providers.

And the growth has been phenomenal: Gocompare.com saw a leap in pre-tax profit in 2010, up from £12 million to £30 million on a turnover of £101.5 million. In contrast, Hayley's old business Confused.com dived from £25.7 million in 2009 to £16.9 million after losing market share – which it blamed on a disappointing media campaign. But Gocompare.com still has some way to go to beat the number one price comparison site MoneySupermarket.com.

The Gocompare.com model has worked well in the UK, and Gocompare.com's future could include expansion into Europe and the rest of the world. However, one of the lessons that Hayley has learned is that launching a new concept is very hard work, so she won't be rushing into expansion. 'Some of our competitors have moved into Europe and are looking at European expansion and product diversification, but we haven't said where we are going to go next.' Ironically, it's easier to be the second business in the market rather than the first as there's less pressure. Whilst all eyes are on whether MoneySupermarket.com can retain its number one position, Gocompare.com only has one way to go and that's up! One thing's for sure: Hayley will ensure her customers are at the heart of any future plans and her bet on a like-for-like comparison site has paid off in spades.

Dropbox

Out-of-the-box success

Founders:	**Drew Houston and Arash Ferdowsi (shown, left to right)**
Age of founders:	**24 and 21**
Background:	**Self-admitted 'computer geeks'**
Founded in:	**2007, USA**
Headquarters:	**California, USA**
Business type:	**Online file-hosting service**

Sometimes the best business ideas come from simple solutions to life's small problems. Conceived in 2007 and officially launched by co-founders Drew Houston and Arash Ferdowsi a year later, Dropbox is a web-based file-hosting service that uses cloud storage to let its users share and back up files using file synchronisation capability.

Drawing comparisons with pioneers Apple, Google and Facebook, Dropbox's growth has been nothing short of stunning. And it grosses far more per employee from its 70-strong team than those luminaries do. Despite the fact that 96% of the company's approximately 50 million users pay nothing for their service, Dropbox is said by analysts to be on course to take in revenue of $240 million in 2011. What's more, it's been said that the company can double its sales in 2012 without recruiting a single new customer, as users exceed their 'freemium' allowance.

But seeing as the company moved into a new 87,000-square-foot headquarters early in 2012, and rumours abound that the company is in the process of raising between $200 and $300 million (£129 and £194 million) in funding at a whopping $5 billion (£3.2 billion) valuation, it's clear that Drew and Arash have no need to be modest.

The precociousness of youth

The story of Dropbox begins with a precocious child who grows into an overachieving teenager. As a mere five-year-old in suburban Boston, Drew began messing about on an IBM PCjr, and not long after, he started writing his first code.

Drew recounts that his mother, a school librarian, sensed his burgeoning computer 'geekiness' and did her best to help him fit in with other kids by refusing to let him skip years in school. Things changed, however, when Drew was a teenager. At just 14, he signed up to beta test an online video game. In the process, he made a detailed list of all of its security flaws. Impressed, the company hired Drew as their networking programmer in exchange for equity in the company. Drew continued to work with small start-ups throughout high school, and when he wasn't working he was still coding.

Drew says he knew then, at secondary school, that he wanted to run a computer company. But inspired by Daniel Goleman's book *Emotional Intelligence*, he knew that just being smart wasn't enough to make a company succeed, so he spent the summer before his first year at Massachusetts Institute of Technology (MIT) reading business books.

'No one is born a CEO, but no one tells you that', Drew has said of that time. 'The magazine stories make it sound like [Facebook founder Mark] Zuckerberg woke up one day and wanted to redefine how the world communicates with a billion-dollar company. He didn't.'

Drew's first hands-on education in managing people came when he rushed the Phi Delta Theta fraternity, and took on a leadership position as treasurer for the sole purpose of gaining that experience. But when fellow fraternity brothers left to pursue their own entrepreneurial visions, Drew was left frustrated. He had the desire and was building his skill set, but he was waiting for that moment of divine inspiration. He needed an idea. And then he got one.

'No one is born a CEO, but no one tells you that.'

In January 2007, Drew boarded a bus going from Boston to New York City. He'd brought his laptop and planned to do some work during the four-hour journey. But as the bus pulled away he realised he had forgotten his USB memory stick, and without those files he wouldn't be able to get anything done. It was actually a frequent problem of his, but this time, on the bus, he had a moment of clarity. There must be a way to sync your important files to devices over the web. Immediately Drew began doing what he did best: writing code.

Driven by frustration

Driven by the frustration of working from multiple computers, Drew sought to create a service that would let people bring all their files anywhere, with no need to email attachments. Drew coded a demo of his idea. Four months later, in June 2007, Drew left Boston for good and flew to San Francisco, where he pitched the idea to Paul Graham of the highly regarded start-up incubator Y Combinator. Paul had seen a demo of Dropbox that Drew posted online and was keen to learn more.

The model Drew pitched was simple: Dropbox makes all of your important files available to you wherever you may be in the world. Using cloud technology, files are synced and accessed from any computer or phone. Working late at the office? Just add the file you've been working on to your Dropbox folder and pick it up later at home. What Dropbox was selling was never again having to remember a USB stick or think about where your files are.

Drew wrote software that users could download and install for free, creating a special folder on the user's computer. Anything added to this Dropbox folder would automatically save to all of that user's computers, as well as to the Dropbox website. The true innovation, however, was its social nature, with users able to invite people to share any folder in their Dropbox, making it essential for a wide range of users, such as teenagers who want to share music, or businesses sharing information and designs with colleagues and clients.

What Dropbox was selling was never again having to remember a USB stick or think about where your files are.

Ultimately, everything hinged around a business model called freemium. Users would pay nothing to sign up for Dropbox, and just by signing up they would get 2GB worth of space. Drew knew this would lure people in. But Drew also knew the nature of the internet and that users would blow through 2GB. At that point, the Dropbox model would offer users upgrades to 50GB and 100GB with monthly fees of $10 (£6.47) and $20 (£12.90), respectively.

The potential was huge. And Paul Graham was impressed. On behalf of Y Combinator, a start-up funding firm, Paul agreed to give the pair $15,000 (£9,700) in initial funding to develop the business further and take it to the next stage. The amount was modest, but Y Combinator as a rule provides very little start-up money, reflecting Paul's theory that with the web and free software available, the cost of starting an IT firm has greatly decreased. In addition to the money, Paul's firm offered advice and the opportunity to build connections. But there was a catch – Paul insisted that for the idea to work, Drew needed a co-founder.

Drew didn't have long to search for the right person. Things were moving quickly. He polished his demo of Dropbox and ultimately decided to show it to his friend and fellow MIT student Arash Ferdowsi. So impressed was Arash that he dropped out of MIT – with only one term left before graduation – so that he could help Drew make Dropbox a reality.

With Arash on board and Paul's funding in the bank, Drew had the tools he needed to move forward. With the $15,000 (£9,700), he rented a flat and bought a Mac, which he spent 20 hours a day reverse engineering in his attempt to make his Dropbox application work on every computer and on the growing number of 'smart' devices such as phones and tablets. Then, three months later, Drew and Arash were invited to a meeting that would accelerate the business even further and change their lives for ever.

So impressed was Arash that he dropped out of MIT – with only one term left before graduation – so that he could help Drew make Dropbox a reality.

After a Y Combinator event, Arash, the son of Iranian refugees, was approached by a man who started speaking to him in Farsi. The man was Pejman Nozad, a famous dot-com-era investor, notable for funding start-ups such as PayPal.

Nozad got to know the young entrepreneurs and believed in their plan. He persuaded them that they needed to think bigger and started representing the pair, telling investors that they were already fielding a number of offers from venture capital firms. 'Basically, he was our pimp', Drew has joked.

It worked. In September 2007, the pair got a meeting with Sequoia Capital, the firm that famously funded internet giants Google and Yahoo! Drew and Arash were seeking only a few hundred thousand dollars, and they admit they were quietly nervous when it became apparent at the meeting that they would be talking about much larger sums.

'On a Friday afternoon, we walked into the Sequoia offices, and on the walls were the original stock certificates of Apple and Cisco. It was daunting', Drew writes. 'I was thinking, "Holy shit, I'm just some kid. What the hell am I doing here?"'

Pitch of a lifetime

Keeping their nerves at bay, the pair made their pitch, and the next day they were visited at home by legendary investor Michael Moritz, who heard the same presentation. Another meeting followed – this time, dinner with fellow investor Sameer Gandhi – and for the first time they began to talk specific numbers. Michael had told his partners to go forward with the deal, and Sameer revealed that they would be investing $1.2 million (£757,000) in Dropbox.

'We got an email a few days later from Sequoia requesting instructions for a wire transfer', Drew continues. 'Arash and I just looked at each other. We thought, "It'd be really embarrassing if we started – or quickly ended – this relationship by not even knowing how to get the million dollars into our bank account."'

Drew recounts the humorous episode of the two of them venturing into their bank and asking if there was a limit to how much one can deposit into a bank account.

'It's hard to describe the feeling of looking at your bank account online and continuously hitting Refresh, watching the balance increase from $60 to $1.2 million (£37 to £753,530)', Drew writes. 'You really have $1.2 million. And now it's up to you to figure out how to use it.'

'We got an email a few days later from Sequoia requesting instructions for a wire transfer. ... We thought, "It'd be really embarrassing if we started – or quickly ended – this relationship by not even knowing how to get the million dollars into our bank account."'

Soon they had more. In total, Drew and Arash raised $7.2 million (£3.6 million) from a combination of Sequoia Capital, Paul Graham at Y Combinator, Accel Partners and a host of other prominent investors, such as Amidzad (Nozad's firm), and brothers Ali and Hadi Partovi, who sold their start-up iLike to MySpace in 2009.

Every other file storage service at the time suffered problems with internet latency, large files or bugs, Drew had told them, and Dropbox was the first to conquer them all. Perhaps crucially, the service supports revision history, so a user's files deleted from the Dropbox folder can be recovered from any of a user's synced computers. Past versions are saved for 30 days; however, users can purchase a 'Pack Rat' option of unlimited version history. Finally, the version history uses an encoding technology that helps conserve bandwidth and time. If a user makes changes to a file, Dropbox, when syncing, uploads only the elements of the file that have been changed, not the whole file.

'I've seen a variety of companies attacking parts of this problem', Moritz later told *Forbes* magazine. 'Big companies would go after this, I knew. I was betting they had the intellect and stamina to beat everyone else.'

Fine-tuning the model

The next step for the pair was fine-tuning their model, which they eventually presented in a private beta launch video on the social news website Digg

A screenshot of Dropbox online.

in March 2008. Hoping to get around 15,000 user requests from the video, Drew and Arash were stunned to find 75,000 people wanting to test their service.

Not wanting to risk the bad press that could ensue from 75,000 people trying still-uncertain software, Drew hand-picked a number of people to test Dropbox through a series of private invitations. The invitation-only strategy was successful in bringing in tens of thousands of new users, and the company added to that figure by drawing some 300,000 new users alone from its newly launched iPhone app.

Using social media sites such as Twitter and Facebook, the Dropbox team netted another 50,000 users almost immediately. Drew and Arash also used Google AdWord placements to help spread the word in a more targeted manner and build viral momentum among an audience it knew was paying attention.

In short, Drew has said, the early growth strategy was simple: go where your first followers hang out and make yourself visible. Dropbox did this with their private beta launch and they continued with a strategy of winning over their niche users first and riding that momentum.

The pair were also quite media savvy. Knowing that journalists are busy people, they've said that part of cultivating Dropbox's momentum was helping reporters find the angle when reporting on their growth. To this end they met journalists in person, and Dropbox has always included a thorough media resources page on its site.

Significantly, Drew and Arash resolved that Dropbox should focus on doing a couple of things well rather than many things poorly. They poured their time into making their service as easy as possible for its users, not asking them to think too much when using it, but openly inviting feedback. This ease of use, and a referral programme that increased sign-ups by some 60% in the first year eventually helped Dropbox surge past the all-important benchmark of a million users.

The early growth strategy was simple: go where your first followers hang out and make yourself visible.

Using a video on a social news site like Digg to introduce themselves was a bit unconventional and is something Drew concedes they couldn't do now. But at the time, the people they were trying to sign up for their service were Web 2.0 geeks who resided on sites like Digg and Reddit – Reddit itself being a fellow Y Combinator start-up.

The buzz to go global

On advice from its investors, Dropbox finally officially launched later in 2008 at the TechCrunch50 technology conference, a global competition for start-up companies. Fifty entrepreneurs are invited to present at the event, and the winner receives $50,000 (£27,000). The event is supported by Sequoia Capital, one of Dropbox's key investors, who thought the young company could make a name for itself.

Dropbox didn't win the competition, but the event provided enough exposure to create buzz. The company had just nine employees when it formally debuted – eight engineers to monitor the servers and deal with customer queries, and one designer – despite boasting a number of registered users soaring well past the million mark.

For the remainder of 2008, Drew, Arash and their small team pulled all-nighters, working out bugs and perfecting the small details, even down to the shades of colour on the company's icons. Registered user numbers continued to grow tenfold that year, as Dropbox weathered the sharp economic downturn that autumn thanks to its small number of staff, limited overheads and a service that was essentially free. By April 2009 they could claim 10 million members, while in their modest offices investors Hadi and Ali Partovi were showing Drew and Arash how to recruit talented staff and market themselves more effectively.

Looking back, Drew says their main challenge that first year was marketing. 'We sucked at it', Drew recalls. He's said that they knew they had a great product, but the company's biggest obstacle was selling a product that solved a problem most people didn't know they had.

But Drew and Arash didn't want to rely on a marketing firm. Nothing can kill momentum like an overly slick marketing message. Instead, they turned to their customers. Research showed Dropbox users were very loyal to the firm, and so Drew and Arash offered 250MB of extra storage free to each customer who gave them a referral.

'Most of our growth is word of mouth or viral, so free users are still valuable: we grow faster, and they refer people who might pay', Drew has said of their strategy. The move, in fact, was so successful that 25% of all new registered users still come to Dropbox this way.

Privacy issues and public problems

The company experienced a few more contentious challenges, however. Dropbox drew criticism for harbouring those who infringe on others' copyright, and as a result it had to adjust its terms in accordance with the Digital Millennium Copyright Act, which establishes a notification-and-takedown system for addressing claims of copyright infringement. To comply, Dropbox has reserved the right to delete or remove any file from users' accounts in response to claims from copyright owners.

The company was also forced to fend off claims that its staff could access its users' files at any time. Questions over its privacy and security policy reached fever pitch when a complaint was filed with the Federal Trade Commission. The complaint attacked one of Dropbox's systems, which checks whether a file has been uploaded before by another user. It was alleged that linking between files to an existing copy exposed users' files to intruders. In response, Dropbox tightened its security measures and clarified its terms of service.

These were only minor issues, however. Dropbox's rapid growth saw the firm expand its team to 20 people to cope with all of the queries and requests coming from its paying customers in 175 countries. By 2010, its team grew to 60, and Dropbox began launching new services targeted towards businesses, such as Dropbox for Teams, and a new 1TB storage option.

As Dropbox expanded, Drew's time began to shift away from coding to more traditional CEO territory: people management. Uninspired by stereotypical cubicle life, Drew wanted to create a new corporate structure and has broken Dropbox's staff engineers into small teams, while just three managers handle the company's thousands of servers.

With the company reportedly looking to expand from 70 to more than 400 staff, Drew has said that the biggest challenge Dropbox faces is internal communication, since messages from the top have typically been shouted across the room. Times have certainly changed for Drew and Arash, who just a few years ago were coding in their small shared flat in San Francisco.

Dropbox pokes fun at its foolproof system.

Perhaps the defining moment for Drew, when it became apparent just how far he'd really come, arrived in December 2009 when he received an invitation to meet his hero, Steve Jobs.

The meeting was at Apple's Cupertino offices, and Steve was interested in buying the plucky start-up. After pleasantries, Steve made his pitch. But Drew told him to stop. He was well and truly flattered, but he wasn't selling. He wanted to grow the company. And as Dropbox surged past the 25 million user mark in the months following and has today breached 50 million, Drew is well on course to achieving his dream.

Where are they now?

After reaching the 25 million user threshold, Dropbox signed deals with mobile carrier Softbank and handset maker Sony Ericsson in a bid to attract more customers in Asia and Europe. As the company cruised past 50 million users in 2011, Drew and Arash announced even bolder plans.

In August 2011, the pair invited seven top venture capital firms with a history in Silicon Valley to visit their offices and make an offer for further investment by the following Tuesday. According to interviews with insiders, just before midnight on Monday, Dropbox's Head of Business Development expressed his concern that only one offer had arrived and suggested that Drew and Arash pull the funding round.

But Drew declined. He would see it through. And as he expected, every firm came back with an offer in the morning. They eventually closed a mammoth deal in September with Index Ventures, Sequoia, Greylock, Goldman Sachs, Benchmark Capital, RIT Capital Partners and Accel Partners that netted the company $250 million (£162 million) on a $4 billion (£2.6 billion) valuation. According to Forbes, Drew's own estimated 15% stake is worth some $600 million (£388 million).

Dropbox's rapid growth has seen it ranked as the world's fifth most valuable web start-up company, falling in line after luminaries like Facebook, Twitter, Zynga and Groupon. And industry observers have noted that people save more files on Dropbox than there are tweets on Twitter.

Drew, who remains CEO, has said he envisions a day in the not too distant future when Dropbox does more than just store, for instance, people's photos. He sees his system taking it a step further and reading the metadata and embedded location information on these photos, which can then be indexed to allow users to arrange all the pictures taken within a 20-mile radius. Named the best young tech entrepreneur by Business Week, there seems to be little doubt he will achieve this and much more.

Google

Google

Organising the world's information

Founders:	**Sergey Brin and Larry Page (shown, left to right)**
Age of founders:	**24 and 25**
Background:	**Stanford PhD computer science students**
Founded in:	**1998, USA**
Headquarters:	**California, USA**
Business type:	**Search engine**

Google. **We all know its name** and use its website probably more than any other. We also know that it is extremely successful and that its founders have become billionaires. Yet amazingly, in 1999 almost none of us had heard of it, let alone used it. Its growth has been more substantial than most of the world's greatest business success stories, and it happened faster, too.

The birth of PageRank

But Google hasn't always been such a goldmine. In fact, when they started, Google's co-founders Larry Page and Sergey Brin weren't even sure how their site would make money.

The pair met at Stanford University in the spring of 1995, where they were both enrolled in its prestigious computer science PhD programme. Located in Silicon Valley, Stanford had already spawned some of the world's most successful technology companies, such as Hewlett-Packard and Sun Microsystems, and the academic environment encouraged risk-taking and entrepreneurship. Its office of technology licensing offered technologists resources, advice and assistance with the patent process to help its students commercialise their research projects in return for a stake in the businesses. It was also a stone's throw from Sand Hill Road, home to some of America's most successful venture capital firms.

Sergey and Larry had both grown up surrounded by science and technology. Larry's father was one of the first-ever recipients of a computer science degree from the University of Michigan. His mother was a database consultant with a master's degree in computer science. Sergey was born in Moscow and went to the USA when his parents moved there; his mother was a scientist at NASA and his father a mathematics professor at the University of Maryland. Sergey had completed his BS in mathematics and computer science at the University of Maryland by the age of 19, while Larry had built a working inkjet printer out of Lego blocks in high school. So by the time they met, both were highly accustomed to computers and how they work. They struck up a strong friendship at Stanford, fuelled greatly by their shared love of academic debate and discourse.

At the time, several rudimentary search tools existed, but a search on one of them would generally yield thousands of results, which were not ranked in any order of relevance. Fellow Stanford PhD students Jerry Yang and David Filo had developed Yahoo! to tackle the problem, but they employed a team of editors to assemble a web directory and were already struggling to keep up with the growing World Wide Web. Convinced there was a better way, Sergey, an expert in extracting information from vast amounts of data, joined forces with Larry, who was studying the leading search engine Alta Vista. Never short of ambition, Larry set out to download the entire web onto his PC to study the relevance of web links, which Alta Vista didn't appear to be taking into account. The project took far longer than expected and cost the computer science department around $20,000 (£12,000) every time they sent out a crawler program to capture online data – but the effort was definitely worth it.

Never short of ambition, Larry set out to download the entire web onto his PC to study the relevance of web links.

They concluded that the number of links pointing to a site was a measure of its popularity. Furthermore, they decided that links could be weighted. For instance, if the BBC (which itself receives high volumes of traffic and has many links pointing to it) links to your website, this is worth more than a link from a less popular site. Naming it after himself, Larry called the algorithm he developed to establish this pecking order PageRank. By adding this to traditional search methods (which matched keywords on pages with those in the search terms) the pair devised a search engine that produced results that were highly accurate and relevant to the user's request. Google was conceived.

Looking for a buyer

The founders did not set out to build a business. Coming from backgrounds where academia was revered, they were more excited to have stumbled across the basis of a killer thesis. They developed a prototype of their search engine, called BackRub, which was renamed Google in 1997. The term was a play on the word googol, a mathematical term for the number 1 followed by 100 zeros, and it represented the vast amounts of data on the web. Working day in, day out from a room on campus, the founders unleashed their creation on Stanford's student body via the university's intranet. Its popularity among this information-hungry population soared through word-of-mouth recommendations, as users quickly discovered how much faster and more relevant its search results were.

Not wanting to get too distracted from their academic pursuits, but certain that they had created something far superior to anything else available at the time, they attempted to sell their technology to Excite, Yahoo! and then market leader Alta Vista for up to $1 million (£630,000) before patenting it. Amazingly, each company passed on the opportunity. Search did not present any obvious revenue-generating opportunities, and Google's goal to produce results in a split second did not make it an ideal space for advertisers. Feeling passionately that they had developed something that people truly needed, Sergey and Larry were left with no choice but to take Yahoo! co-founder David Filo's advice and take Google to market themselves.

By amassing email feedback from their academic peers, they refined their offering before seeking funding to make it scalable. In August 1998, they met private investor Andy Bechtolsheim, a co-founder of Sun Microsystems, who had sold another business to Cisco for hundreds of millions of dollars. Despite the lack of a clear business model, Bechtolsheim was so taken with the idea that he wrote out a cheque to Google Inc. for $100,000 (£60,000) on the spot, compelling Sergey and Larry to incorporate the company. Google was born.

Scaling it up

Bechtolsheim was particularly impressed with Sergey and Larry's plans to rely solely on the strength of their product and word-of-mouth recommendations to market the brand, instead of blowing huge sums on advertising. Instead, they planned to invest in IT as no other company had done before. From the outset, Sergey and Larry had been extremely efficient in their use of computers. They were downloading, indexing and searching the internet using a network of off-the-shelf PCs they had custom built and linked together themselves. On these computers ran the software and algorithms they had also designed to crawl through and rank web pages. The intention was to continue with this strategy, scaling it up cost-effectively by adding more and more PCs to the network to ensure their lightning-fast search results kept up with the growing number of websites and users.

The well-known Google search page.

Google's stated mission is 'to organise the world's information and make it universally accessible and useful.'

Following Bechtolsheim's endorsement, several friends and family members also backed the pair, who were able to raise a total of $1 million (£630,000). After running their operations from a garage for a while, where they hired their first member of staff, the duo moved into offices in California in 1999. A mention in *PC Magazine*'s top 100 websites created a huge surge in user numbers, and before long, Google was dealing with upwards of 500,000 searches each day.

Struggling to maintain the level of IT investment they needed to keep up, the team was before long forced to seek further backing. Luckily for them, the economic climate worked in their favour. Google's story is set against the backdrop of the dot-com rise (and subsequent fall). Following the buzz created by the stock market flotation of internet browser producer Netscape in 1995, which valued the company at $3 billion (£1.89 million) after the first day of trading, Wall Street stockbrokers were on the prowl for more internet success stories.

In 1999, Google closed a deal with two of the world's most prestigious venture capital firms, both based on Sand Hill Road in Silicon Valley: Sequoia Capital, which had backed Yahoo!; and Kleiner Perkins Caufield & Byers, which had backed Amazon and many others. In an unprecedented move, the renowned venture capitalists agreed to invest equally in Google, with neither having a controlling interest. So eager were they to back the search pioneer while they had the chance (despite it still not having a successful business model) that each firm put up $12.5 million (£7.5 million), while Sergey and Larry remained in sole charge of the company they had created – a non-negotiable condition for them.

Going global

Following the buzz this created, Google experienced a major growth spurt. Larry and Sergey continued in their method of custom-building server racks using parts from low-cost PCs and stacking them one on top of the other, getting maximum value per square foot in their data centres. At this stage, their business model was to earn income by licensing their search technology to other partners. This wasn't bringing in sufficient revenue, so they began to consider other ways to turn their growing search engine into a sustainable business.

They were initially hesitant to allow advertisers on to the site because they worried that users would doubt the search results' impartiality, and Sergey and Larry remained resolute that they would never allow companies to pay to rank more highly, as other search engines had done. They came up with a compromise which was to revolutionise not only their own business, but also their competitors' – and the world's advertising industry. Their idea was that whenever someone searched for a topic, they would display small text ads relevant to the subject of the search alongside the more prominent 'natural search engine results'.

Sergey and Larry remained resolute that they would never allow companies to pay to rank more highly. ... They came up with a compromise which was to revolutionise the world's advertising industry.

This soon evolved into the current pay-per-click model, whereby Google would earn money whenever a user clicked on one of these 'sponsored links'. The rate paid per click was set by the advertiser in a fair, automated online auction process.

This worked spectacularly well for several reasons: it was extremely simple and quick for an advertiser to set up; it could be tested for a tiny investment (far smaller than any other advertising method); it enabled advertisers to present their message to a very highly targeted audience; it was free unless someone clicked on the advertiser's link; it was easy to measure how successful it was; and, above all, it worked. Advertisers got excellent results from people clicking on their ads.

In 2000, the founders hired Dr Eric Schmidt as Chief Executive to take over the day-to-day running of the business. Although Sergey and Larry were hesitant at first for fear of losing control of the company they had created (after all, this was a condition of the investment to which they had reluctantly agreed), Schmidt's appointment proved to be extremely successful. In particular, his business expertise played a key role in Google's overseas expansion. One of the first things he noticed was that, while 60% of its searches came from outside the USA, just 5% of ad revenues came from overseas advertisers. While the searches had been available in foreign languages for some time, and the business was truly serving a global audience, it had yet to make money from this. Under Schmidt's supervision, sales offices were duly established in London, Hamburg, Tokyo and Toronto. Revenue soared.

Google's stated mission is 'to organise the world's information and make it universally accessible and useful.' Hardly a modest ambition! As its revenue grew, it started adding new services to deliver more of this mission. By 2004, in addition to the core search engine, it offered Google Images, a huge library of searchable images, and Google News, a service that aggregated stories on any particular subject from around the world. It also introduced Gmail, a web-based email service.

Going public

In August 2004, the founders reluctantly listed the search engine on the NASDAQ stock exchange, raising $1.2 billion (£756 million). Going public was actually the last thing Sergey and Larry wanted to do. Apart from the fact that their independence had helped them weather the dot-com bust, they were extremely hesitant to make their financial information available to competitors.

Up until 2004, analysts had grossly underestimated just how big the search giant had become, and the last thing Google wanted was for the world to know how much money they were making, or more information on how they were making it. However, they now had so many investors that US law required them to disclose their financial information. Given that they would have to spill the beans anyway, they felt it prudent to take the company public and give their early employees and investors a tangible return.

No other company in history has achieved such brand awareness without spending heavily on advertising and marketing.

But shortly before its IPO (initial public offering), a number of factors coincided to bring down Google's share price. First, the company had to deal with backlash from rival Overture, a subsidiary of its largest competitor, Yahoo! Overture pioneered the idea of selling ads to accompany search results using a pay-per-click model, and accused Google of infringing its patents. Conscious of the negative effect of the ongoing legal battle in the run up to its stock market debut, Google's founders gave Yahoo! 2.7 million shares in an out-of-court settlement.

Secondly, Google's recent entry into the email market with Gmail was steeped in controversy. The founders sought to offer a service that was far better than anything else out there. Using their search technology, you could easily search for and find a stored message within Gmail, and Google offered what was then a colossal 1GB of space with an account. However, their plans to make money through contextual ads, which were generated by scanning messages and matching ads to keywords, were slammed by privacy advocates.

The combination of factors meant that Google's IPO valued shares at just $85 each (£43). But this didn't last for long. Despite these setbacks, Google's share price rose to $100 (£63) by the end of the first day of trading, valuing the company at $23.1 billion (£11.3 billion). As with many new companies in Silicon Valley, many of Google's early employees had been given share options instead of high salaries, which helped keep costs down for the young business while it was trying to become profitable. This made early employees millionaires when the company went public.

Part of Google's phenomenal growth has come from a scheme it created called AdSense. This allows other websites to install a Google search box on their site; when users click on the contextual ads that Google supplies, the partner website earns some of the fee advertisers pay to Google. AdSense has been enormously popular with other websites, including giants such as AOL and the *New York Times*. AdSense is typical of Google's progressive approach and its belief that working alongside competitors can grow the market for all.

Continued growth

Google has used its success to make a number of significant acquisitions. Examples include its $1.65 billion (£897 million) purchase of user video clip phenomenon YouTube in October 2006 and its purchase of online advertising network Doubleclick in April 2007. The latter was bought for $3 billion (£1.5 billion), lengthening its reach into the display advertising market on the web.

The company's founding principles have also played a key part in the company's success, not least the founders' determination to make Google a great place to work. Its motto, 'Don't be evil', is world famous, as is the award-winning culture that Sergey and Larry have fostered. On site at its Californian headquarters, staff can make use of a wide range of facilities, including pool tables, swimming pools and volleyball courts, as well as being well fed with free gourmet food.

Engineers are actively encouraged to spend 20% of their time working on their own projects. Both Google News and Froogle, an online shopping service, are the result of this initiative. Google now has sales offices all over the world, and this culture of creativity pervades them all. As a result, the company receives more than 1,300 job applications every week.

Its motto, 'Don't be evil', is world famous, as is the award-winning culture that Sergey and Larry have fostered.

No other company in history has achieved such brand awareness without spending heavily on advertising and marketing.

Technicians hard at work in the Google office, California.

Where are they now?

At the height of its success in 2007, shares in Google were being sold for $741.80 (£370), but their price began to tumble amid fears that its ad revenue was falling (newspapers reported fewer people were clicking on its ads). But, true to form, Google laid waste to those claims when it brought home $1.3 billion (£700 million) in profit between January and March 2008, on revenue of $5.1 billion (£2.7 billion).

In April 2011, a Google share would set you back $577 (£373). Its market capitalisation (the current value of all its shares) at that time reached a staggering $185.6 billion (£120 billion). Annual revenues hit just shy of $30 billion (£18.9 billion) for 2010.

Google's website now processes hundreds of millions of searches every day. Google's homepage has retained its design simplicity, mostly steering clear of Flash features, despite the fact that it could potentially be a source of considerable extra income. As a result, it loads quickly, improving the customer experience. It is estimated that Google's network now consists of considerably more than 500,000 servers, a computing power unmatched by any other company. Its employees still assemble and customise the PCs the company uses to carry out its searches. No enterprise has more computing power than Google.

In 2011, Google announced that Larry would be resuming the post of Chief Executive and Eric Schmidt would take a step back. The trio, including co-founder Sergey, have run the company collaboratively very successfully for the past 10 years, but in a blog post, Larry announced that they'd all agreed to clarify their 'individual roles so there's clear responsibility and accountability at the top of the company.'

It's not clear what prompted the change, but one thing's for sure; Google will continue to grow and grow.

Contributing authors

Thank you to the following:

ASOS	Georgina-Kate Adams
Cheapflights	Sam Thorp
Dropbox	Jeff Meyer
eBay	Kim Benjamin
Electronic Arts	Carol Tice
Etsy	Carol Tice
Flickr	Gareth Platt
Gocompare.com	Marcus Austin
Google	Steph Welstead
Groupon	Carol Tice
LinkedIn	Kim Benjamin
Made.com	Trevor Clawson
Match.com	Ryan Platt
Mind Candy	Gareth Platt
MoneySupermarket.com	Lianne Slavin
Mumsnet	Kim Benjamin
Neon Play	Ryan Platt
The NET-A-PORTER Group Limited	Marcus Austin
Pixar	Carol Tice
Spotify	Gareth Platt
TripAdvisor	Jeff Meyer
Twitter	Carol Tice
Wikipedia	Kim Benjamin
Wonga	Georgina-Kate Adams
Zynga	Carol Tice